NEW SCIENCE LIBRARY

presents traditional topics from a modern p
those associated with the hard sciences—physics, biology, and
medicine—and those of the human sciences—psychology, sociology, and philosophy.

The aim of this series is the enrichment of both the scientific and
spiritual view of the world through their mutual dialogue and
exchange.

New Science Library is an imprint of Shambhala Publications.

General Editor   Ken Wilber

Consulting Editors   Jeremy Hayward
Francisco Varela

Wayne Untereiner

The New Biology

Discovering the Wisdom in Nature

ROBERT AUGROS & GEORGE STANCIU

Illustrations by Michael Augros

NEW SCIENCE LIBRARY
Shambhala
Boston & London
1988

NEW SCIENCE LIBRARY
An imprint of
Shambhala Publications, Inc.
Horticultural Hall
300 Massachusetts Avenue
Boston, Massachusetts 02115

9 8 7 6 5 4 3 2 1

First paperback edition

Printed in the United States of America

Distributed in the United States by Random House
and in Canada by Random House of Canada Ltd.

The Library of Congress catalogues the hardcover edition
of this work as follows:

Augros, Robert M.
  The new biology.

  Includes bibliographical references and index.
  1. Biology.   2. Ecology.   3. Evolution.
I. Stanciu, George N., 1937-   . II. Title.
QH313.A78 1987   574   86-28058
ISBN 0-87773-364-3
ISBN 0-87773-439-9 (pbk.)

Cover art: Max Ernst's *The gramineous bicycle garnished with bells the dappled fire
damps and the echinoderms bending the spine to look for caresses* (Cologne, 1920 or
1921). Botanical chart altered with gouache, 29¼" × 39¼". Collection, The
Museum of Modern Art, New York. Photo © 1987 Museum of Modern Art.

Contents

Acknowledgment

The authors wish to thank the Earhart Foundation, Ann Arbor, Michigan, for its generous support through a series of research grants that helped make this book possible.

THE NEW BIOLOGY

Introduction

In the first quarter of this century, relativity and quantum physics demonstrated the limits of Newtonian mechanics. These momentous innovations transformed forever the science of physics. Parallel events have yet to occur in the life sciences, however. Biologist Edmund Sinnott, for example, acknowledges the modern progress in his field but notes that "there has been no revolution here as that which shook the physical sciences so profoundly."[1] Physicist Henry Margenau agrees: "Biologists have not yet experienced the transcendental leaps beyond customary ideas which Einstein and Heisenberg forced physicists to take."[2] For the most part, contemporary biology is still working within the paradigm of Newtonian mechanics. As biologist Ludwig von Bertalanffy puts it, "Today biology is still in its pre-Copernican period."[3]

At the turn of the century, who could have suspected that some of the most fundamental assumptions of physics were about to be reversed, that the very concepts of matter, gravity, time, and space—all things taken for granted everywhere and hardly ever reflected on—would soon be radically modified? Today, mounting evidence calls for a revision of the most fundamental principles in the life sciences, including the definition of life, how biology relates to the other sciences, the role of evolution in biology, the place of man in nature, what is meant by a scientific explanation, and the very concept of nature.

The search for a new paradigm has already begun in some disciplines. Bertalanffy comments: "The numerous attempts appearing today to find a foundation for theoretical biology point to a fundamental change in the world picture which is taking place now that the view based on the classical physics has reached its limits."[4] Current upheavals in evolutionary theory illustrate the point: conventional Darwinian mechanisms are under attack. Steven Stanley, paleobiologist of Johns Hopkins University: "Today the fossil-record is forcing us to revise this conventional view."[5] Even the synthetic theory of evolution developed by Ernst Mayr and others is being severely criticized from within biology. Paleontolo-

1

gist Stephen Jay Gould of Harvard declares, "The synthetic theory
...as a general proposition, is effectively dead, despite its persistence as textbook orthodoxy."[6] But if evolution is the single theory
that unifies all biology, any major revision in it would require a
readjustment in virtually every biological science and a reassessment of the whole framework of the life sciences.

In addition, within the past few decades several new fields have
arisen in biology, some of them yielding profound discoveries that
do not fit into the Newtonian program. For example, the modern
science of animal behavior, founded in the 1930s by Konrad Lorenz,
Niko Tinbergen, and Karl von Frisch, is not based on the machine
models of classical physics. Similarly, several ecologists, including
Daniel Simberloff and Paul Colinvaux, are challenging the notion
that nature is a competitive struggle.

In this context, Mayr has declared, "It is now clear that a new
philosophy of biology is needed."[7] Our goal in the present book is to
make a contribution toward formulating the new biology, by
unifying and synthesizing the work already done in disparate fields
and supplementing it with our own work, using the new physics as a
guide throughout. For example, the revolutions of relativity and
quantum theory forced physics to outgrow the narrow confines of
mechanism. In some areas of current biology mechanical models
work beautifully, but in others they fail miserably. We shall
carefully distinguish between these areas and, where necessary,
suggest alternatives to the mechanistic approach.

Though self-contained, this book is the second in a series. It
continues and further develops the same themes as our previous
work, *The New Story of Science,* in which we examine the origins of the
new world view in physics and neuroscience. The present work is
not a comprehensive survey of general biology, nor does it treat
exhaustively even those subjects it touches on. Our intention is
merely to outline, by examples, arguments, and expert testimony,
the contours of the new paradigm for biology, illustrating its
implications in a few key areas. We hope this will prove useful both
to the biologist and to the nonbiologist.

Finally, it is impossible in one volume to give the reader an
adequate notion of life's vastness and overwhelming splendor. If our
meager representation at least intimates these qualities of nature

and perhaps evokes the reader's wonder, we shall consider our efforts successful. We apologize to Mother Nature, as it were, for our inability to do justice to her richness, her beauty, and her wisdom.

1

Physics As the Paradigm

Most biologists today consider biology to be an extension of physics. Biologist Peter Medawar writes: "Biology is not 'just' physics and chemistry, but a very limited, very special and profoundly interesting part of them. So with ecology and sociology."[1] Biologist E. H. Mercer agrees: "Most scientists in practice behave as if they believed that only matters of convenience or convention separate physics from biology; or to put it another way, they act on a belief that there is really only one science."[2]

This view rests on the argument that science is analysis and analysis requires the resolution of a subject into its simplest elements. Such a procedure generates a scheme that relates the sciences to each other (see Figure 1.1).[3] Within this scheme, the laws that govern crowds, classes of persons, and societies are based on the qualities and characteristics of the individual. The causes of an individual's actions arise from anatomy, physiology, and the biochemistry of brain mechanisms. These subjects are in turn resolvable to the laws of chemistry and physics. This process of analysis finally stops with high-energy physics, which studies the ultimate particles.

Mercer assigns the origin of this scheme for the sciences: "Inevitably the idea spread that all the sciences could be brought together and integrated in terms of particle dynamics using Newtonian methods, and a universal scientific materialism came into being."[4] According to the materialist program, once the simplest particles are reached, all else can be understood by composition. Physicist Heinz Pagels writes:

"In its crudest form, material reductionalism maintains that there is a series of levels. At the bottom level are the subatomic particles, and from these the chemical properties of atoms and molecules are obtained. Molecules form living and nonliving things, and from the behavior of molecules and cells it is possible to determine the

5

behavior of individual humans. They in turn establish a social order and institutions. Finally at the top level of the ladder are historical events. The claim is that in principle, history is materially reducible to subatomic events."[5]

Because the principles of physics have universal application in living and nonliving things, the other natural sciences are thought to be connected to physics by deduction. Mercer speaks of "the prevailing view that biology is a derived science whose principles can be deduced from the basic laws of physics and chemistry."[6]

This schema is as old as modern science itself; Descartes affirms that all disciplines are really one continuous science: "Philosophy as a whole is like a tree whose roots are metaphysics, whose trunk is physics, and whose branches, which issue from this trunk, are all the other sciences. These reduce themselves to three principal ones, viz., medicine, mechanics, and morals."[7] Descartes proposes this conception of the sciences together with a completely mechanistic account of living things. Speaking of the motion of the blood and of local motion in animals, he says, "The laws of mechanics...are identical with those of Nature."[8] Hobbes also resolves politics and psychology to physics.[9] And later the British Royal Society was founded with the same program in mind. Its first secretary, Henry Oldenburg, describes the Society in a letter to Spinoza:

"In our Philosophical Society we indulge, as far as our powers allow, in diligently making experiments and observations, and we spend much time in preparing a History of the Mechanical Arts, feeling certain that the forms and qualities of things can best be explained by the principles of Mechanics, and that all the effects of Nature are produced by motion, figure, texture, and the varying combinations of these."[10]

Newton gave new impetus to the mechanistic program and laid its foundation in physics. Without Newton's laws of motion the program would have been just a dream. In the preface to his *Principia*, Newton speaks of the ideal of the mechanistic program: "I derive from the celestial phenomena the forces of gravity with which bodies tend to the sun and the several planets. Then from these forces, by other propositions which are also mathematical, I deduce the motions of the planets, the comets, the moon, and the sea. I wish we could derive the rest of the phenomena of Nature by the same kind of reasoning from mechanical principles, for I am induced by many reasons to suspect that they may all depend upon certain forces by which the particles of bodies, by some causes hitherto unknown, are either impelled toward one another and cohere in regular figures, or are repelled and recede from one another."[11]

Pursuing Newton's ideal, mathematician Pierre Laplace enunciated the logical consequence of atomic determinism: "An intelligence, which at a given moment knew all of the forces that animate nature, and the respective positions of the beings that compose it, and further possessing the scope to analyze these data, could condense into a single formula the movement of the greater bodies of the universe and that of the least atom: for such an intelligence nothing could be uncertain, and past and future alike would be before its eyes."[12]

The mechanistic program persists today, not in physics, but in biology, psychology, and the social sciences. The difficulty of applying it to particulars in these areas is attributed to the complexity of the Laplacian calculation, not to any inherent flaw in the program itself. Mercer writes: "The sheer magnitude of the reductionist proposal is not an objection to its validity; in fact no one seriously believes it can or will be carried out—indeed it may be beyond us; a demonstration of its theoretical possibility, it is felt, would suffice to establish its truth in principle. The insistence that all biology, psychology, sociology, and history be interpreted deterministically has stimulated an enormous amount of research and continues to influence both private, scientific, and even national policies."[13]

There have been many famous attempts to implement the mechanistic program in various disciplines. In economics Malthus clearly uses a mechanical model taken from physics. He writes that in economics we must "consider man as he really is, inert, sluggish, and averse from labour unless compelled by necessity."[14] This is a paraphrase of Newton's first law of motion: "Every body continues in its state of rest ... unless it is compelled to change that state by forces impressed upon it."[15] Malthus conceives man after the manner of a Newtonian mass, adding, "The first great awakeners of the mind seem to be the wants of the body.... The savage would slumber for ever under his tree unless he were roused from his torpor by the cravings of hunger or the pinchings of cold." Most people, he says, need "stimulants to exertion."[16] The model is from mechanics: Man is an inert mass that must be activated by external forces.

Karl Marx attempts a similar materialistic scheme to account for all human activities: "In the social production which men carry on they enter into definite relations that are indispensable and independent of their will; these relations of production correspond to a definite stage of development of their material powers of production. The sum total of these relations of production constitutes the economic structure of society—the real foundation, on which rise legal and political superstructures and to which correspond definite forms of social consciousness. The mode of production in material life determines the general character of the social, political, and spiritual processes of life. It is not the consciousness of men that determines their existence, but, on the contrary, their social existence determines their consciousness."[17]

Freud models his psychology on mechanistic biology. He begins with an assumption that "mental processes are essentially unconscious,"[18] the unconscious being an uncontrollable mechanical force. It follows that "man is a creature of weak intelligence who is ruled by his instinctual wishes."[19] The mechanical model is evident when Freud speaks of "the premises upon which psychoanalysis rests—the existence of unconscious mental processes, the special mechanisms which they obey, and the instinctive propelling forces which are expressed by them."[20] And he argues that there is an aggression instinct in man by using "biological parallels."[21]

Behaviorism, in attempting to resolve all human behavior to biological factors or conditioning, makes the sharpest denial of man's agency. B. F. Skinner: "A scientific analysis of behavior must, I believe, assume that a person's behavior is controlled by his genetic and environmental histories rather than by the person himself as an initiating, creative agent; but no part of the behavioristic position has raised more violent objections. We cannot prove, of course, that human behavior as a whole is fully determined, but the proposition becomes more plausible as facts accumulate."[22]

Though controversial and unprovable, determinism appears to be the only available scientific approach to man. This leads Skinner to a denial of consciousness in man, a denial even more radical than Freud's: "Mental life and the world in which it is lived are inventions. They have been invented on the analogy of external behavior occurring under external contingencies. Thinking is behaving. The mistake is in allocating the behavior to the mind."[23]

Malthus, Marx, Freud, and Skinner agree on one thing: man is not an agent in his own right, but is acted upon by inner and outer forces beyond his control. In the full rigor of the mechanistic scheme, man cannot act for a conscious purpose.

Zoologist Edward Wilson attempts to implement part of the schema in Figure 1.1 by resolving social behavior to biological principles through what he calls "the new discipline of sociobiology, defined as the systematic study of the biological basis of all forms of social behavior, in all kinds of organisms, including man."[24] Wilson expects in the future that "the mind will be more precisely explained as an epiphenomenon of the neuronal machinery of the brain."[25] He describes how the more basic disciplines will absorb the derivative ones:

"The discipline abuts the antidiscipline; the antidiscipline succeeds in reordering the phenomena of the discipline by reduction to its more fundamental laws; but the new synthesis created in the discipline profoundly alters the antidiscipline as the interaction widens. I suggested that biology, and especially neurobiology and sociobiology, will serve as the antidiscipline of the social sciences. I will now go further and suggest that the scientific materialism embodied in biology will, through a reexamination of the mind and the foundations of social behavior, serve as a kind of antidiscipline to the humanities."[26] Thus, "having cannibalized psychology, the new neurobiology will yield an enduring set of first principles for sociology."[27]

Lastly, ethologist Richard Dawkins, in *The Selfish Gene*, proposes that man is not a cause but an effect, and that life and mind are merely the outcome of genes that "swarm in huge colonies, safe inside gigantic lumbering robots, sealed off from the outside world, communicating with it by tortuous indirect routes, manipulating it by remote control. They are in you and in me; they created us, body and mind; and their preservation is the ultimate rationale for our existence. They have come a long way, those replicators. Now they go by the name of genes, and we are their survival machines."[28]

There have been many other attempts to implement the mechanistic scheme of the sciences, but the above illustrate the program with some of its expectations and consequences. When a biologist

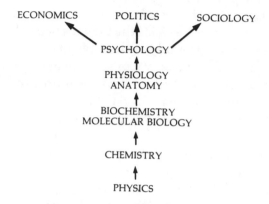

Figure 1.1. The materialistic scheme of the sciences. The sciences are seen as studying various structures and properties of matter. Biology investigates those particular arrangements of matter that cause living phenomena; psychology, politics, and sociology examine the behavior that results from the configurations matter takes in the human brain. All sciences are conceived to be ultimately reducible to physics.

seeks to make his science an extension of physics, it pertains to the physicist to judge whether the attempt is well advised. But physicists long ago passed judgment on the mechanistic program within physics itself. Einstein wrote: "Science did not succeed in carrying out the mechanical program convincingly and today no physicist believes in the possibility of its fulfillment."[29]

Nevertheless the mechanistic program is still pursued in biology. Physicist Henry Margenau: "It is still widely believed that a complete knowledge of physics, chemistry, and biology will ultimately explain the phenomena of life and account for consciousness and the mind. The later are said to 'reduce' to the former when all details are understood. Reductionism is the philosophy that affirms this view. Its simplest form is materialism, the doctrine asserting that all human experience is ultimately understandable in terms relating to physics of matter, more specifically the theories of prequantum physics."[30]

This belief creates an incongruity between contemporary physics and the life sciences. Zoologist William Thorpe: "Physicists are implying that, fundamentally and in its totality, inanimate matter is not mechanical; whereas molecular biologists are saying that whenever matter is recognized as being alive, it is completely mechanical (that is, it is reducible to a rather superficial nineteenth-century type of physical chemistry).... [Physicist David] Bohm issues a timely warning that molecular biologists should consider the fact that, in the nineteenth century, physics theories were far more comprehensively and accurately tested than is possible for current theories of molecular biology. Despite this, classical physics was swept aside and overturned, being retained only as a simplification and approximation valued in a certain limited macroscopical domain. It is not improbable that molecular biology, undoubtedly magnificent though its achievements are, will sooner or later undergo a similar fate."[31]

The mechanistic model in biology does break down at the most basic level. Physicist Freeman Dyson explains: "Every student of molecular biology learns his trade by playing with models built of plastic balls and pegs. These models are an indispensable tool for detailed study of the structure and function of nucleic acids and enzymes. They are, for practical purposes, a useful visualization of the molecules out of which we are built. But from the point of view of a physicist, the models belong to the nineteenth century. Every physicist knows that atoms are not really little hard balls. While the molecular biologists were using these mechanical models to make their spectacular discoveries, physics was moving to a quite different direction.

"For the biologists, every step down in size was a step toward increasingly simple and mechanical behavior. A cell is more mechanical that a bacterium. But twentieth-century physics has shown that further reductions in size have an opposite effect. If we divide a DNA molecule into its component atoms, the atoms behave less mechanically than the molecule. If we divide an atom into nucleus and electrons, the electrons are less mechanical than the atom."[32]

The failure of the mechanistic program in physics ushered in a new world view. Physicist Richard Feynman declares that if you believe that atoms are like little solar systems, "then you are back in 1910."[33] The same profound changes open the possibility today for a new biology. The entire mechanistic scheme rests on Newton and presupposes a certain conception of matter. Newton describes the ultimate particles of matter as "massy, hard, impenetrable, moveable particles of [various] sizes and figures." He assigns the properties of these particles as "extension, hardness, impenetrability and inertia."[34] We note that atoms are imagined as existing in the same manner as large bodies like apples or billiard balls.

The new understanding of matter is dramatically different. The most profound innovations came from quantum physics. Werner Heisenberg: "It is true that quantum theory is only a small sector of atomic physics and atomic physics again is only a very small sector of modern science. Still it is in quantum theory that the most fundamental changes with respect to the concept of reality have taken place, and in quantum theory in its final form the new ideas of atomic physics are concentrated and crystallized."[35] After years of experiment and analysis it was discovered that "it was not possible to formulate the laws of quantum mechanics in a fully consistent way without reference to the consciousness," in the words of Eugene Wigner.[36] This is called the principle of observership. Max Born defines it more completely: "No description of any natural phenomenon in the atomic domain is possible without referring to the observer, not only to his velocity as in relativity, but to all his activities in performing the observation, setting up instruments, and so on."[37]

Dyson amplifies the point: "When we are dealing with things as small as atoms and electrons, the observer or experimenter cannot be excluded from the description of nature.... The laws of subatomic physics cannot even be formulated without some reference to the observer.... The laws leave a place for mind in the description of every molecule."[38]

This new understanding of matter does not lead to universal

skepticism or relativism since the contribution of the observer is significant only at the smallest scale where "observing" the particle necessarily means doing something to it. Weizsäcker explains how we must speak of the atom's indeterminacy: "Hence I may not say: 'The atom is a particle' or 'It is a wave,' but 'It is either particle or wave, and I decide by the disposition of my experiments, in which of the two ways it manifests itself.'"[39] It is crucial to note that the indeterminacy inheres in the atom itself, not just in our understanding of it.

Atoms do not have the kind of existence that we find in apples and billiard balls. Heisenberg notes: "In the experiments about atomic events we have to do with things and facts, with phenomena that are just as real as any phenomena in daily life. But the atoms or the elementary particles themselves are not as real; they form a world of potentialities or possibilities rather than one of things or facts."[40] Potentiality, the key concept, resolves these apparent contradictions in experimental results. The atom, of course, is not at the same time a wave and a particle, but the experimenter can actualize this dual potentiality of the atom in either direction.

Given a particle's intrinsic potency and indeterminacy, it is a mistake to imagine it as a body moving through space. That would confer on it a being it does not have. Margenau offers an example: "The word 'orbit,' still used for simplicity, must of course not be taken literally. It refers to a certain probability distribution for the electron's position which has the spatial shape of a diffuse ring or shell about the proton."[41]

Insistence on a sensible or imaginable model was a great attraction of the old physics and at the same time a serious limitation. Weizsäcker writes: "The physical world view of the nineteenth century...took the forms of our perception, in so far as they correspond to classical physics, as absolute, and therefore thought that a process which was not perceptible to the senses had been understood only after it had been reduced to a model after the pattern of the perceptible. We recognize how this conception, too, derives from the thought of a unified picture of the world. This picture was a grandiose attempt, and it was natural that physics should follow it as far as possible. But the advance of our knowledge has decided against it."[42]

Pagels explains that the new physics is understandable though not picturable: "Grasping quantum reality requires changing from a reality that can be seen and felt to an instrumentally detected reality that can be perceived only intellectually. The world described by the quantum theory does not appeal to our immediate intuition as did the old classical physics. Quantum reality is rational but not visualizable."[43]

The distinction between the picturable and the nonpicturable serves to illustrate the division between the macroscopic and the microscopic worlds. Pagels describes how quantum indeterminacy is negligible in large objects but reigns at the lowest level: "For a flying tennis ball, the uncertainties due to quantum theory are only one part in about ten million billion billion billion (10^{-34}). Hence a tennis ball, to a high degree of accuracy, obeys the deterministic rules of classical physics. Even for a bacterium the effects are only about one part in a billion (10^{-9}), and it really doesn't experience the quantum world either. For atoms in a crystal we are getting down to the quantum world, and the uncertainties are one part in a hundred (10^{-2}). Finally, for electrons moving in an atom the quantum uncertainties completely dominate and we have entered the true quantum world governed by the uncertainty relations and quantum mechanics."[44]

Atomic materialism from Democritus down to the present day has always assumed that the ultimate particles exist in the same manner as large scale objects. Heisenberg comments: "The ontology of materialism rested upon the illusion that the kind of existence, the direct 'actuality' of the world around us, can be extrapolated in the atomic range. This extrapolation is impossible, however."[45] On this impossible extrapolation rests the entire reductionist schema of the sciences outlined above. Consequently, deriving laws for plants, animals, or human beings from the laws of ultimate particles is impossible in principle.

The consequences of quantum theory reaffirm the priority of the everyday world we all experience, as Heisenberg points out: "Previously, physics had attempted to treat processes accessible to our senses as secondary and derived and to explain them in terms of events on an atomic scale. These events were considered to be the 'hidden' objective reality. However, we now recognize that events accessible to our senses (with or without the aid of scientific apparatus) can be considered to be 'objective.'"[46]

With atomic materialism matter was the source of all action and mind was a passive by-product. The new physics reverses this perspective: matter is passive, potential, and incomplete while mind is a source of action. This leads Dyson to declare that "Our consciousness is not just a passive epiphenomenon carried along by chemical events in our brains, but is an active agent."[47]

Built into the new physics is the recognition that the agent has free will. So, far from being "unscientific," acknowledging free choice in man is necessary for the study of matter, and indeed for all experimental science. Weizsäcker points out that "freedom is a pre-requisite of the experiment. Only where my action and thought are not determined by circumstances, urges or customs but by my free choice can I make experiments."[48] Though we may in some cases act automatically and without reflection, there remains an area where free choice operates and this is an ultimate datum.

Thus modern physics asserts that the human mind is an agent, an independent, irreducible source of action. We must therefore revise the schema of the sciences, taking into account this recognition of mind as a cause. Historically, the mechanistic model has been fruitful in the strictly physical sciences such as chemistry, astronomy, and geology. Here the mechanistic program has the greatest area of legitimacy, recognizing, of course, the limits set by relativity and quantum theory.

Concerning man, the new physics implies that mind and choice are irreducible elements. They are real causes of human action and cannot be resolved to material forces. Because man performs actions that matter cannot share in, namely, understanding and willing, the human sciences are autonomous and cannot take their first principles from physics and chemistry. Heisenberg cautions: "If we go beyond biology and include psychology in the discussion, then there can scarcely be any doubt but that the concepts of physics, chemistry, and evolution together will not be sufficient to describe the facts."[49] Man's understanding and will belong to the independent realm of the human sciences: psychology, politics, ethics, and economics.

The revised schema of the sciences shown in Figure 1.2 takes into account the two ultimate realities, matter and mind. All the sciences must incorporate or acknowledge these two realities, albeit in varying degrees. As we have seen, matter cannot be understood

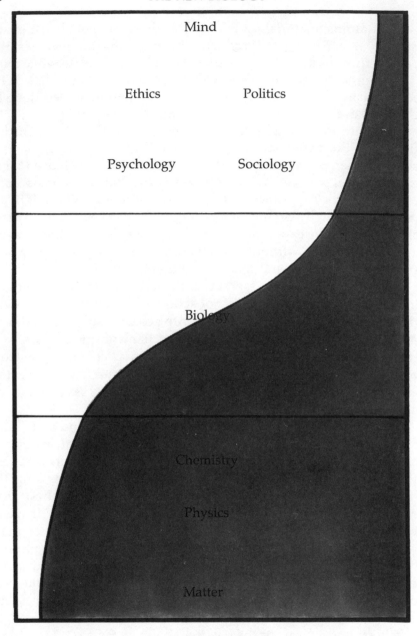

Figure 1.2. The new schema of the sciences. Both ultimate realities, matter and mind, are incorporated in varying degrees into all the sciences. Biology occupies a middle ground between physics and human sciences.

without introducing mind. Hence, physics, the science of matter, must necessarily include mind, not, of course, as part of its subject matter but as an indispensable precondition for certain of its fundamental principles.* And since man is composed of matter and mind, the human sciences must include reference to matter, although their chief subject is the mind and its works.

Biology occupies a middle ground between physics and the human sciences. This suggests that some of the principles of biology are reducible to physics and others are not. So while the skeletal structure of a hummingbird is understandable in terms of physics, its mating behavior is not. The rules of grammar apply to all great works of literature, but one cannot deduce Shakespeare or Milton from them. Nor is grammar alone sufficient to distinguish tragedy from comedy, the epic from the novel and other forms. In a similar way, living things in all their variety cannot be deduced from physics and chemistry, nor are the actions of plants and animals reducible to physical and chemical laws alone, even though they never violate those laws. Biologist François Jacob puts it succinctly: "Biology can neither be reduced to physics, nor do without it."[50] In the revised schema of the sciences, biology will incorporate in some way an equal mix of matter and mind. The exact nature of this mix will be worked out in the chapters that follow.

*For example, we have argued in *The New Story of Science*, chap. 4, not only that mind is central to relativity and quantum theory, but that a Mind is responsible for the origin of matter and that reference to the human mind as a goal of the universe can explain many physical constants, from the subnuclear to the cosmological, that are otherwise inexplicable.

2

Life

Modern biology textbooks are characteristically silent when it comes to the definition of life. James E. Lovelock, an expert on life at low temperatures, when contemplating how to design an instrument to test for life on other planets, was struck by the degree to which biologists avoid the question of what life is:

"After my visits to the Jet Propulsion Laboratories, I had time to do more thinking and reading about the real character of life and how one might recognize it anywhere and in any guise. I expected to discover somewhere in the scientific literature a comprehensive definition of life as a physical process, on which one could base the design of life-detection experiments, but I was surprised to find how little had been written about the nature of life itself.... Data galore had been accumulated on every conceivable aspect of living species, from their outermost to their innermost parts, but in the whole vast encyclopaedia of facts the crux of the matter, life itself, was almost totally ignored. At best, the literature read like a collection of expert reports, as if a group of scientists from another world had taken a television receiver home with them and had reported on it. The chemist said it was made of wood, glass, and metal. The physicist said it radiated heat and light. The engineer said the supporting wheels were too small and in the wrong places for it to run smoothly on a flat surface. But nobody said what it was."[1]

Many life scientists are reluctant to speak about the nature of life in general. Biologist William S. Beck recounts a revealing incident: "I was present at a meeting of one of the most distinguished of biochemistry departments. We were having tea.... The discussion was interrupted by a message from a local philosophical society asking if the department would provide a speaker to participate in a forthcoming symposium on the nature of life. All assembled understood biochemistry and heredity and genes and enzymes, but no one felt he had anything to say about life. The request was politely declined.

"One of the remarkable and frustrating aspects of modern biology is the fact that the roaring tide of specialization has left no one who feels qualified to hold forth on the problem of life itself. Biology has its taxonomists, botanists, bacteriologists, and biochemists, each an expert in his own domain, but no one wants to tackle the single overriding question common to all. Much has been written on the subject, but happily or unhappily, little by working biologists, who are chained to empiricism and not to speculation."[2]

Jacob maintains that "the operational value of the concept of life has continually dwindled and its power of abstraction declined. Biologists no longer study life today. They no longer attempt to define it. Instead they investigate the structure of living systems, their functions, their history."[3] But one wonders how they can do that without some way to recognize which systems are living and which are not.

Some biologists take the further step of denying the possibility of definition. John Kendrew, for example, comments on disputes over whether viruses are living: "These arguments are only important if one supposes that there is a fundamental distinction between living things and nonliving things, some kind of boundary on one side or the other of which everything must be placed. Personally I do not think there is any evidence of such a boundary, or any difference in essence between the living and the nonliving, and I think most molecular biologists would share this view."[4] The limit of this skepticism is reached when the term *life* is rejected outright by some, as in N. W. Pirie's paper "The Meaninglessness of the Terms Life and Living."[5]

A paradox to say the least: biology, by etymology "the science of life," is pursued by persons uncomfortable with the concept of life, who find it impossible to define, if not meaningless, and who would prefer to abandon the notion entirely. If biologists take this skepticism seriously, how are they to identify the objects of their study? Biologist Barry Commoner in the essay "In Defense of Biology" points out the consequences of abandoning the notion of life, when he criticizes a work of popularization. The book, he says, "opens with the following sentence: 'Modern science has all but wiped out the borderline between life and non-life.' Since biology is the science of life, any successful obliteration of the distinction between living things and other forms of matter ends forever the usefulness of biology as a separate science. If the foregoing sentence is even remotely correct, biology is not only under attack; it has been annihilated."[6] How did contemporary biology get itself into such a bizarre state? History reveals the answer.

The Machine Model

The modern conception of life and the living thing are rooted in Cartesian philosophy. Descartes begins his philosophy by dividing the universe into two irreconcilable categories, matter and mind. The realm of matter, in which he places both plants and animals, acts according to rigid, mechanical laws. "The laws of Mechanics ... are identical with those of Nature."[7] Thus he introduces the machine model to biology: "Since art is the imitator of nature, and since man is capable of fabricating various automata in which there is motion without any cogitation, it seems reasonable that nature should produce her own automata, far more perfect in their workmanship, to wit all the brutes." Descartes even speaks of "the machine of the human body."[8]

Since Descartes' day the machine model has endured, although it has taken many different forms. Bertalanffy briefly traces the history of some of the forms: "Depending on the state of the art, the model found different interpretations. When in the 17th century Descartes introduced the concept of the animal as a machine, only *mechanical machines* existed. Hence the animal was a sort of complicated clockwork. ... Later on the steam engine and thermodynamics were introduced, which led to the organism being conceived as a *heat engine*, a fact to which we owe the calculation of calories, for example. As it turned out, however, the organism is not a heat engine, transforming the energy of fuel first into heat and then into mechanical energy. It rather is a *chemical-dynamic* machine, directly transforming the chemical energy of fuel into effective work, a fact on which, for example, the theory of muscle-contraction is based. Lately, self-regulating machines came to the fore, such as the thermostat, missiles aiming at a target and the servomechanisms of modern technology. In parallel, the organism became a *cybernetic machine*. The most recent development are *molecular machines*."[9]

The tradition is still strong to this day, especially among molecular biologists. Jacques Monod, for example, explicitly credits Descartes and declares, "Anything can be reduced to simple, obvious, mechanical interactions. The cell is a machine; the animal is a machine; man is a machine."[10]

The similarities between machines and living things are apparent: both organisms and machines are organized wholes that use physical and chemical laws to accomplish certain tasks. But the similarities are superficial and mask profound differences. Jacob points out some of the contrasts: "In a watch, each part is the instrument of movement of the other parts, but a wheel is never the efficient cause that produces another wheel. A part exists *for* another but not *by* another. The cause that produces wheels is not to be found in the nature of wheels, but outside them, in a being capable of putting his ideas into effect. A watch cannot produce parts, or rectify the movement itself when it is out of order. An organized being is, therefore, not simply a machine, since a machine has only a force of movement, while the organism contains in itself a force of formation and regulation that it communicates to the material of which it is made."[11]

No machine rebuilds its own parts. All organisms, however, constantly renew their tissues and cells right down to the molecules. A dramatic illustration is the transformation of a caterpillar into a butterfly or moth. Entomologist Peter Farb describes the frenzy of activity that goes on in the pupa or chrysalis: "Lifeless as they may seem, pupae are engaged in furious rearrangement of their tissues. Among moths, the extra legs along the caterpillar's abdomen are lost. Where the stumpy legs of the thorax had been, the long, slender legs of the adult now develop. Mouth parts change from the chewing to the sucking type. The four wings develop, as do reproductive organs. Most of the muscular system is transformed. At certain stages during the breakdown of old structures and the build-up of new, the pupa's contents may be largely liquid."[12]

Not only is the adult butterfly radically different in appearance with its dozen or more new organs, it also has different habits of behavior and often lives in a different environment than the larva. All these astounding changes occur in the pupa where the larva degenerates to a fluid and devours itself by using phagocytes, rapidly rebuilding a new organism. It takes only twelve days for a monarch caterpillar to transform itself into a butterfly able to fly twenty miles per hour. And the material in one caterpillar is just

Figure 2.1. Complete metamorphosis of the painted lady butterfly. These four forms of the same individual insect are so diverse that the adult butterfly seems almost a different species from the caterpillar. The chrysalis is like a second egg, yielding a winged adult completely unlike the sluggish, segmented larva, both in habits and diet. In contrast to the transformation of a caterpillar into a butterfly, no machine rebuilds it own parts.

enough to make one butterfly. (See Figure 2.1.) No machine approaches such a performance.

Furthermore, as Jacob mentioned, machines do not repair themselves. All living things, however, are capable of self-repair to some degree, as when they heal from minor injuries without external aid. Many animals can grow new body parts to replace lost or damaged ones. Some have more amazing powers: cut a starfish or a flatworm in half, and each part generates a whole new organism. What machine can duplicate such a feat? Plants, of course, have this power to the fullest degree. Biologist Edmund Sinnott: "In plants, even more than in animals, pieces of tissue or even single cells, if isolated from the rest of the individual, show an ability to restore the whole again. The power of cuttings to strike root has been used since the dawn of horticulture to produce new plants abundantly from old ones."[13]

Another difference is that machines do not grow from seeds or eggs but are composed of unchanging parts, assembled from the outside. Consequently, when a machine begins to function it already has all its parts. Not so the living thing. From its beginning it grows, not only in size but with an increasing differentiation of parts, organs, and new functions. Bertalanffy writes: "Of all the wonders which life presents to us in such plenty, that of development is surely the greatest. Let us recall what it means: on the one hand we have this little drop of jelly which, as a fertilized ovum, represents the germ of an organism; on the other is the wonderful edifice of the complete living creature, with its myriads of cells, its endlessly complicated organs, characters, and instincts."[14]

Hair, teeth, nails, bones, fat, blood, skin, muscles, sense organs, digestive system, nervous system, circulatory system, endocrine system—an astonishing variety of new equipment arises from the tiny, undifferentiated, fertilized ovum of an animal, each tissue, each organ, and each system made of different materials, but all exquisitely coordinated and suited to their sundry tasks! No machine even remotely imitates the growth and development of the humblest organism. Plants exhibit the same powers to no less a degree than animals. Sinnott describes the development of a flower:

"Around the tip of the minute dome that is to give rise to a flower bud appear circles of knob-like outgrowths such as those which make a leaf. The outer ones develop into sepals, the next into petals, the next into stamens and in the centre appear the ovary and its parts. In many species, as the bud enlarges, these various floral structures are packed and folded and twisted tightly together, much like the tissue of a parachute but in a far more complex fashion. In the bud of an iris, just before it opens, one finds the three petals packed closely in a counterclockwise spiral, the three stamens and the three stigma lobes tucked inside them and the whole firmly enclosed by the sepals. When the bud opens all these parts unwrap themselves and open out into the iris blossom. The opening of an umbrella is simplicity compared to this. How these packed and folded parts grow from their minute beginnings so precisely that in the opening of the leaf and flower nothing is missing or is wrongly placed is one of the wonders of development."[15]

Yet another difference: machines have only a unity of order, not a unity of substance. A horse, through growth, determines its *own* shape and structure; consequently, its organs, tissues, and cells are identifiably horse organs, horse tissues, and horse cells. The horse is characteristically horse right down to its macromolecules, with its own distinctive DNA, hemoglobin, enzymes, and proteins. Given a cell, a good cytologist would be able to identify what organism it came from and even what function it performed. But an isolated ball bearing or length of copper wire, since they are not characteristic of any particular kind of machine, would offer an engineer no clue as to their origin. Every part of the living being, down to its macromolecules, bears the signature of its owner.

Biologist J. S. Haldane observes that the unity of structure in living things presupposes a unity of metabolic functions: "The living structure is evidently organized: that is to say every part of it bears a definite relation to every other part. As, however, the structure is the outcome of metabolic activity, it follows that the metabolic activity of the living body is also organized, every aspect of it bearing a definite relation to every other aspect. That this is actually so has become more and more clear with the advance of physiology, particularly in recent times."[16]

Thus all the parts of the living body, even at the molecular level, cooperate in the organism's actions. Biologist A. I. Oparin offers the striking example of animal movement: "In the muscles of the animal carrying out this movement, the protein fibriles are orientated in a particular way relative to one another. Such a structure, however, cannot be likened in any way to that of a machine. In a machine the structural elements do not play any part whatsoever in the chemical transformation of the energy source. If the component parts of the machine were themselves to undergo chemical transformation during their work, this would, of course, lead quickly to the destruction of the whole mechanism. On the other hand, the elements of construction of the living body, the protein fibriles in this case, themselves take a direct part in the metabolic reactions which serve as the source of that energy which is transformed into a mechanical movement."[17] (See Figure 2.2.)

In taking food, the living thing again gives evidence of its profound unity. "The organism maintains its form, structure and chemical composition unchanged while its material is continually changing," writes Oparin.[18] Nutrition requires the breakdown of one substance and the buildup of another. The organism has the amazing ability to convert external matter into its own substance without turning into the alien substance. Lions feeding on zebra do not become zebralike. On the contrary, the food becomes the organism. Plants even manufacture their own substance from inorganic materials. The unity the organism maintains despite the constant flux of incoming nutrients and outgoing waste products is not just an equilibrium of physical and chemical forces. It costs the organism a continual expenditure of energy to resist the relentless tendency to disorganization. This differs from nonliving flowing systems such as rivers, storms, or fires. Oparin explains: "The peculiarity which distinguishes life qualitatively from all other forms of motion of matter (and in particular from inorganic flowing systems) is that, in the living body, the many tens and hundreds of thousands of individual chemical reactions, which, in their sum, make up the metabolism, are not only strictly co-ordinated in time and space, not merely co-operating harmoniously in a single sequence of self-renewal, but the whole of this sequence is directed in an orderly way towards the continual self-preservation and self-reproduction of the living body as a whole."[19] A machine converts its fuel into heat, motion, and chemical by-products, but not into its own substance as happens in the organism.

Oparin also points out the unusual way the living body exploits the laws of physics and chemistry in generating its own energy: "If the transformation of energy took place in the same way in

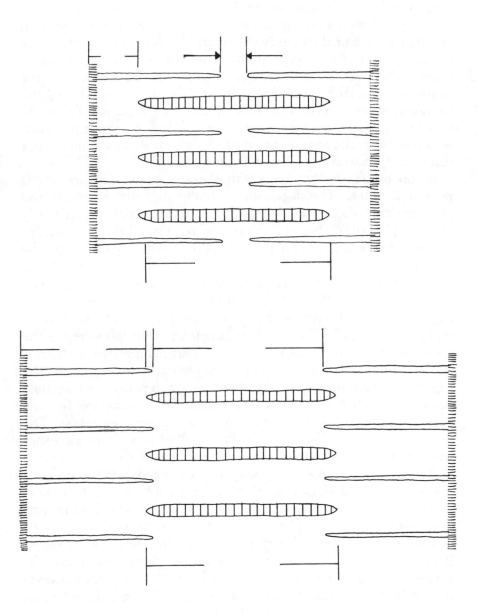

Figure 2.2. These schematic diagrams show protein fibriles in muscle tissue before and after contraction. The fibriles take part in the metabolic reactions that produce the energy for mechanical movement. If the component parts of a machine were to undergo chemical transformation during their work, it would destroy the machine.

organisms as it does in heat engines, then, at temperatures at which living things can exist, the coefficient of their useful activity would fall to an insignificant fraction of one percent. It is, in fact, amazingly high, considerably higher than that obtained in present-day engines. The explanation of this is that the oxidation of sugar, or any other respiratory fuel, in the organism takes place not as a single chemical act, but by a series of individual reactions co-ordinated in time.

"If the oxidation of organic materials in the organism took place suddenly, then the living body would be unable to make rational use of all the energy set free in this way, especially if it was given off in the form of heat. In the oxidation of only 1 mole (180 grams) of sugar about 700 kcal. are liberated. The instantaneous liberation of this amount of energy would be associated with a sharp rise in temperature, the denaturation of proteins and the destruction of the living body. This same energy effect, which is brought about by the organism under ordinary conditions of low temperature, depends on the fact that in the process of biological oxidation, sugar is not converted into carbon dioxide and water suddenly, but slowly, by stages. A process of this sort not only gives the possibility of surmounting the energy activation at ordinary temperatures, it also enables the living body to make rational use of the energy which is gradually set free. Thus, the more highly organised the metabolism, i.e., the better the co-ordination between the separate reactions comprising it, the higher the coefficient of useful activity."[20]

At normal temperatures many ordinary chemical reactions take place much too slowly to maintain life processes. But if to speed up the reactions the organism were heated, cell tissues would be damaged. And such heat production would be far too costly for the organism. The answer to this problem is enzymes, protein catalysts produced by the organism itself. They speed up reactions enormously even at low temperatures. For example, a by-product of many necessary metabolic steps in a cell is hydrogen peroxide (H_2O_2), a toxin that, if not decomposed quickly, will oxidize important organic compounds in the cell. Without a catalyst present, 1 mole (34 grams) of hydrogen peroxide requires 44,800 calories of heat to decompose. If platinum is present in the solution, it will need only 11,700 calories to decompose. But with the enzyme *catalase* present, the same quantity of hydrogen peroxide decomposes using less than 2,000 calories. The average cell manufactures about 2,000 different enzymes, each of which is specific for catalyzing one particular chemical reaction. Thus, the cell produces chemical tools, tailor-made for its own needs.

Another fundamental difference between organism and machine is that organisms are natural things, whereas machines are artificial things; no natural science studies watches, locomotives, or dishwashers. Artifacts are man-made and assembled from without. Organisms are made by nature and develop from within. Monod speaks of the "radical difference between any artifact, however highly perfected, and a living being." He explains:

"An artifact (whether a honeycomb, a dam built by beavers, a paleolithic hatchet, or a spacecraft) results from the application to the materials constituting it of forces *exterior* to the object itself. . . . A living being's structure results from a totally different process, in that it owes almost nothing to the action of outside forces, but everything, from its overall shape down to its tiniest detail, to 'morphogenetic' interactions with the object itself. It is thus a structure giving proof of an autonomous determinism: precise, rigorous, implying a virtually total 'freedom' with respect to outside agents or conditions—which are capable, to be sure, of impeding this development, but not of governing or guiding it, not of prescribing its organizational scheme to the living object."[21]

External conditions have only an indirect effect on the living being. A seedling may wilt in excessive heat or fail to grow normally in the absence of certain nutrients, but no external condition directs the pattern of its growth. Whether it produces a dandelion or a rose is determined from within.

The division of the artificial and the natural also distinguishes living beings from machines designed to mimic life functions. Oparin makes the point well: "The actual principles of construction of any machine now in existence reflect the character of the person who made it, his intellectual and technological level, his aims and his methods of solving the problems in front of him.

"This also applies fully to the various 'cybernetic toys' which are now being made, the point of which is simply to imitate living things, such as Grey Walter's 'tortoise,' Shannon's 'mouse,' Ducrocq's 'fox' and Ashby's 'homeostat,' constructions which have been wittily described by Grey Walter as 'machines which can serve no useful purpose.'"[22]

A further difference is that the parts of a machine can be completely separated, then reassembled, so that the machine again runs normally. But the organs of an animal cannot be separated without inducing irreversible death. Georges Cuvier, the father of paleontology, once remarked, "The machines that are the subject of our researches cannot be dismantled without being destroyed."[23] Biologist J. Shaxel agrees: "Living processes and living materials as such simply do not exist save as parts of single whole organisms."[24]

The cell, too, differs radically from any machine, first by incessant activity. A machine can be turned off indefinitely without damage. Lacking power, none of its parts will move on their own. But even a hibernating animal must continue to metabolize stored nutrients. If it stops doing so, it dies. As long as it lives, the engine must always be running, as it were. Animals and plants that are frozen and temporarily cease all metabolism ought to be considered only potentially alive when in such a state. Biologist Paul Weiss remarks, "A living system that does not behave is dead; life is process, not substance."[25]

Oparin agrees: "The organisation of life is fundamentally dependent on a regular sequence of metabolic reactions and the form and structure of living bodies are flowing in nature. For this reason organisms can only exist for any length of time as a result of the continuous accomplishment of chemical transformations, which constitute the essence of living, and the cessation of which would lead to the disruption of the living system and the death of the organism."[26] Weiss points out the essential mobility of life is not conveyed by photographs or diagrams of the cell:

"It is impossible to convey a reasonably accurate conception of a living cell by illustrations on a printed page or by museum models, even when supplemented by verbal description. As a matter of fact, the frozen immobility of those text book illustrations has led to such abstruse misconceptions of a living cell that any portrayal would have to dwell more on what the actual cell is not, than on what it is.... What we perceive as static form is comparable to a single still frame taken out of a motion picture film. Taken all by itself, a static picture fails to reveal whether it portrays a momentary state of an on-going process or a permanent terminal condition. Unless this ambiguity is constantly borne in mind, one runs the risk of mistaking the static picture of the cell for evidence of a mosaic of well-consolidated structures."[27]

The average cell carries out hundreds of chemical reactions every second and can reproduce itself every twenty minutes or so. Yet all this occurs on such a tiny scale: over 500 bacteria could fit into the area occupied by the period at the end of this sentence. Jacob marvels at the minute laboratory of the bacterial cell, which "carries out some two thousand distinct reactions with incomparable skill, in the smallest space imaginable. These two thousand reactions diverge and converge at top speed, without ever becoming tangled, and produce exactly the quantity and quality of molecular species required for growth and reproduction, with a yield close to one hundred percent."[28]

In light of this remarkable activity of every cell in a living body we must conclude with biologist Jakob von Uexküll that "the cell is not a machine, but a machinist."[29] Speaking of an illustration of a cell, Weiss compares and then contrasts the cell with a factory:

"Now, to break down in your minds the illusion of fixity evoked by this fixed specimen, let me point out that practically all you see in this picture is fleeting; and that goes even more so for what you do not see. A cell works like a big industry, which manufactures different products at different sites, ships them around to assembly plants, where they are combined into half-finished or finished products, to be eventually, with or without storage in intermediate facilities, either used up in the household of that particular cell or else extruded for export to other cells or waste disposal. Modern research in molecular and cellular biology has succeeded in assigning to the various structures seen in the picture specific functional tasks in this intricate, but integrated, industrial operation. There is a major flaw, however, in the analogy between a cell and a man-made factory. While in the latter, both building and machinery are permanent fixtures, established once and for all, many of the corresponding sub-units in the system of the cell are of ephemeral existence in the sense that they are continuously or periodically disassembled and rebuilt, yet always each according to its kind and standard pattern. In contrast to a machine, the cell interior is heaving and churning all the time; the positions of granules or other details in the picture, therefore, denote just momentary way stations, and the different shapes of sacs or tubules signify only the degree of their filling at the moment. The only thing that remains predictable amidst the erratic stirring of the molecular population of the cytoplasm and its substructures is the overall pattern of dynamics which keeps the component activities in definable bounds of orderly restraints. These bounds again are not to be viewed as mechanically fixed structures, but as 'boundary conditions' set by the dynamics of the system as a whole."[30]

Jacob also acknowledges similarities between cell and factory but insists even more on the fundamental differences: "The bacterial cell is obviously best described by the model of a miniaturized chemical factory. Factory and bacterium only function by means of energy received from the exterior. Both transform the raw material taken from the medium by a series of operations into finished products. Both excrete waste products into their surroundings." But he adds, "If the bacterial cell is to be considered as a factory, it must be a factory of a special kind. The products of human technology are totally different from the machines that produce them, and therefore totally different from the factory itself. The bacterial cell, on the other hand, makes its own constituents; the ultimate product is identical with itself. The factory produces; the cell reproduces."[31]

All the properties of the organism we have discussed so far—its astonishing unity, its capacity to build its own parts, its increasing differentiation through time, its power of self-repair and self-regeneration, its ability to transform other materials into itself, its natural action from within, and its incessant activity—all these not only distinguish the living being from the machine but also demonstrate its uniqueness amid the whole of nature. "For these features we have no analogue in inorganic systems," writes Bertalanffy.[32] The organism is *sui generis*, in a class by itself. If so, then with Bertalanffy we must conclude that "mechanistic modes of explanation are in principle unsuitable for dealing with certain features of the organic; and it is just these features which make up the essential peculiarities of organisms."[33]

The model of the machine, if it excludes differences, will constitute an obstacle to understanding life. Oparin recalls the history of mechanism in biology: "For a number of years the overriding wish to identify the organism with a mechanism forced many scientists to ignore all the increasing factual evidence and look for some rigid, unchanging, static structures in the living body so that these structures themselves might be regarded as the specific bearers of life."[34]

If we insist on considering the organism a machine, then we will never be able to discover what is peculiar to living things because clearly machines, no matter how complex, are not alive. The same holds for molecules. Oparin: "Life is a property of any organism, from the highest to the lowest, but it does not exist in inorganic natural objects, no matter how complicated their structure may be."[35] The embarrassment and skepticism regarding the notion of life and the inability to define it that we saw at the beginning of this chapter follow ineluctably from the insistence on the machine model for living things.

From these contrasts of organism and machine, it is not difficult to gather a definition. Life is the capacity for self-motion. Nutrition and growth, found in all living things, are both self-initiated, self-directed changes. As we have seen, no machine can initiate and direct such changes in itself. Higher organisms, of course, can move themselves in higher and more perfect ways than mere nutrition and growth, for example, the capacity for voluntary local movement directed by sense awareness that we see in the higher animals. But all living things, and only living things, share the capacity for some kind of self-movement.

This does not mean that searching for mechanisms is always mistaken. Bertalanffy: "The refutation of the machine theory by no means excludes *every* physico-chemical explanation of life phenomena."[36] An animal's heart resembles a pump in many respects, and it is useful to examine how it meets the requirements of physics, respecting all the laws for flowing liquids. The heart differs, however, from any merely mechanical pump because it grows, repairs itself, and adjusts to the animal's needs. In a word, it is alive. No harm results from calling the animal a "machine," or the oak tree an "edifice," as long as we realize we are using a metaphor. The machine metaphor can be useful for certain purposes provided we never mistake the metaphor for the thing.

Nor does recognizing the inadequacy of this metaphor force one into vitalism. It is not necessary to postulate a separate, nonmaterial entity that directs the plant's vital operations. The plant does the directing. The activities of an organism, at least the nonconscious activities, are essentially matter in motion. Therefore, to seek a natural principle for their explanation is reasonable. Jacob argues that "The two kinds of synthesis carried out by the living cell—

successive rearrangements and polymerization—are not fundamentally different from those carried out in the laboratory by the
organic chemist. There is no particular mystery about transformations that occur in the cell; no unknown material; no reaction or
chemical bond that appears beyond the reach of laboratory techniques."[37]

Oddly enough, the same faulty assumption lies behind both
mechanism and vitalism. Mechanism argues that since the living
thing is a body, then it must be a machine; vitalism argues that since
the organism is not a machine, it must be run by some nonbodily
principle. Both sides equate body with machine. This notion derives
from seventeenth-century physics, wherein the whole of nature
was considered a vast machine. But mechanism's monopoly on
scientific explanation has been overthrown by twentieth-century
physics. So it makes sense to look to modern physics for new
inspiration as to how life fits into the rest of nature.

The Uniqueness of Organic Form

Twentieth-century physics has given us a radically new picture of
matter. Physicist Erwin Schrödinger describes the former picture
that dominated science for centuries and still dominates the popular
imagination:

"Democritus and all who followed on his path up to the end of the
nineteenth century, though they had never traced the effect of an
individual atom (and probably did not hope ever to be able to), were
yet convinced that the atoms *are* individuals, identifiable, small
bodies just like the coarse palpable objects in our environment. It
seems almost ludicrous that precisely in the same years or decades
which let us succeed in tracing single, individual atoms and particles,
and that in various ways, we have yet been compelled to dismiss the
idea that such a particle is an individual entity which in principle
retains its 'sameness' for ever."[38]

As we saw in Chapter 1, matter at the particle stage is spoken of in
modern physics in terms of probability waves and potentialities, not
rigid, mechanical structures. Speaking of atoms and small molecules, Schrödinger offers this contrast: "The *old* idea about them was
that their individuality was based on the identity of matter in
them.... The *new* idea is that what is permanent in these ultimate
particles or small aggregates is their shape and organization."[39]

Form dominates matter, giving it actuality, completing it and making it a specific kind of thing with definite properties. Heisenberg speaks of the simplest forms that matter can acquire: "Experiments have shown the complete mutability of matter. All elementary particles can, at sufficiently high energies, be transmuted into other particles, or they can simply be created from kinetic energy and can be annihilated into energy, for instance into radiation. Therefore, we have here actually the final proof for the unity of matter. All the elementary particles are made of the same substance, which we may call energy or universal matter; they are just different *forms* in which matter can appear.

"If we compare this situation with the Aristotelian concepts of matter and form, we can say that the matter of Aristotle, which is mere 'potentia,' should be compared to our concept of energy, which gets into 'actuality' by means of form, when the elementary particle is created.

"Modern physics is of course not satisfied with only qualitative description of the fundamental structure of matter; it must try on the basis of careful experimental investigations to get a mathematical formulation of those natural laws that determine the 'forms' of matter, the elementary particles and their forces."[40]

New forms predominate at each level of organization in nature. At the chemical level, for instance, we know that water is not a mere mixture or aggregate of hydrogen and oxygen gases. Such a mixture would be highly explosive whereas water is not—it puts out fires. The mere mixture of the two gases in a flask would admit of mechanical separation. Not so with water. Water, then, is not an aggregate of two substances; it has a new unity of its own. The independent unities of hydrogen and oxygen are sacrificed and absorbed into the higher level of water's form. This is not a mere accidental rearrangement of the old parts but a brand new substance. Strictly speaking, the elements hydrogen and oxygen are not *actual* parts of water. They are there only potentially in the water and can be recovered actually only by breaking down, that is by destroying, the water, just as the hydrogen and the oxygen are lost when water is generated. The same holds for any other chemical compound as opposed to a mixture. In sodium chloride both the sodium and the chlorine give up their characteristic properties in forming a new unity. The physical properties of NaCl differ from those of sodium and chlorine.

What are commonly considered the "parts" of compounds, then, are not parts in the way that bricks are parts of a building, where each retains its own individuality and properties and undergoes no transformation of substance. The unity of a chemical compound is not the unity of a heap. On the contrary, the form induced into the transformed parts is the source of a new unity of substance.

Heisenberg spoke of the "natural laws that determine the 'forms' of matter."[41] Chemistry has demonstrated that not just any elements have the potential to take on the form of a given compound. Water cannot be generated from the union of oxygen with nitrogen. Further, the right materials do not combine in just any proportion to produce the new substance. Water is always formed from twice as much hydrogen by volume as oxygen. These elements fused in equal portions produce not water but hydrogen peroxide.

Furthermore, even the right ingredients, united in the right proportions, do not generate a substance unless combined in the right order. Two or more substances may have identical chemical compositions but different arrangements of parts. Such substances, called isomers from the Greek roots *iso* and *meron*, meaning "equal part," have different physical, chemical, and biological properties. For example, two chemical substances have the molecular formula C_2H_6O. One is ethyl alcohol, the familiar intoxicant, which is a liquid that boils at 78.5°C. The other is dimethyl ether, a poisonous gas, with a boiling point of -23°C. It is manufactured industrially for use as a refrigerant. If one studies the models in Figure 2.3, it soon becomes evident that the given ingredients can be combined in two and only two ways that respect the laws of chemical valence requiring four bonds for carbon, two for oxygen, and one for hydrogen. Chemists Harold Hart and Robert Schuetz comment: "Corresponding to these two possible arrangements, two and only two substances have been found with the formula C_2H_6O. One is ethyl alcohol (grain alcohol), a liquid at ordinary room temperature; the other is dimethyl ether, a gas. Because of the different arrangement of the atoms within the molecules, these compounds exhibit different physical and chemical properties. The *structural* formulas A and B [see Figure 2.3] tell us that these substances are different, whereas the molecular formula C_2H_6O does not."[42]

Isomers clearly illustrate that the structure or form is primarily responsible for a substance's identity, not the material components.

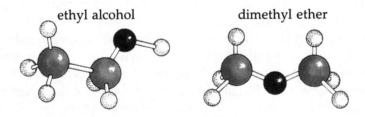

A B

Structural Formulae

CH_3 CH_2 OH CH_3 O CH_3

Abbreviated Chemical Formulae

ethyl alcohol   dimethyl ether

Three-Dimensional Models

Figure 2.3. Ethyl alcohol and dimethyl ether. Two carbon atoms, six hydrogens, and one oxygen can be combined in two and only two ways according to chemical valence laws. The result is two compounds with the same molecular formula (C_2H_6O) but with different structures and different properties. The structure of form is primarily responsible for a substance's identity, not the material components.

Incidentally, we must not forget the difference between the models and the compounds that they help us think about. For while the balls and pegs are rearranged without any change in the units, the atoms are restructured only by being themselves transformed. If each atom retained its individuality, no amount of rearranging would generate a new substance. However useful these models are for visualizing molecules, they mislead if taken literally. Recall physicist Freeman Dyson's admonition given in Chapter 1: "From the point of view of the physicist, the models belong to the nineteenth century. Every physicist knows that atoms are not really little hard balls."[43]

The same relations of potential and actual operate at the subatomic level when particles unite to form the elements. A hydrogen atom is not simply a proton and an electron. It is a new unity, a new form, imposed on the proton and electron and into which they lose their separate identities. Hydrogen has different properties from either the proton or the electron. A sign of this new unity is that a hydrogen atom has less mass than the combined masses of one electron and one proton. So to change hydrogen into a proton and an electron, energy is required. Such a process actualizes the particles that are potentially in the hydrogen atom.

Many other examples might be given, but these are adequate to show that the source of unity, novelty, and agency at every level is *form*. This lesson from physics and chemistry resolves a long-standing debate in biology between reductionists and emergentists. Reductionism, which we discussed in Chapter 1, expects to deduce all phenomena including life and man, from the laws that govern elementary particles. Those who call themselves emergentists consider this expectation naive and a gross oversimplification. Ernst Mayr argues: "Attempts at a 'reduction' of purely biological phenomena or concepts to laws of the physical sciences has rarely, if ever, led to any advance in our understanding. Reduction is at best a vacuous, but more often a thoroughly misleading and futile, approach.... Systems almost always have the peculiarity that the characteristics of the whole cannot (not even in theory) be deduced from the most complete knowledge of the components, taken separately or in other partial combinations. This appearance of new characteristics in wholes has been designated *emergence*."[44] Mayr offers instances of irreducibly biological phenomena: "Species, competition, territory, migration, and hibernation are examples of organismic phenomena for which a purely physical description is at best incomplete and usually biologically irrelevant."[45] Medawar agrees: "There is simply no sense in saying that politico-sociological concepts like electoral reform and the foreign exchange deficit can be 'interpreted in terms of biology,' and it is hardly less than idiotic to say that they can be interpreted in terms of physics and chemistry, though if the axiom of reducibility were true it would follow that they were so."[46]

Positively stated, emergentism wishes to acknowledge the genuine novelty in nature at each successive level of organization, to affirm that there are real distinctions between things, and to respect the hierarchy of natural beings. Medawar puts it simply: "Each higher-level subject contains ideas and conceptions peculiar to itself. These are the 'emergent' properties."[47] Life, sensation, and mind are considered to be among these.

But what, then, is the *source* of the new being? If the complex is explained in terms of the simple, then this is reductionism. If the properties of the higher level have no explanation, then they are irrational and without cause. Mayr himself admits that "emergence is a descriptive notion which, particularly in more complex systems, seems to resist analysis."[48]

The reductionist maintains that since a connection or explanation exists between levels, nothing really new can emerge at higher levels. The emergentist holds that since real novelty exists, there can be no connection with what came before. The former destroys the distinction of things; the latter, their intelligibility.

But both schools assume a false model of how the levels are related. They assume that natural entities are nothing but aggregates of the smallest particles, which themselves are totally actual. If, however, we understand the components at each level to be potential, not actual, we can retain both novelty and rationality. The higher form is new and different, not a mixture or a compounding of lower forms, but is *understandable* in terms of them (at least up to the level of the plant). The higher form actualizes the potentiality of lower forms. For example, the form of sodium chloride can be understood by referring to the form of sodium and the form of chlorine. It does not have the same properties that they do, but its properties are based on theirs and are developments of them at a new level. Thus, the emergence of table salt from the union of

sodium and chlorine is neither hollow nor irrational. The salt is a
genuinely novel substance and yet eminently intelligible. Likewise,
the form of sodium is intelligible in terms of the potentialities of
protons, neutrons, and electrons. A good atomic physicist can tell
you why sodium has the physical and chemical properties it exhibits.
Feynman observes that "fundamental theoretical chemistry is really
physics."[49] This in no way diminishes the uniqueness of sodium or
salt.

These principles are readily applied to living things. The organism
is best understood if seen as the culmination of a long hierarchy of
natural forms. In the series from subatomic particles to elements, to
molecules, to compounds and minerals, to viruses, to organisms, we
notice as we proceed from small to large there arises more actuality,
more stability, more perfect agency, and greater variety of kinds.

For example, only six stable subatomic particles exist: the photon,
the proton, the electron, the neutron, and two kinds of neutrinos.*
These do not grow or reproduce. They do not have an "inside," and
like all nonliving things, they act only when they are acted upon
from without. Their sphere of agency is severely limited though
within it great power is available. Stars exploit this power source
and through thermonuclear combustion produce light and heat
with heavy elements as by-products. Astronomers speak of the "life
cycle" of stars, but a star's "life" is strictly determined by the amount
of matter it begins with. A cloud of hydrogen with a mass of one-
twentieth or less of the sun's mass coheres but its internal gravity is
too weak to generate pressures sufficient to trigger thermonuclear
combustion. This results in an "almost star" like the planet Jupiter
which generates more energy than it receives from the sun but falls
short of the pressures needed to set off nuclear reactions. A star
cannot truly grow or reproduce itself It is more an aggregate than a
unity.

The interaction of subatomic particles produces the nearly
hundred naturally occurring elements which exhibit far more
variety and agency than the proton, electron, neutron, or neutrino.
At a higher level of organization we find compounds, organic
molecules, and minerals, each with its own special properties and

*Strictly speaking, the free neutron is not stable; its mean lifetime is about sixteen
minutes.

powers. On the large scale, quantum uncertainty disappears, hence, more stability.

By virtue of its structure, a complex organic molecule has an "inside" of sorts, but it cannot interact with anything without losing its identity. At this level a wider range of activity is possible but the molecule itself does not have the needed equipment to develop what is available. As Oparin remarks: "Any organic substance can react in very many different ways, it has tremendous chemical possibilities, but outside the living body it is extremely 'lazy' or slow about exploiting these possibilities."[50]

Crystals increase in size by mere addition from the outside, involving no transformation of substance as in plant and animal growth. Jacob comments on the attempt to account for organic functions by analogy to crystals: "This is an old analogy, already invoked more than two centuries ago to explain the shape, growth and reproduction of organized beings. It had been necessary to abandon this comparison, however, once the structure of a perfect crystalline solid was brought to light. Such a crystal requires the same pattern to be repeated in three dimensions. It is a regular arrangement of atoms from the centre to the surface. Being inaccessible, the interior of the structure has no function. The crystal can develop only by the addition of components to its surface. It does not reproduce."[51]

Moreover, as in the "growth" of a fire, no internal principle limits the increase in crystals. Crystallographer Elizabeth Wood writes: "Crystals are made up of exceedingly small structural units, repeated, side by side, indefinitely in all directions. A perfect crystal is a *homogeneous* body. Any small bit of it is just like every other small bit of it."[52] If there is no difference of parts in a crystal, then clearly one part cannot act on another. Finally, because crystals form from the outside their structures are limited in number, dictated by geometry. Mathematics states that there are only thirty-two possible classes of crystal symmetry. The 230 types of crystal structures that occur in nature all fall into one of them.

Viruses represent a much higher level of organization. About a thousand times larger than a protein molecule, the average virus is visible only through the techniques of electron microscopy. Viruses prefigure certain life functions and are considered by some to be rudimentary living things. Closer inspection, however, indicates otherwise. Viruses carry out no true life activities. Linus Pauling notes:

"After the particles are formed they do not grow. They do not ingest food nor carry on any metabolic processes. So far as can be told by use of the electron microscope and by other methods of investigation, the individual particles of the virus are identical with one another, and show no change with time—there is no phenomenon of aging, of growing old. The virus particles seem to have no means of locomotion, and seem not to respond to external stimuli in the way that large living organisms do."[53] Viruses have no cell membrane to receive materials selectively from without, no way to assimilate food, and no way to produce energy—all functions of even the simplest cell. Hence, the virus is closed in on itself.

Pauling mentions reproduction as the only living activity viruses appear to perform. But here also it is not genuine reproduction as found in animals and plants where the parent, without self-destruction, produces another being like itself, either by changing itself as when a paramecium divides into two, or by producing a seed or egg that can independently develop into an adult of the same species. Viruses have no eggs or seeds, and they do not multiply by division. They are necessarily parasitic. Because they have no metabolism, viruses have no control over themselves and therefore cannot replicate themselves outside of a living cell. The process of replication occurs not by the virus devouring the cell and changing its materials into more viruses. On the contrary, the virus, or at least its nucleic acid, is absorbed into the cell whose materials and energy sources the foreign nucleic acid comandeers. And, unlike reproduction in plants and animals, replication in viruses requires the disintegration of the "parent" virus. Pauling suggests that the virus is nonliving: "If ... we require that living organisms ... have the property of carrying on some metabolic reactions, then the plant viruses would be described simply as molecules (with molecular mass of the order of magnitude of 10,000,000) that have such a molecular structure as to permit them to catalyze a chemical reaction, in a proper medium, leading to the synthesis of molecules identical with themselves."[54]

That viruses are nonliving jibes with other evidence as well. They have the machinelike capacity of being disassembled and reassembled without loss. In 1955 at the University of California, biochemists Heinz Fraenkel-Court and Robley Williams separated tobacco mosaic by chemical means into its component parts, RNA and protein. In the separated state, the protein was completely inactive and the activity of the nucleic acid greatly reduced. When the two components were put back into one container, the parts recombined to form an active virus, similar in structure to the original one and able to cause tobacco blight.

Viruses, like machines, are constructed from the outside. Living things grow from within, even the simplest bacterium, as Jacob notes: "It is not inconceivable . . . that in the future the thousands of chemical species contained in the bacterial cell may be synthesized one by one. But there is no chance of seeing *all* these compounds being assembled correctly and a bacterium emerging fully armed from a test-tube."[55]

For the same reasons, the form of a virus is determined by the requirements of physics and chemistry; true growth in animals and plants produces forms not explicable by physical laws alone. Molecular biologist Salvador Luria points up the contrast: "Scrutiny of the organization of shells of many viruses with the electron microscope proves that their protein molecules are assembled according to well-known principles of solid geometry, the same ones employed by roof builders to construct quasi-spherical shells of maximum strength using uniform building elements. The shells of viruses bear close resemblance to Buckminster Fuller's domes.

"The perfect geometric shape of virus shells is in its way as remarkable as the symmetrical shape of a starfish or a sea urchin. But the shape of these animals and of all complex organisms is achieved through an elaborate process of development, involving cellular interactions whose complex mechanism is not yet understood. The shape of a virus is simply the outcome of the assembly of protein molecules tending, like all molecular structures, to reach a state of minimal energy."[56]

It is easily demonstrated that only things that have grown from within can incorporate the kind of fivefold symmetry found in starfishes and sea urchins. Such symmetry is geometrically impossible for anything that increases from without.

Viruses take on mathematically predictable shapes. Mercer comments: "On geometrical and energetic grounds a viral coat of identical particles can be constructed in either of two arrangements:

a cylinder having helical symmetery or a self-closing shell."[57] Thus the adenovirus that infects the human respiratory tract is an icosahedron, while the tobacco mosaic virus is a helix of RNA protected by about 2,000 identical protein subunits. (See Figure 2.4.)

Viruses, then, fall just short of life. They are too small to incorporate life functions, and they do not have a sufficient diversity of parts. Thus in biology, as in physics, a quantum principle obtains: below a certain degree of organization, life cannot exist. Life's unique kind of organization is widely recognized. Niels Bohr: "Analogies from chemical experience will not, of course, any more than the ancient comparison of life with fire, give a better explanation of living organisms than will the resemblance, often mentioned, between living organisms and such purely mechanical contrivances as clockworks. An understanding of the essential characteristics of living beings must be sought, no doubt, in their peculiar organisation, in which features that may be analysed by the usual mechanics are interwoven with typically atomistic traits in a manner having no counterpart in inorganic matter."[58]

Activity is closer to the essence of life than structure, since structure exists for the sake of activity. The key to the living thing is the excellence of its agency. An organism can change itself; it can act or not act on its own initiative, not as determined by outside forces. The animal or plant is not always growing or reproducing, even when food is abundant. Nonliving things do not have control over their activities; they are either always in action or are put into action from the outside. No machine turns itself on. It must be switched on, or plugged in, or at least put into contact with its energy source. Even mechanisms with built-in thermostats and timers must be set in advance, either by the manufacturer or by the user. Ethologist Niko Tinbergen remarks, "One of the striking things about living creatures is that they do no *more* than is required. Unlike most machines, they do not have to be switched on and off by an outside manipulator; something is built into them that does this at the proper time."[59]

With the organism, acting or not acting, however conditioned by outside circumstances, comes from within. Living things move themselves, not merely with local motion of parts but by producing *qualitative* changes in those parts. Animals and even plants display a surprising degree of self-regulation regarding temperature, for

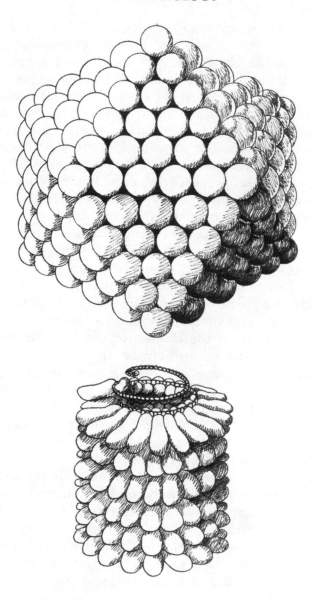

Figure 2.4. Three-dimensional models of adenovirus and tobacco mosaic virus showing identical inter-changeable units. The perfect geometrical shape of a virus is simply the outcome of the assembly of protein molecules, tending like all molecular structures to a state of minimal energy. In contrast to true growth in a plant or an animal, a virus increases from without.

example. In field and laboratory tests when the temperature was 30°C or lower, monkey flower leaves were warmer than the surrounding air. When the air temperature was above 30°C, the leaves were cooler. Other plants yielded similar results.[60] Inanimate objects simply take on the temperature of the environment. Living things, on the other hand, show their autonomy by balancing metabolic heat with evaporative cooling to suit their own requirements. A living being can change itself and thus has control over its actions in a way never found in the inanimate world. Sinnott sees self-regulation as life's hallmark: "This quality of directive self-regulation, whatever its final relation to chemical and physical processes may prove to be, is a uniquely biological phenomenon, and an understanding of it, I believe, will prove a clue to the character of life itself."[61]

The unique unity, organization, and activity of the organism arises from its unique *form*. This natural form is not a ghost: in the plant this form acts only in and through the physical and chemical properties of matter and is *not* separable from matter. This natural form perishes if the unity or structure of the organism is destroyed.

In sum, the organism can reproduce itself without destruction. It can grow—that is, increase in quantity—while retaining its characteristic form. It can even grow new diversity of parts. It can change other things into its own substance without losing its identity. All these actions—reproduction, growth, self-regulation, nutrition—demonstrate the organism's agency. In a very real way, even the plant is a master of the material world, utilizing physical laws and inorganic powers to achieve its own goals. For these many reasons, among all natural beings, the organism is highest.

3

Animals and Man

If an animal is something more than a plant, it must have some new capacity or ability that goes beyond the vegetative functions. That capacity seems to be sense perception. The machine model, however, does not allow for sense perception or conscious awareness in animals. Biologist Donald Griffin reports that "Most biologists and psychologists tend, explicitly or implicitly, to treat most of the world's animals as mechanisms, complex mechanisms to be sure, but unthinking robots nonetheless."[1] Descartes, who first proposed that animals were nothing but intricate machines, saw no need of appealing to conscious awareness to explain their behavior: "Since art is the imitator of nature, and since man is capable of fabricating various automata in which there is motion *without any cogitation*, it seems reasonable that nature should produce her own automata, far more perfect in their workmanship, to wit all the brutes."[2] In his *Treatise on Man*, Descartes develops a strictly mechanistic theory of animal behavior, postulating that invisible but corporeal particles called animal spirits are excited by the movements of the senses and course through tiny pores into the brain, where they flow through nerves to instigate muscle contraction, thereby causing the movements of the animals, all according to the laws of mechanics and all without the intervention of awareness on the animal's part.[3] He compares the animal body to the apparatus of a pipe organ and to fountain statues which, powered by hydraulic mechanisms, give the semblance of self-initiated movement.[4]

In his *Description of the Body*, Descartes argues that there is no more need of a soul in animals to explain their movements than there is for "a soul in a clock which causes it to show the hours."[5] All takes place according to the disposition and arrangement of the animal's parts. Only for the human soul, which he equates with the intellect in man, does Descartes admit the existence of feelings, sensations, and emotions.[6]

Descartes' theory became biology's investigative program for animal behavior. In 1874, biologist T. H. Huxley wrote an essay defending the Cartesian hypothesis:

"Brute animals are mere machines or automata, devoid not only of reason, but of any kind of consciousness.... Descartes' line of argument is perfectly clear. He starts from reflex action in man, from the unquestionable fact that, in ourselves, co-ordinate, pur-posive, actions may take place, without intervention of conscious-ness or volition, or even contrary to the latter. As actions of a certain degree of complexity are wrought by mere mechanism, why may not actions of still greater complexity be the result of a more refined mechanism? What proof is there that brutes are other than a superior race of marionettes, which eat without pleasure, cry without pain, desire nothing, know nothing, and only simulate intelligence as a bee simulates a mathematician?"[7]

Descartes and Huxley hold that our own internal experiences of sensations, memories, emotions, and images are irrelevant for a scientific understanding of animal behavior. If animals have none of this interior life then our own experience of it cannot illuminate their actions.

Huxley maintains that even if awareness exists in animals, it will arise only as a side effect of mechanism and will be incapable of causing anything in the animal's behavior: "The consciousness of brutes would appear to be related to the mechanism of their body simply as a collateral product of its working, and to be as completely without any power of modifying that working as the steam-whistle which accompanies the work of a locomotive engine is without influence upon its machinery. Their volition, if they have any, is an emotion indicative of physical changes, not a cause of such changes."[8]

And if all that animals do can be explained without reference to consciousness, why should man be an exception? Huxley sees no reason to exempt ourselves: "To the best of my judgment, the argumentation which applies to brutes holds equally good of men; and, therefore...all states of consciousness in us, as in them, are immediately caused by molecular changes of the brain-substance. It seems to me that in men, as in brutes, there is no proof that any state of consciousness is the cause of change in the motion of the matter or the organism.... The feeling we call volition is not the cause of a voluntary act, but the symbol of that state of the brain which is the immediate cause of that act."[9]

We here witness the beginnings of behaviorism, which persists as
a strong current in psychology and in animal studies to this day. In
light of this we can understand why many modern psychologists
feel that the existence of consciousness, even our own, is uncertain.
D. O. Hebb, for instance, states that "The existence of something
called consciousness is a venerable *hypothesis*: not a datum, not
directly observable." Lawrence S. Kubie maintains, "Although we
cannot get along without the concept of consciousness, actually
there is no such thing." And K. S. Lashley declares, "There is not
direct knowledge of an experiencing self.... The knower as an
entity is an unnecessary postulate."[10] This also explains psychologist Gordon Allport's observation that "For two generations,
psychologists have tried every conceivable way of accounting for
the integration, organization and striving of the human person
without having recourse to the postulate of a self."[11] These
statements are reminiscent of Laplace's retort to Napoleon's query
concerning the role of God in mechanics—"Sire, I have no need of
that hypothesis"—except that in the present case we are told that
our own minds are scientifically superfluous. Just as it generates a
biology without life, the machine model generates a psychology
without mind or conscious awareness.

The mechanistic approach to man and animals is premised on
materialism. Even emergentists who repudiate reductionism nevertheless retain materialistic presuppositions concerning the nature of
the mind. Ragnar Granit, for example, states: "Like so many other
biologists, I think of mind or conscious awareness as an emergent
property in the evolution of life. This implies that it exists *in nuce* in
properties of matter, just as does the insulin molecule or the double
helix containing DNA."[12] And as Mayr points out, "Emergentism is
a thoroughly materialistic philosophy."[13]

Thus, regarding animal behavior, the central issue that orients all
else is materialism. Can matter and its properties account for
conscious experience, that is, for feelings, sense perceptions, memories, and emotions? Sir Charles Sherrington, the founder of modern
neurophysiology, after a lifetime of research on the brain and the
nervous system, thought not: "A radical distinction has therefore
arisen between life and mind. The former is an affair of chemistry
and physics; the latter escapes chemistry and physics."[14] As we saw
in Chapter 2, the vegetative processes of nutrition, growth, and cell

metabolism occur only by means of the physical and chemical properties of matter, even though the plant has a unity and self-regulation not shared by any inanimate body. Sherrington contends that actions of conscious awareness, however, transcend the mechanisms of physics and chemistry.

Textbooks typically gloss over the profound differences between sense awareness itself and its necessary physiology, giving the impression that descriptions of structures and of physical-chemical events suffice to explain sensory perception. But molecular biologist Gunther Stent points out, for example, that "physiological studies really leave the central problem of visual perception untouched.... No matter how deeply we probe into the visual pathway, in the end we need to posit an 'inner man' who transforms the visual image into a percept."[15] The sensible qualities a person perceives never appear in the brain as such. The brain itself is shrouded in complete silence, even while the person hears the deafening roar of a jet aircraft engine. Likewise, the brain, encased as it is in the skull, is covered with darkness and produces no light even while the person perceives the brilliance of the sun's glare. Our brains do not become colder when we touch snow or harder when we touch iron. The brain is chemically and physically *isolated* from the odors, sounds, flavors, textures, temperatures, and colors that exist outside the skull. Not a single sugar molecule passes from the chocolate candy in the mouth to the gustatory region of the cerebral cortex—and yet we perceive the sugar's sweetness notwithstanding. The brain tissue itself takes on none of the sourness of a tasted lemon or the acrid odor of the skunk's spray that we smell.

The study of structure does not dissolve the mystery of sensation but deepens it. When we hear, for instance, sound waves are caught by the external ear and funneled into an inch-long channel to the ear drum, which passes vibrations onto the small bones of the inner ear. These in turn convert the vibrations into hydraulic pressure waves in the liquid-filled cochlea where differences in pressures are detected by extremely sensitive hairs (see Figure 3.1). These hairs respond to movements as slight as the width of an atom and translate them into electrical currents that traverse the cell below the hairs and discharge tiny amounts of a chemical agent onto auditory nerves that carry impulses to the brain, where the resulting spatiotemporal patterns give rise to the sensation of

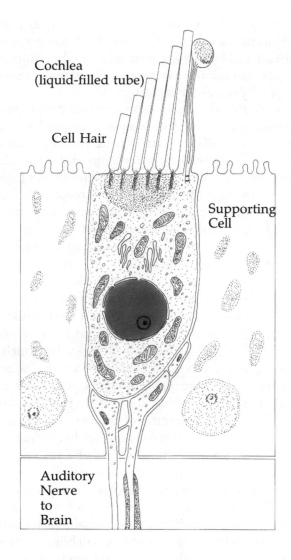

Cochlea
(liquid-filled tube)

Cell Hair

Supporting
Cell

Auditory
Nerve
to
Brain

Figure 3.1. A hair cell inside the cochlea of the
ear. A tweak at the top sends an electrical current
to the bottom, where a chemical messenger is
released onto nerve endings. The many mechanical, electrical, and chemical changes themselves
are not the sensation of sound. The sensible
qualities a person perceives never appear in the
brain as such. The brain itself is shrouded in
silence.

sound. After so many mechanical, electrical, and chemical translations, it is amazing that we perceive anything of the external world.

The brain, then, receives no sense qualities of external objects in a physical or chemical way. Nothing enters it from the sense organs except nerve impulses.[16] If we could shrink ourselves down to the size of a nerve cell, what would we see within the brain? A tour guide might point out to us the intricate chemical changes at the synapses, making possible the transmission of a nerve impulse from one neuron to the next; we might see electron transport, ion interactions, and the furious chemical activity of enzymes within each cell. But nowhere could we see or taste the sparkling burgundy being enjoyed right now by the brain's owner, even if the guide pointed out a particular series of electrical impulses that correlated with those sensations. Nowhere could we see the person's remembrance of his first day at school as a child, or the unicorns prancing through his imagination as he listens to the second movement of Beethoven's Seventh Symphony. No emotions would be discernible either. We would never recognize this particular spatiotemporal pattern of neuronal activity as anger at having received a traffic ticket, or that complex electrical pattern in the nerve cells as joy, or fear, or despair. At every level we meet only with the physical correlates of sensations and emotions, never with the experiences themselves.

Physicist Erwin Schrödinger argues that neither anatomy nor physiology can account for sense awareness since they are common to both conscious and unconscious activities: "Not every nervous process, nay by no means every cerebral process, is accompanied by consciousness. Many of them are not, even though physiologically and biologically they are very much like the 'conscious' ones, both in frequently consisting of afferent impulses followed by efferent ones, and in their biological significance of regulating and timing reactions partly inside the system, partly towards a changing environment."[17]

In the same vein, after showing that "sensation of colours cannot be accounted for by the physicist's objective picture of light-waves," Schrödinger adds: "Could the physiologist account for it, if he had fuller knowledge than he has of the processes in the retina and the nervous processes set up by them in the optical nerve bundles and in the brain? I do not think so. We could at best attain to an objective knowledge of what nerve fibres are excited and in what proportion, perhaps even to know exactly the processes they produce in certain brain cells—whenever our mind registers the sensation of yellow in a particular direction or domain of our field of vision. But even such intimate knowledge would not tell us anything about the sensation of colour, more particularly of yellow in this direction—the same physiological processes might conceivably result in a sensation of sweet taste, or anything else."[18]

For all the above reasons, neuroscientist Sir John Eccles declares, "Conscious experiences...are quite different in kind from any goings-on in the neuronal machinery; nevertheless the events in the neuronal machinery are a necessary condition for experience, though...they are not a sufficient condition."[19] At no level does physics or chemistry explain sense perception or emotion. The latter pertain to a whole new order of reality. And here an appeal to emergent properties of matter avails nothing. Thermonuclear combustion, for example, might be considered an emergent property of matter that does not show itself until a critical quantity of mass is reached. But gravity, the force responsible for the necessary pressures, is present even at the smallest scale of electron, proton, and neutron. At that level, gravity, though for most purposes negligible, is nevertheless present. The gravity necessary to spark the furnace of a star is merely a matter of degree. Applied to the animal, this model assumes that sensory awareness exists to a small degree in molecules, atoms, and electricity but emerges full-blown in the nervous system of the animal. However, molecules, atoms, and electricity do not possess sensory awareness in a slight degree; they do not possess it at all. Consequently, sensory awareness is not an emergent property of matter.*

Nor can we argue that the animal is contained in the potentialities of lower forms of matter as water is contained in the potentialities of hydrogen and oxygen. For in the case of chemical and mineral forms, new properties at the higher levels are the same in *kind*. The properties of water differ from those of hydrogen and oxygen, but water has the same kind of properties: boiling point, freezing point,

---

*For a fuller development of the immaterial element in sense perception see *The New Story of Science*, pp. 9-17, 109-112.

density, chemical activity. But sense perceptions, imaginings, remembrances, and emotions are outside the order of physical and chemical properties. Therefore, attempting to explain them by the properties of matter is like an astrologer trying to explain human actions by reference to the stars and planets—there is no middle term.

We saw in Chapter 2 that the plant stands above inanimate matter, yet all its processes respect and even utilize the laws of physics and chemistry. Every chemical reaction that goes on inside the plant could, at least in principle, be duplicated in a test tube. Everything the plant does is matter in motion. The living organism itself, however, cannot be assembled from without. Thus *what* the plant produces is not unique but *how* it produces it is, the physical and chemical results proceeding from a unified, coordinated, self-regulating entity.

The animal stands higher than the plant in two ways. First, something the animal produces, namely sensation, transcends the order of matter in motion. Sensory awareness and emotions are in principle not reproducible outside of an animal. Second, the animal possesses a unity, a coordination and a self-regulation superior to the plant since the animal can direct itself in a conscious manner by means of its perception of the world. It is clearly a superior agent. Plants have no genuine awareness of the world, though they can react to certain physical stimuli and even mimic sensation by their tropisms—for example, turning their leaves toward the sun.

Sensation, then, is neither reducible to matter nor does it emerge out of matter. Therefore, the form that renders the animal capable of feelings and perceptions is vastly superior to the plant's form, which is limited to vegetative activities.

These conclusions do not drive us into Cartesian dualism. Despite the transcendence found in sensory perceptions and emotions, a bodily organ is still indispensable for all these activities of the animal. Without an eye and an optic nerve and a visual cortex, there is no sight. The electrical and chemical activities are not themselves sensations; yet they make sensations possible—necessary but not sufficient conditions as, Eccles puts it. This explains why drugs or brain damage can temporarily or permanently inhibit sensory capacities.

It should be noted that when we speak of animal perception,

nothing obliges us to ascribe the same degree of awareness to all species. Some clearly possess fewer sense powers than others; the interior life of a barnacle must be minimal as compared with that of a chimpanzee. And widely differing degrees exist within the same category of sense faculty. Many worms and shellfish, for example, exhibit a sensitivity to light diffused through their skin. They cannot see objects as such, but detect light in a way analogous to the way we feel warmth. Contrast this with a vertebrate's eye, which employs a lens to focus a sharp image of the object seen, in three dimensions and in color. And between these two extremes lie a whole range of differing degrees of vision found in different species.

Animal Behavior

If animals experience conscious awareness, then they are not machines and their behavior cannot be reduced to mechanical causes alone. Many techniques are available to study what animals experience. In higher animals sensation is evident. An animal with a pair of eyes almost identical to our own in structure clearly experiences some sort of vision. This conclusion can be nuanced by experiment to test the acuity of the animal's vision, its color perception, its depth perception, its capacity to distinguish shapes, and its night vision. Experimental techniques include not only blindfolding the animal and checking results, but also inserting surgically a tiny electrode into the animal's optic nerve. The electrical pulses that correlate with the animal's seeing can be displayed on an oscilloscope screen so that we can in a more direct way see what stimuli the eye is reporting to the brain and how intense they are. The problem is more difficult when an animal's eyes are very different from our own or when it has sense organs that we do not have. Do bees perceive polarized light? Can bats hear sounds above the range of our hearing? Such questions must be answered by experiment.

The sensory powers of vertebrates are evident because of their similarity to our own. But invertebrates also perceive those things necessary for their livelihood. Ethologist Niko Tinbergen developed experimental proof that the digger wasp, for example, employs olfactory, visual, and tactile clues to hunt and to identify its prey, the honey bee.[20] He also showed that this wasp memorizes the landmarks around its nest, allowing it to return easily after hunting flights. The experiments, some of which are illustrated in Figure 3.2, clearly demonstrate memory and shape recognition in the digger wasp.[21] Similar evidence has established memory and shape discrimination in bees, octopuses, fish, and birds. Not only do the highest animals possess superior sensory equipment, but their use of it is more sophisticated. Certain primates can translate visual images into tactile ones, a procedure called cross-modal perception. Koehler reports that chimpanzees shown objects they could see but not touch were able to select matching objects from an unseen mixture of articles in a bag.[22] Davenport and Rogers established experimentally that "Orang-utans and chimpanzees can discriminate between two objects on the basis of tactile cues and select the one that matches a visually presented sample," even when a wide variety of three-dimensional objects unknown to the subjects is used.[23] Crossmodal perception requires the comparison of data from two different external senses, and is beyond the ability of many animals. The octopus, for example, is unable to direct its own tentacles by sight alone. Biologist Helena Curtis notes:

"If an octopus sees a crab behind a glass partition, it will rush directly toward it, flushed with excitement, and when it reaches the glass, will press itself against the pane, writhing its tentacles. One of the tentacles may chance over the top of the glass and reach the crab. The octopus, however, will continue to respond to the visual stimulation of the crab and press excitedly against the glass as if it were in pursuit of the prey. Apparently the impulses received from the tactile stimulation of the arm are not integrated with those received from the eye, nor is the movement of the arm detectably influenced by the fact that the octopus can see its arm and the prey."[24]

The higher animals clearly experience emotions. Biologist Wolfgang Kohler speaks of his experience with chimpanzees: "Their range of expression by gesture and action is very wide and varied, and, beyond all comparison, superior, not only to that of lower apes, but also to the orang-utan's. Much is easily comprehensible to us human beings—for example, rage, terror, despair, grief, pleading, desire, and also playfulness and pleasure."[25]

Some animals show evidence of imagination. Bees and ants use internal maps to orient themselves.[26] And we have good reason to

Figure 3.2. Evidence of shape perception in insects. The digger wasp always memorizes salient features around its nest so as to find it easily when it returns. In one experiment, Tinbergen set a circle of pine cones around the nest that the wasp learned to recognize (*upper left*). When he moved the circle of cones, the wasp searched in the center and could not find the nest only a foot away (*upper right*). When he arranged the cones in a triangle around the nest and set up a circle of stones nearby, the wasp searched inside the circle, proving that it was guided by the shape and not by the cones themselves (*bottom*). (After Tinbergen, 1965)

believe that even dreams, which are acts of the imagination, are found in higher animals. Ethologist Donald Griffin: "Sleeping dogs sometimes move and vocalize in ways that suggest they are dreaming; their movements resemble those of feeding, running, biting, and even copulation. They sometimes snarl or bark. Some observers of sleeping animals have concluded that these motions and vocalizations accompany dreams related to recent experiences. Human sleepers show two distinct types of EEG potentials. The first, a relatively low-frequency pattern, characterizes deep sleep; the second, called REM sleep, is more irregular and is usually accompanied by rapid eye movements, which can be recorded separately by electrodes located near the eyes. When human subjects are awakened from one of these types of sleep, they are much more likely to report that they were dreaming during REM sleep.... Comparable recordings from sleeping birds and mammals show very similar patterns of REM sleep...indicating that mammals and birds may dream."[27]

Animals are also able to select which among many incoming stimuli will be registered in consciousness. We all have experience of this: by concentrating our attention on one voice among many in a noisy room, we can effectively tune out other distracting sounds. Figure 3.3 shows how with an electrode we can monitor what an animal is actively aware of and record when that awareness shifts from one thing to another. The animal possesses a superior agency, having a say in which sensory information impinging on its faculties will become part of its consciousness and influence its behavior. The animal is an agent; brutes are not simply moved by external forces, as Descartes thought.

This brings us to a related question. It is one thing to recognize that an animal hears, sees, remembers, imagines, and has emotions, another to understand *what* it sees, what its perceptual world is like. The theoretical capacity of the sense organs themselves does not define an animal's world, but rather the interpretation of perceptions by the animal on the basis of instinct and previous experience. Tinbergen says of animals that "though all share one world, all may be said to live in different worlds, since each perceives best only that part of the environment essential to its success."[28] Ethologist Jacob von Uexküll, among the first to document the remarkable specificity of animal perception, gives the example of birds: "A jackdaw is

Figure 3.3. Animals select from incoming stimuli only those that are most pertinent. A cat sitting calmly hears a ticking metronome. Its perception can be recorded on a graph if an electrode is inserted into its brain and connected to a meter. When the cat sees a mouse, however, it concentrates its attention solely on the mouse and tunes out the irrelevant ticking (shown by flat graph). (After Tinbergen, 1965)

utterly unable to see a grasshopper that is not moving. . . . A jackdaw simply does not know the shape of a motionless grasshopper and is so constituted that it can only apprehend the moving form. That would explain why so many insects feign death. If their motionless form simply does not exist in the field of vision of their enemies, then by shamming death they drop out of that world with absolute certainty and cannot be found even though searched for."[29]

The question of what an animal *could* see, given such and such an eye, is a secondary one. The crucial point is what the animal in fact *looks* at, what it *looks for*, and *how* it looks for it with that eye. An animal may respond to certain stimuli in one situation but not in another. Tinbergen distinguishes between potential and actual stimuli:

"A mere knowledge of the potential capacities of the sense organs never enables us to point out, in any concrete case, the actual complex of stimuli responsible for the release of a reaction. From a study of sensory capacity we can infer what changes in the environment can or can *not* be perceived by the animals, but a positive answer about what *does* release the observed reaction is impossible. This turns upon the peculiar fact that an animal does not react to all the changes in the environment which its sense organs can receive, but only a small part of them. This is a basic property of instinctive behavior, the importance of which cannot be stressed too much. For instance, the carnivorous water beetle *Dytiscus marginalis*, which has perfectly developed compound eyes . . . and can be trained to respond to visual stimuli, does not react at all to visual stimuli when capturing prey, e.g., a tadpole. A moving prey in a glass tube never releases nor guides any reaction. The beetle's feeding response is released by chemical and tactile stimuli exclusively. . . . For instance, a watery meat extract promptly forces it to hunt and capture every solid object it touches. . . .

"The occurrence of such 'errors' or 'mistakes' is one of the most conspicuous characteristics of innate behavior. It is caused by the fact that an animal responds 'blindly' to only part of the total environmental situation and neglects other parts, although its sense organs are perfectly able to receive them (and probably do receive them), and although they may seem to be less important, to the human observer, than the stimuli to which it does react."[30]

One study at Massachusetts Institute of Technology began by inserting tiny electrodes into a living frog's optic nerve so that the

electrical impulses traveling to the frog's brain became measurable.
Using this technique, the investigators formed a good idea of what
the frog sees and how it sees. For example, when a small object is
brought into the frog's field of vision and left immobile, the frog's
eye sends electrical impulses to the frog's brain for a few minutes,
but then ceases to do so. After a short time, then, the object is no
longer there as far as the frog is concerned. Its eye is wired to cancel
out stationary objects after a few minutes. The researchers report:
"The frog does not seem to see or, at any rate, is not concerned with
the detail of stationary parts of the world around him. He will starve
to death surrounded by food if it is not moving. His choice of food is
determined only by size and movement. He will leap to capture any
object the size of an insect or worm, providing it moves like one. He
can be fooled easily not only by a bit of dangled meat but by any
small object."[31]

Furthermore, the frog characterizes an object visually by four
kinds of specialized nerve fibers that measure sustained contrast,
net convexity, moving edges, and net dimming. The frog's eye has
only two categories: "my predator" and "my prey"; the frog's sex life
is conducted solely by hearing and touch.[32]

Each animal investigated in this way shows different categories of
perception closely aligned with its way of life. Thus the science of
animal behavior, founded in the 1930s by von Frisch, Lorenz, and
Tinbergen, begins by discovering what the animal experiences, its
degree of awareness, what it attends to, and how its perceptions
account for its actions. Such a science seeks to understand the
animal's instincts, that is, what it learns and what it knows without
learning; how it communicates with members of its own species; the
emotions the animal experiences, how they are provoked, and with
what effects. The science of animal behavior provides the ultimate
cause of an animal's movements, while the physical sciences explain
the mechanics of those movements. Biologist E. S. Russell contrasts
this kind of animal science with mechanism:

"In such work the animal is accepted as a living whole, showing
certain characteristic activities, which can be accurately observed
and recorded, which can be modified experimentally, submitted to
scientific study. It is true that the point of view adopted is quite
different from that of the physical investigator; the fact that *the
animal is an active and striving agent* is taken at its face value, and the

psychologist is not afraid to assume that the animal has its own perceptual world, the existence of which can be deduced from its behavior. His conception of organism is much richer, less abstract, than that formed by the mechanist."[33]

This is not to say that physics and chemistry bring no light to the study of animals. On the contrary, they have a great deal to contribute. A book like *How Life Learned to Live* by Helmut Tributsch illustrates how illuminating the application of those sciences is to biology in general and to animal behavior in particular. Tributsch writes, "Almost all the basic principles of mechanics, dynamics, thermodynamics, optics, and acoustics had already been in the service of life for millions of years before the human mind learned to understand and master their function."[34] For example, how can the albatross fly for hours without flapping its wings? Tributsch explains how the bird exploits "the aerodynamic lift generated by the friction between air and waves," effectively getting a free ride by soaring and gliding at the right moments.[35]

Why are fish such efficient swimmers? Apart from their aerodynamic shape, the slime on their bodies reduces turbulent friction with the water by 66 percent.[36]

Since nature uses jet propulsion for movement in water-dwelling creatures, such as the squid, why not among land animals or flying creatures? Physics says that the recoil generated is proportional to the mass of the expelled medium. This works well with water, but the acceleration required to generate significant recoil with air, since its mass is so much less than that of water, would exceed biological conditions.[37]

How can a mosquito sustain its rapid wing beats without exhausting its muscles? Tributsch answers, "The wings of the insect are kept in motion by periodic elastic deformations of the thorax. Resilin prevents the loss of motion energy with every wingbeat at the moment of braking on the point of reversal. Its elastic properties cause the flight mechanism to act like a rubber ball, which retains its kinetic energy when bouncing off the ground though it simultaneously reverses direction."[38] So the mosquito expends energy only for moving its wings in one direction, the reversal being provided free by elastic bounce.

What prevents a fish from sinking to the bottom if it is heavier than water, or floating to the top if it is lighter than water? A constant struggle against buoyancy or against gravity would put a taxing drain on a fish's available energy. The answer is a tribute to nature's economy of energy. About half of all osseous fish have flotation bladders, which fill with more or less gas (metabolically produced) according to the fish's changing needs. Other fish solve the problem with a greater proportion of high-buoyancy fat stored in their tissues.[39]

Tributsch offers dozens of other applications of physical principles to animal behavior. There is no question about the value of this approach. The only question is whether such a study exhausts the whole of animal life. Is anything left out if we study animal movements exclusively from the viewpoint of physics and chemistry? Such a perspective does not reach the central core of the animal—its interior life, its sensory awareness, learning, communication, and emotions. Physics and chemistry can explain how an animal is able to move but not why it moves here rather than there. To understand that, we must know something about what the animal is perceiving.

Even instinctual actions are conscious actions, triggered and directed by the animal's perceptions. Some argue that because animals make apparently senseless errors when circumstances are changed from the normal that they must be acting unconsciously. They point out warbler parents dutifully feeding a cuckoo chick to the detriment of their own young, or a tern brooding a flash bulb substituted for one of its eggs. Conscious behavior does not exclude the possibility of deception, for we do not think a human being acts mechanically or unconsciously if he is deceived by a counterfeit ten-dollar bill. The above examples, like the starving frog surrounded by immobilized insects, teach us a great deal about the highly specialized ways animals perceive their prey, their enemies, or their young, but they do not demonstrate unconsciousness. On the contrary, because the pattern of the cuckoo chick's gaping mouth presents the hapless warbler parents with a superstimulus, they prefer to feed the cuckoo instead of their own young. That the sensed clues the birds key on can misfire in abnormal situations is no proof of unconsciousness or stupidity.

Furthermore, after a flight, terns find their eggs by first finding their nest site, so for them what is in the nest is by definition an egg. Birds such as the murre that lay eggs without a nest have a much keener perception of their eggs and do not mistake just any round objects for them. Terns and gulls lack this precision because they do not need it normally. Thus, a blind spot in one species' perception is seldom universal. But the general rule holds: what an animal does not perceive, it need not know.

Nor do animals act with the rigidity of machines. Even the actions of arthropods exhibit a good deal of flexibility. Tinbergen remarks of the digger wasps he studied that "There is a greater degree of plasticity in the behavior of these animals than I had been led to expect."[40] Ethologist W. S. Bristowe describes how web-weaving spiders vary their stereotypical behavior to adjust to novel situations.[41] This self-direction is most apparent in the behavior of higher animals. In the territorial behavior of higher animals, territories are generally maintained by males and only during the breeding season. This behavior in the wildebeest, for example, is triggered by the male hormone testosterone. But as mammalogist Richard Estes points out, territoriality is not reducible to mere chemical machinery: "What is most amazing about territoriality is that it is not only physiological but also psychological—as proved by the fact that a territory owner switches off virtually all displays of sex and aggression whenever he leaves his property."[42] A male wildebeest that leaves his home area for a drink is meek and nonaggressive when he passes through the territories of other males.

The layman is frequently under the impression that individual animals of the same species are identical and without personality. This would be true if they were machines, but it is contradicted by the testimony of all experienced ethologists, at least with respect to higher animals. For example, animal researcher Dian Fossey studied African gorillas for five years and learned to identify individual animals by their habits and emotional dispositions: "I know many of them as individuals, each with a distinctive personality. And, mainly for identification in my notes, I have given them names."[43] Jane Goodall says the same after living two years in close contact with wild chimps: "Chimpanzees show as much individuality as man himself."[44]

Another denial of animal consciousness comes from the attempt to reduce all animal behavior to conditioned responses. Behaviorism, taking its principles from Descartes, gained great impetus from

Pavlov's experiments. Both Pavlov and Descartes use the machine model to reduce animal behavior to a series of reflex actions that occur without consciousness or perception. If your hand accidentally touches a very hot object or a live electrical wire, the energy passing through nerves to your spinal cord will trigger a neural arc that contracts appropriate muscles to pull your hand away. This procedure would take place in the same way in an unconscious person. The reflex act is automatic and mechanical, requiring no perception, awareness, or voluntariness. A frog with its brain removed still responds with appropriate leg movements to push away an acid-soaked gauze touched to its back. Accordingly, Descartes, Huxley, and Pavlov ask, why have recourse to awareness to explain anything the animal does?

If an animal moved only when touched with a live electrical wire, or when hit in the knee joint with a hammer, or when subjected to some other excessive physical stimulus, then the reflex theory would be plausible as a universal explanation of animal behavior. But animals exhibit a great deal more autonomy than that. In a reflex action the physical stimulus is the full and adequate cause of the resulting movement. The amount of electricity jolting the hand is sufficient to jump the neural arc and contract the muscles. If less powerful, it would not cause the reflex action. Such a model is useless, however, if we want to understand conscious behavior. Why, for example, does the male three-spined stickleback attack anything red that approaches its nest during the breeding season? The minuscule amount of energy coming to the fish's eye from a few square centimeters of red cannot trigger a neural arc that would contract muscles for attack. For strictly mechanical reasons, then, the attempt to reduce the fish's movements to reflex actions fails. The male attacks red objects because it is defending its spawning territory from other males, which it *recognizes* by a special sign: their red underbellies. By virtue of its perception, the fish itself directs its organs of motion to the appropriate action for driving out the intruder. This shows that the animal, not the external stimulus, is the agent. The patch of red does not cause the attack but occasions it. Tinbergen distinguishes between the measurable electric or chemical stimulus of reflexology and the sign stimulus that releases an animal's instinctive actions.[45]

In a similar way the honey dance of a bee is not a sufficient *physical* cause for the bee's co-workers to leave the hive and fly in a particular direction for a fixed distance to find an abundance of food. Their behavior makes sense only if real information has been communicated to them through the dance. That presupposes the dancer and its co-workers possess some degree of awareness. Bees are not unconscious robots. The same principle holds for animal migration, courtship displays, care of young, hunting, eating habits, self-defense, communication, and fighting, in a word, all true actions of the animals as opposed to metabolic or mechanical and unconscious activities taking place within the animal. All such behavior requires conscious self-direction. If, as we saw above, sense perception itself transcends matter, then so must animal behavior. It is not merely difficult to derive animal behavior from DNA coding, or reflex acts, or physiology; it is impossible. The root cause of every truly animal action is some kind of awareness.

In denying animal consciousness, behaviorism logically excludes all autonomy of the animal as well. This theory rejects the concept of instinct and conceives of animal behavior as caused entirely from the outside. Theoretically one should be able to condition virtually any animal to respond with any action one chooses (provided only that the animal is physically capable of it) and trigger that action by any stimulus (provided only that it is able to affect the animal). Any animal, any stimulus, any response. Behaviorism conceives the animal not as having a given nature, but as pure plasticity.

The denial that animals are autonomous agents can be tested experimentally. The proprietors of Animal Behavior Enterprises, psychologists Keller Breland and Marian Breland, have had more than fourteen years' experience in training for various commercial purposes over six thousand individual animals of thirty-eight different species, including reindeer, cockatoos, porpoises, and whales. The Brelands' business is a perfect test case because they began it as enthusiastic behaviorists.[46]

The Brelands from the start encountered a "persistent pattern of discomforting failure...breakdowns of conditioned operant behavior."[47] For example, trying to condition a raccoon to pick up two coins and put them into a metal box to receive an immediate food reward, the Brelands ran into difficulty: "Not only could he not let go of the coins, but he spent seconds, even minutes, rubbing them together...and dipping them into the container. He carried on this behavior to such an extent that the practical application we had in mind—a display featuring a raccoon putting money in a piggy bank—simply was not feasible. The rubbing behavior became worse and worse as time went on, in spite of nonreinforcement."[48] Chickens supposed to deliver to a spectator a plastic capsule containing a toy would, after a few successful performances, begin to stab at the capsules and pound them up and down on the floor of the cage. Pigs trained to deposit large wooden coins in a piggy bank for immediate food rewards would do well for a few weeks but then begin dropping the coins repeatedly, rooting them, tossing them into the air, and rooting them again indefinitely. The Brelands at first thought lack of hunger caused this strange, unconditioned behavior: "However, the behavior persisted and gained in strength in spite of severely increased drive [hunger]—[the pig] finally went through the ratios so slowly that he did not get enough to eat in the course of a day. Finally it would take the pig about 10 minutes to transport four coins a distance of about 6 feet. This problem behavior developed repeatedly in successive pigs."[49]

Similar problems arose with "porpoises and whales that swallow their manipulanda (balls and inner tubes), cats that will not leave the area of the feeder, rabbits that will not go to the feeder, the great difficulty in many species of conditioning vocalization with food reinforcement, problems in conditioning a kick in a cow, the failure to get appreciably increased effort out of ungulates with increased drive, and so on."[50] A clear failure of the assumption "any animal, any stimulus, any response." Hunger does not seem to be the only thing that "drives" animals. The Brelands conclude that these long-term results "represent a clear and utter failure of conditioning theory," and point to the primacy of instinct:

"Here we have animals, after having been conditioned to a specific learned response, gradually drifting into behaviors that are entirely different from those which were conditioned. Moreover, it can easily be seen that these particular behaviors to which the animals drift are clear-cut examples of instinctive behaviors having to do with natural food-getting behaviors of the particular species. . . .

"The chicken that hammers capsules is obviously exhibiting instinctive behavior having to do with breaking open of seed pods or the killing of insects, grubs, etc. The raccoon is demonstrating so-called washing behavior. The rubbing and washing response may result, for example, in the removal of the exoskeleton of a crayfish. The pig is rooting or shaking— behaviors which are strongly built into this species and are connected with the food-getting repertoire."[51]

How fundamental instinct is—it can predominate over conditioning. "The general principle seems to be that wherever an animal has strong instinctive behaviors in the areas of the conditioned response, after continued running the organism will drift toward the instinctive behavior to the detriment of the conditioned behavior and even to the delay or preclusion of the reinforcement," the Brelands observe.[52] Accordingly they criticize the postulates of behaviorism:

"Three of the most important of these tacit assumptions seem to us to be: that the animal comes to the laboratory as a virtual *tabula rasa*, that species differences are insignificant, and that all responses are about equally conditionable to all stimuli.

"It is obvious, we feel, from the foregoing account, that these assumptions are no longer tenable. After 14 years of continuous conditioning and observation of thousands of animals, it is our reluctant conclusion that the behavior of any species cannot be adequately understood, predicted, or controlled without knowledge of its instinctive patterns, evolutionary history, and ecological niche."[53] The Brelands mention that they gained more useful information from ethologists such as Lorenz and Tinbergen than from the reports of conditioning laboratories.[54] Their experience convincingly argues that the animal is an autonomous agent.

Are Animals Intelligent?

Animals are clearly conscious agents, but is consciousness the same as intelligence? Animals undeniably act on the basis of sense perception, emotion, and instinct, but do they reason or deliberate? Do they possess intellectual understanding? Certain observations and experiments seem to point to affirmative answers to these questions, especially with regard to primates. Three reasons have led some ethologists and psychologists to conclude that animals have intellectual powers, at least in some degree.

First, many species seem capable of abstracting universal concepts. In tests conducted by Hayes and Nissen, a home-raised chimpanzee discriminated between dozens of categories using photographs and sorted various objects according to size, shape, and color.[55] Nissen comments: "This achievement of infrahuman primates approximates conceptualization as it is known in man."[56] Griffin reports experiments in which monkeys consistently selected among three objects the single item that was unlike the other two. It looks as if the animals grasped the abstract concept of dissimilarity.[57]

Second, many animals seem to reason and draw conclusions from what they perceive. For example, Wolfgang Kohler's classic experiments demonstrated the chimpanzee's power of insight and apparent capacity to make inferences. Apes used sticks to reach food suspended from the ceiling; others piled boxes on top of one another to solve the same problem. One animal even led the experimenter to a place under the banana and then leaped onto his shoulders to grab the fruit![58] Jane Goodall observed unprompted chimpanzees in the wild strip sticks of leaves and insert them into termite mounds, then withdraw the sticks to feast on the insects clinging to them.[59] Such animals appear to comprehend the relation of means and end. In Japan a wild female macaque was observed throwing a rice-sand mixture into the water. The sand sunk but the rice floated and was scooped up to be eaten. This apparently deliberate action was copied by other monkeys and became a permanent part of the troop's behavior.[60]

Third, some primates have been taught what appears to be rudimentary symbolic communication. Various psychologists have developed five major projects in this area, pursuing two different strategies, sign language and symbol system. In 1969, Beatrice Gardner and R. Allen Gardner trained Washoe, a female chimpanzee, in American Sign Language. After three years' training the animal used more than eighty-five signs.[61] Francine Patterson followed this sign language approach with Koko, a female gorilla.[62] Herbert Terrace's project trained a male chimpanzee to sign. His animal, Nim, acquired a 125-word vocabulary after four years.[63] Using another strategy David Premack tried to train a chimpanzee to use plastic symbols to compose sentences.[64] And a team directed by Duane Rumbaugh habituated another chimp, Lana, to push buttons on a computer-controlled console, signifying her desires in Yerkish, an artificial language specifically designed for the experiment.[65] Some argue that the animals in these five projects acquired a command of true language and therefore must possess the ability to grasp meanings and universal concepts.

Do these experiments and observations demonstrate intellectual comprehension in animals? Regarding conceptualization, animals sort objects by their different appearance to the eye or according to the different ways they affect other senses. Not just apes but a wide variety of animals including mammals, birds, mollusks, and insects can distinguish shapes and patterns.[66] If a dragonfly could not distinguish between large and small objects, between moving and stationary objects, what use would its vision be? But all these judgments are perceptual, not intellectual. There is no reason to suppose that the digger wasp understands the definition of a circle just because it discerns that shape from others during experiments (see Figure 3.2). Matching to sample does not demonstrate conceptualization or intellectual powers; it demonstrates only the ability to discriminate stimuli at the sense level. Even the cross-modal perception of apes discussed earlier does not transcend the level of sense perception.

One cause of confusion about abstract universal concepts is that sense powers do possess a certain kind of universality. Socrates' eyes see not only this red in front of him but *any* red, and not just red but *all* colors. This kind of universality, without which the sense powers would be useless, is not to be confused with the universality of intellectual concepts. To see this red and by vision alone perceive its difference from other colors is not to define what redness is or to understand what all colors have in common, tasks impossible for the eye.

The difference between intellectual concepts and sense images is demonstrated most clearly when no sense percept can solve the problem. Psychologist Jean Piaget, who has studied children's cognitive development for over forty years, devised many such tests. He describes one that is ingenious yet simple: "An open box containing about twenty brown wooden beads and two or three white wooden beads is presented to the subject. After he has manipulated the beads he is asked whether there are more wooden beads or more brown beads in the box. The great majority of children below seven years can only say, 'There are more brown ones.'"[67] The young child who answers that there are more brown beads is deciding on the basis of sense images and percepts rather than on the logical relations between universal categories. This test and similar ones could easily be adapted to animals of several species.

In fact, Piaget's extraordinary work with its valuable distinctions and fertile principles would with great profit be applied to the area of animal psychology. To gain insight into a mind limited to sense perception, motor habits, memory, and associations, without the capacity to understand the nature or reason of anything, it makes sense to begin with the animal most studied and most known to us: the human infant. Piaget describes the baby before six months of age: "From the perceptual point of view, from the time a child starts to smile (from the fifth week on), he recognizes certain persons as distinct from others, etc. We must not, however, assume that he conceptualizes a person or even an object. Persons and objects are tangible and animated apparitions which he recognizes as such, but this proves nothing with respect to their substantiality, or as to the dissociation between the self and the external world."[68]

Piaget discovered that at this stage the child perceives objects but not their permanence, or what he calls their substantiality. He recounts one observation made with his son at age seven months: "At his feeding time I offered the child his bottle filled with milk, but as he stretched out his hands I moved the bottle behind my upraised arm. If the bottle remained partly in sight, the baby would reach around my arm to seize it. But when my arm hid the bottle, the child would begin to cry as though it had vanished completely!"[69] On another occasion Piaget observed a baby chasing a ball around a room: "When the ball rolled under the armchair, he retrieved it without difficulty. But after it had rolled under the sofa where he could not see it, he soon stopped looking there and ran back to look for it under the armchair! We must conclude that he had not yet constructed the concept of a permanent object; the ball existed only as a sort of semi-object, midway between perceptual and substance. There was a beginning of localization, necessary to give an object permanence, but the localization was linked to the place of the child's previously successful action, not yet to the object itself."[70]

In a similar way animals act without understanding the substance or the *what* of a thing. It is extraordinarily easy to misinterpret their actions, however. For instance, a person observing a flock of birds mobbing a cat that has captured one of their number might assume the birds had understood the situation and had chosen an appropriate course of action. Not so. Lorenz reports that on one occasion when returning home from a swim he was suddenly attacked by the normally friendly flock of jackdaws that nested on the roof of his home. The birds screeched their sharp, metallic mobbing call and hailed agonizing pecks on Lorenz's hand. He had just withdrawn from his pocket his black bathing suit. This was sufficient to trigger the jackdaw's mobbing instinct. Lorenz remarks: "Of all the reactions which, in the jackdaw, concern the recognition of an enemy, only one is innate: any living being that carries a black thing, dangling, or fluttering, becomes the object of a furious onslaught."[71] Lorenz notes that his large, old-fashioned camera never provoked any reaction even though it was black, "but the jackdaws would start their rattling cry as soon as I pulled the black paper strips of the pack film which fluttered to and fro in the breeze. That the birds knew me to be harmless, and even a friend, made no difference whatever: as soon as I held in my hand something black and moving, I was branded as an 'eater of jackdaws.'"[72]

When Lorenz held in his hands a featherless nestling jackdaw, none of the other birds attacked or paid any particular attention. When the nestling's feathers developed, however, so that the bird became black, Lorenz's hand was furiously attacked by the parents if he tried to pick up the young bird.[73] This demonstrates that the birds did not act like human beings in similar situations; namely, by first understanding the danger, then deciding what to do about it. The birds' reaction, though triggered by sense perception, is rigidly determined by instinct. The jackdaws perceive black, they perceive flapping, but the amazing thing is they cannot perceive bathing suit or film or even jackdaw, as Lorenz's test proved.

Because animals do not grasp the substance or the *what* of anything, their innate responses are keyed to a few external stimuli. A deaf turkey hen pecks all her own chicks to death as soon as they are hatched. The poults' distressed cheeping is the only stimulus that can inhibit the hen's natural aggression in defense of the nest. The cheeping alone evokes a maternal reaction in the hen. Without the cheeping, the young turkey is judged by instinct to be an enemy and is attacked. A hen with normal hearing will attack a realistic stuffed chick if it emits no sound and is pulled toward the nest by a string. Conversely, she will respond maternally to a stuffed weasel if it has a built-in speaker that produces the cheeping of a turkey poult.[74]

Kohler reports similar reactions in his chimpanzees: "I tested them with some most primitive stuffed toys, on wooden frames, fastened on to a stand, and padded with straw sewn inside cloth covers, with black buttons for eyes. They were about forty centimeters in height, and could perhaps be taken for caricatures of oxen and asses, though most drolly unnatural. It was totally impossible to get Sultan, who at that time could be led by the hand outside, near these small objects, which had so little real resemblance to any kind of animal. He went into paroxysms of terror, or threatened recklessly to bite my fingers, when I, whose dangerous possibilities were well-known to him, tried to draw him towards the toy, as he struggled and strained backwards. One day I entered their room with one of these toys under my arm. Their reaction-times can be very short; in a moment a black cluster, consisting of the whole group of chimpanzees, hung suspended from the farthest corner of the wire-roofing, each individual trying to thrust the others aside and bury his head deep in among them."[75]

How remarkable that the apes perceived the shape, size, color, and design of the stuffed toys but could not see what they *were*—harmless cloth and wood. Psychologist Francine Patterson discovered the same thing while training her female gorilla: "Although Koko has never seen a real alligator, she is petrified of toothy stuffed or rubber facsimiles. . . . I have exploited Koko's irrational fear of this reptile by placing toy alligators in parts of the trailer I don't want her to touch."[76]

Animals, then, deal with phenomenal appearances, not with what things are. They do not distinguish between sense qualities of a thing and what the thing is. Consequently, they are incapable of understanding causes. Associating in memory one thing with another is not the same as understanding a cause. Piaget's studies of children again shed light on this point. Children begin to pick up objects and examine them at about four and a half months. In one experiment Piaget covered his own son's crib with a transparent canopy and put several toy rattles on top of the covering. A cord attached to the middle of the cover dangled into the child's crib (see Figure 3.4). The baby discovered the cord by accident and was soon pulling it harder and harder to watch the toys dance above him,

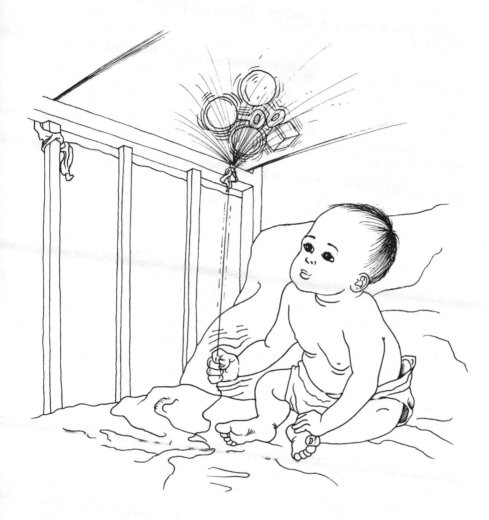

Figure 3.4. A cord attached to the middle of a transparent cover hung down into the baby's crib. The child pulled it repeatedly, enjoying the sound of rattles on top of the cover. Then the experimenter removed the rattles and, unseen, emitted a series of whistles that attracted the baby's attention. When the experimenter stopped the whistles, the baby pulled the cord, looking in the direction of the whistles. This demonstrates that the baby was reacting by means of a sensorimotor association rather than an intellectual grasp of cause and effect. Animals behave according to the same principle.

apparently understanding the relation between the cord and the canopy of toys. But Piaget asks: "Does an infant of this age perceive a physical connection between the cord and the covering of the crib and comprehend a physical cause and effect? Or does he merely make a more general and subjective connection, at once egocentric and phenomenalistic, between the 'action of pulling the cord' and the interesting sensory results in the form of the sight and sound of the bouncing toys?"[77]

To answer this question, Piaget removed the rattles and then, from a hidden position, interested the baby in a toy swung from a long stick above the canopy. The child watched, smiled, and cooed at the toy. Then Piaget stopped the movement, whereupon the baby seized the cord and pulled it! Another test confirms this result: "The baby may even respond in the same manner to a distant sound. Hiding myself behind a screen in a corner of the room, I whistle a certain number of times at regular intervals until the baby has acquired a sufficiently lively interest to stretch his head and looks in the direction of my corner. Then I stop whistling. The baby's eyes explore the corner for a moment; then he pulls the cord hanging in his crib, looking back to the corner from which the whistles came!"[78]

Thus the baby has not yet grasped the relation of cause and effect or of means and end as such but merely makes a confused association between an action (pulling the cord) and prolonging interesting experiences. All this occurs without any recognition of mechanics, distance, or points of contact.

Apes behave in a similar manner when presented with strings attached to food not immediately accessible. Kohler recounts that in experiments where food outside the cage could be had by pulling the right cord, his chimpanzees did not bother making observations but just grabbed something and pulled. "When hungry," Kohler adds, "the chimpanzee will pull the rope, while looking at the objective, even when he *must and obviously does see* that there is no contact between them."[79] Here the animal is clearly acting on the basis of an association between pulling the rope and getting food, and not by virtue of understanding cause and effect or means and end. Later experiments by psychologist Herbert Birch confirm the same findings: six chimpanzees were habituated to the technique of string pulling in a single string situation (thirty trials), but none of the animals performed significantly above chance in tests with two strings where one was clearly unconnected to the food.[80] Kohler doubts whether the "concept" of connection is for the apes anything more than visual proximity.[81]

Kohler gives several examples where the best tool easily loses relevance for the animal when not visible simultaneously, or almost simultaneously, with the objective. In cases where a stick was needed to get the food, Kohler remarks, "I have used every means at my disposal to attract Tschego's attention to the sticks in the background of her cage . . . and she did look straight at them; but in doing so, she turned her back on the objective, and so the sticks remained meaningless to her."[82] Birch makes similar observations.[83] This indicates no knowledge of means and end as such. The problem is on the purely sensory plane for the animal. Apes frequently demonstrate that they do not comprehend a clearly insufficient means. Birch records one animal making twenty-six consecutive futile sweeps at food with a stick obviously too short. After several violent temper tantrums, by accident the ape hit into its reach the string joined to a sufficiently longer stick.[84]

But perhaps most revealing are the errors the animals make. Kohler witnessed what he called "crude stupidities" in his chimpanzees where the animals should have been able to survey the situation.[85] For example, one chimpanzee, Sultan, piles up boxes beneath the place where the fruit was on the *previous* trial, not under where it hangs now.[86] This is like the baby Piaget observed looking for a ball not under the sofa where it was lost but under a chair where he had found it the time before. On another occasion, after testing his animals with boxes for four weeks, Kohler puts the food *outside* the cage and leaves within reach a stick able to retrieve it. The result: "Sultan drags a box to that spot at the bars, opposite which the objective is lying (outside), and turns first one side, then the other towards the bars quite stupidly; fetches more boxes, and begins as if to build."[87] (See Figure 3.5.)

The same kind of "stupidities" are committed by other apes.[88] With the fruit outside the bars, Grande, another chimp, drags stones about the cage as an aftereffect of repeated experiments in which stones served as footstools.[89] Rumbaugh, Rumbaugh, and Boysen, who conducted experiments in 1978, also note similar errors. Even after their apes had been thoroughly trained in the use of several tools, they repeatedly tried the wrong one when all were

Figure 3.5. The chimpanzee associates piling up boxes with getting the banana. But he does not understand cause and effect, as is seen when he piles the boxes *against* the bars to get the banana outside the cage.

available at once in a tool box: "keys were inserted into long tubes, locks were poked with sticks, sponges were twisted on bolts" to get at the food bait.[90]

If the apes were capable of an intellectual understanding of cause and effect, they would not make mistakes of this kind. But their actions make perfect sense if they are based merely on motor habits and acquired associations. For example, a man who trades in his manual shift automobile for one with an automatic transmission will for some time feel a definite inclination to shift his new vehicle manually in accordance with his previous habit. In a sense this inclination is not really an error because there is no judgment. Reason is not the source of the inclination; in fact reason contradicts it. In the same way the infant in the crib pulls the cord to hear the whistles and the ape puts a box against the bars to get food outside the cage. It is worth noting that none of these animal "errors" would have come to light if before each new series of tests Kohler and the other experimenters had cleared the area of irrelevant equipment. The element of association is evident in Kohler's remark: "When frequent experiments were being made with the boxes (as footstools) the chimpanzees would drag their implements eagerly to the accustomed testplace if I merely showed myself at the door at the usual time."[91] All these examples indicate that though primates sometimes *use* tools, they do not *understand* them.

Though animal experiments of this sort are customarily called "problem solving," we should recognize that the animal itself is not trying to solve any kind of intellectual problem; it is simply trying to get food or some other desired object. Consequently, the animal often pays little attention to its own behavior and frequently cannot repeat it own successful "solution" even a few minutes later.[92] The experimenter is trying to solve an intellectual problem: he wants to arrange an experiment that will yield valid insights into the animal's behavior. Chimpanzees, on the other hand, are notorious for losing interest in the "problem." Likewise, "learning" in animals means acquiring habits and associations, not understanding reasons or causes. Being trained or conditioned is not equivalent to intellectual comprehension.

Typically, the apes do a good deal of blundering around before attaining the desired object. Sometimes their activity leads them to "solve" the problem accidentally. But experimenters, Kohler and

Yerkes[93] among others, claim that some solutions represent true insight by the animal, not just chance behavior. What we have seen in no way excludes such a possibility. Piaget explains that a motor habit can be applied to a new object or situation and thus has a certain extendability.[94] Thus a baby will investigate a new object by putting it through a routine of motor manipulations, squeezing it, shaking it, dropping it, putting it into the mouth. In this way the infant comes to discover in a purely sensorimotor fashion the properties of the new object and can eventually use it to accomplish new tasks. Likewise, primates before using an object must first acquire sensorimotor experience of it either through spontaneous handling or through being trained. Ethologist Benjamin Beck describes the process in one experiment with baboons: "The tool use was learned by instrumental trial-and-error, resulting fortuitously from exploratory manipulation of the tool."[95] Once this is accomplished, the animal may be able to extend the newly acquired motor skill to a new situation. There is no objection to calling this "insight" as long as we realize it requires no intellectual understanding.

The extendability of motor habits ought not to be confused with the universality of principles that are understood. A world of difference separates understanding a thing and acquiring a motor skill related to the same thing. For example, learning to ride a bicycle is not an intellectual problem but a question of learning certain motor skills. Gaining these skills does not require that the cause or reason of anything be understood. One can train a circus bear to ride a bicycle, but this does not mean the bear understands why the bicycle is a stable vehicle. In fact, most human bicyclists are unaware of the complex physics and mechanics that make the vehicle function. David E. H. Jones begins a charming scientific paper on the physics of the bicycle with these words: "Almost everyone can ride a bicycle, yet apparently no one knows how they do it. . . . The apparent simplicity and ease of the trick conceals much unrecognized subtlety and I have spent some time and effort trying to discover the reasons for the bicycle's stability."[96] Jones explains that the bicycle has several secrets, including the rider's skill, the gyroscopic effect created by the spinning wheels, center of gravity lowering torque, and castoring forces.[97] Once understood, however, the principle of the gyroscope, for example, can explain the fly wheel of an automobile, the stability of a child's top, and even the precession of the earth's axis as it rotates, causing a change in the polestar over a period of thousands of years. Once the mind has grasped a cause, its applicability is unlimited, but acquiring a bicycle-riding skill simply allows one to ride other bicycles.

In light of the above, what should be our expectations regarding the ability of animals to learn language? First, we note that all animal actions, including tool use and "insight," are accountable by principles found in human infants *before* language begins. Second, if animals, even primates, have no grasp of the what or why of things, it is difficult to see how they could use true language. And third, though chimpanzees in the wild do request food or tickling of one another, they use nonverbal sounds and unsystematic gestures only.[98] If animals possessed the capacity for symbolic communication, one would expect them to use it in the wild without prompting or training. Primatologist Emil Menzel found by experiment that an untrained chimpanzee cannot convey the location of food hidden in a field to other apes either by gesture or sound.[99]

Considering these points, we can better understand the disappointing results of the various attempts to teach animals language. A pet dog that wants to go out for a walk may, without training, bring its leash to its master. This is not language but association and memory. In a similar way chimpanzees can learn to associate plastic tokens or keyboard buttons with objects or actions they desire, and even acquire limited habits of sequencing. But this again is not language. To an English-speaking person, the word *banana* does not mean "something I *do* to experience a sweet taste." But when the chimpanzee Sarah was trained, she was not given the banana until she put a piece of plastic on a language board.[100] The token is not for her a word or symbol that signifies the definition of a particular fruit. On the contrary, placing the token is a contrived motor action she must go through to receive a piece of fruit.

As for animals learning sign language, psychologist Herbert Terrace organized one of the most elaborate projects. At a cost of over $250,000, with four years' labor, Terrace and sixty other teachers trained an infant male chimpanzee in American Sign Language. This project, the best documented of its kind to date, produced over forty video-tape hours of Nim signing and more than 2,000 teachers' reports.[101] Analyzing the 19,000 recorded signs produced by Nim, Terrace found "no evidence of lexical regularities," no sentences, and no grammar.[102] Neither did Nim give evidence of syntax, not even linking an adjective to a noun. Terrace proposes that the Gardners' chimp Washoe signing "water bird" on seeing a swan was merely the sign for *water* that was seen and the sign for *bird* without any syntactical connection. After an extensive analysis of Nim's signing, Terrace concludes, "each instance of presumed grammatical competence could be explained adequately by simple nonlinguistic processes."[103]

Moreover, Nim always combined signs in a series of repetitions with little new information and much redundancy. His longest combination of signs, for example, was "Give orange me give eat orange me eat orange give me eat orange give me you." Also, only 10 percent of the animal's signs were unprompted or unasked for by teachers, in marked contrast with young children's speech, which is more than 80 percent spontaneous and increases steadily in length, richness, and complexity.[104] "By age three," Terrace writes, "a child stops imitating its parents' utterances; by four, Nim's imitations grew to 54 percent."[105]

More significant was Nim's motivation. Terrace notes: "With few exceptions, it did not appear that Nim discovered the 'power of the word' in the same sense that a child does. The exceptions all concerned one function of language: that of *demanding* something. *Hug, play, dirty, sleep, eat,* and so on were all requests that something happen to Nim."[106] It is not accidental that Nim put "Nim" or "me" into twenty out of twenty-one of his most frequent three-sign combinations.[107] For the chimp the signs are not words but merely means of getting what he wants. A striking example—Nim used the sign for dirty not only to indicate a need to use the toilet, but even when he had no such need but was simply bored or did not like a new teacher or wanted to get out of an unpleasant situation. He had learned this sign would provoke immediate action by the trainer. Nim used the sign *sleep* in the same way, even when fully alert and not sleepy.[108]

An acquired motor habit associated with a particular object or action is not a word. If language were merely a vast repertoire of motor associations, there would be no reason to say that animals cannot talk. Piaget's distinctions between the year-old infant's sensorimotor schemata and true intellectual concepts that come later illuminate this whole discussion of animal language: "Sensorimotor intelligence seeks only practical adaptation, that is, it aims only at success or utilization, whereas conceptual thought leads to knowledge as such and therefore yields to norms of truth. Even when the child explores a new object or studies the displacements he provokes by a sort of 'experiment in order to see,' there is always in these kinds of sensorimotor assimilations . . . a practical result to be obtained. . . . There can be no question of attributing to him the capacity of arriving at pure proofs or judgments properly so called, but it must be said that these judgments, if they were expressed in words, would be equivalent to something like 'one can do this with this object,' 'one can achieve this result,' etc. . . . the sole problem is to reach the desired goal, hence the only values involved are success or failure, and to the child it is not a matter of seeking a truth for itself or reflecting upon the relations which made it possible to obtain the desired result. Sensorimotor intelligence is limited to desiring success or practical adaptation, whereas the function of verbal or conceptual thought is to know and state truths."[109]

Terrace discovered the same thing in chimpanzees: "The function of the symbols of an ape's vocabulary appears to be not so much to identify things or to convey information . . . as it is to satisfy a demand that it use the symbol in order to obtain some reward."[110] No grammar, no sentences, no words. Animals can *use* signs or symbols instrumentally and motorially, but they do not *understand* them. Contrast this with the average child of three, who has a vocabulary of 1,000 words; who daily creates sentences of increasing subtlety and richness to inquire about, wonder about, and describe the world; who engages in symbolic play, transforming himself and the objects around him by imagination into a realm of make-believe; who represents both the real and the pretend by his drawings and works of art. All these activities of the child are evidence of an intellect at work. We should not be surprised, on the other hand, when the chimpanzee turns out to be an animal after all.

After a thorough survey of the evidence, linguists Thomas Sebeok and Jean Umiker-Sebeok conclude, "Real breakthroughs in man-ape communication are still the stuff of fiction."[111] And Noam Chomsky, the founder of modern linguistics, adds, "It's about as likely that an ape will prove to have language ability as that there is an island somewhere with a species of flightless birds waiting for human beings to teach them to fly."[112]

The same holds for the much-celebrated intelligence of dolphins. After experiments and observations, researcher Sheri Lynn Gish, for example, dismisses notions that dolphins possess a complex, symbolic, "humanoid" language, claiming that most studies have been descriptive, not quantitive, and have made "tremendous assumptions."[113] Animals are clearly not machines, but neither are they slightly diminished human beings. Intellectual understanding is not found in any degree in any animal but man. The human capacity to understand the what and the why of things is unique in the animal kingdom. With respect to this faculty, man is different in *kind* from animals, not in degree. The difference between apes and other animals is one of degree, since they possess the same kinds of powers to a greater or less extent. But a greater gap separates man from ape than that which separates any two other natural creatures.

Much of the current literature about animals confuses intelligence with consciousness. Consequently, some argue that animals must be intelligent since they are consciously aware of things, while others argue that since animals do not possess intellectual understanding they must be unconscious robots. Both sides have part of the truth: animals do have consciousness but they—even the great apes—lack intellectual understanding. No harm results in applying the words *intelligence* and *understanding* to animals, as long as we recognize that we are extending the meanings of these words to include any purposeful, conscious activity. In this sense Piaget speaks of sensorimotor intelligence in the year-old infant: "It is an entirely practical intelligence based on the manipulation of objects; in place of words and concepts it uses percepts and movements organized into 'action schemata.'"[114] This kind of intelligence also characterizes animals. The ape, then, is not capable of anything different *in principle* than the one-year-old child.

A Nonmechanical Model

In contrast to behaviorism, modern ethology as pioneered by Konrad Lorenz, Niko Tinbergen, and Karl von Frisch is a fine example of nonreductionist science. Reductionism results from using a model that is too narrow: the machine model falls short of the animal, just as animal behavior is simply inadequate as a key to human behavior. The way to avoid the narrowness of reductionism is to find a model that lacks nothing. A model that contains all could not fall short and would eliminate the necessity of reducing or explaining away.

Does such a model exist? If the inadequate model came to biology from the mechanistic physics of the seventeenth century, then perhaps the nonmechanistic physics of the twentieth century can offer guidance in finding the new model. The two great revolutions of modern physics are relativity and quantum theory; both incorporate the centrality of the observer. Physicist Max Born writes: "No description of any natural phenomenon in the atomic domain is possible without referring to the observer, not only to his velocity as in relativity, but to all his activities in performing the observation, setting up the instruments, and so on."[115] Physicist John Wheeler comments: "The observer is elevated from 'observer' to 'participator.' What philosophy suggested in times past, the central feature of quantum mechanics tells us today with impressive force. In some strange sense this is a participatory universe."[116] And physicist Eugene Wigner adds: "It was not possible to formulate the laws of quantum mechanics in a fully consistent way without reference to the consciousness."[117]

The centrality of the observer, then, is a key feature of modern physics. This principle suggests as its biological counterpart that we ourselves are the key to understanding life and living things. Taking man as the exemplar for biology has much to recommend it, since all levels of nature are reflected in him: intellect and will, senses and emotions, voluntary movements, vegetative and metabolic functions, and matter. We do not have every organ that every animal possesses, but to everything that exists in the animal there corresponds something in us, allowing us to comprehend the animal's faculties by analogy from our own experience. And man enjoys the fullest sense of agency, acting for goals he himself selects. The lesser kinds of agency characteristic of animals and of plants are also found in him. Looking at the rest of nature as represented in man is much more reasonable than trying to understand all things on the basis of matter alone. The more contains the less, not the reverse.

The centrality of the observer is more manifestly a principle of biology than of physics. E. S. Russell explains: "Biology occupies a unique and privileged position among the sciences in that its object, the living organism, is known to us not only objectively through sensory perception, but also in one case directly, as the subject of immediate experience. It is therefore possible, in this special case of one's own personal life, to take an inside view of a living organism. Naturally the direct intuitive understanding obtained by this immediate experience of living cannot form the subject-matter of biology, which is an objective science, and we must be very chary of reading into the activities of other organisms the motives and modes of experiences which we discover in ourselves. Nevertheless introspective knowledge does give us an insight into the reality of the living organism which cannot be other wise obtained, and supplies us with a standard by which to test our conceptions of the living thing."[118]

Weizsäcker agrees that knowledge of ourselves as living creatures gives us insight into other living things: "I am a living creature which must behave simultaneously as acting and perceiving. In this context something of the meaning of the behavior of other living things, with whom I am involved in a network of living interactions, is already given me. A stone, to be sure, I know only as object, but a man is necessarily my 'fellow man.' His expressions are carriers of meaning which I can understand because I am myself a man, and it is both practical necessity and ethical obligation, which stirs spontaneously in me, that I should not take them solely as objects, but do my best to understand them. Now the sphere of biology is shot through with both these modes of interpretation and is unable wholly to dispense with either. An amoeba is for me scarcely more than an odd physical object. A saddle horse is for me first of all a partner in the game of life, with whom my inner contact is stronger than with many people. Between both extremes there is any number of intermediate stages."[119]

Our certitude of being alive comes from our own internal experience of seeing, tasting, hearing, remembering, imagining, feeling emotions, self-directed movement, understanding, reasoning, and choosing. We could never recognize these as living functions in other persons or in animals unless we first experienced them in ourselves. If we did not experience dreams ourselves, we would never suspect that dreams occur in animals, no matter what their behavior during sleep, and no matter how much data we collected on rapid eye movement. If we never directed our movements in accordance with knowledge, we would have no reason to distinguish conscious actions from unconscious reflex actions in animals.

Participants at an international workshop titled "Animal Mind—Human Mind" held in 1981 recognized human experience as the foundation for animal studies. Griffin reports: "Many of the participants agreed that a good starting point would be to consider what we know of our own thinking, subjective feelings, and consciousness, and then move on to inquire whether other species experience anything similar. Such an approach was once considered fallaciously anthropomorphic. But it seems now to be widely if not universally recognized that this is a serious objection only if one has already assumed in advance that conscious thinking *is* uniquely human, and the accusation of anthropomorphism is then merely a reiteration of the prior conviction."[120] It is, of course, erroneous to attribute to animals human understandings, deliberation, and free choice, but neither should we fall into the opposed extreme of considering animals as machines. Robotomorphism is no less mistaken than anthropomorphism.

Historically, modern biology's neglect of internal experience is partly explained by its imitation of a physics that relied exclusively on external observation and measurement. But that model was Newtonian physics where mind plays no intrinsic role. Modern physics, as we have seen, affirms the reality of mind and the essential participation of the observer.

The internal experience we have of our own living activities is rejected by some as "subjective," and therefore unreliable for the purposes of science. Regarding hallucinations or other purely private phenomena not accessible to others, their claim would be justified. But we speak here of activities anyone can immediately verify in himself: to sense, to remember, to feel fear or joy, to understand, to choose. This experience is universal and must serve as the constant guide and standard when investigating these abilities in man or in animals. What does it matter that one man cannot experience another man's sensation of red? He has his own. Whatever is verifiable in everyone's internal experience is just as much a fact of biology or psychology as the rat's performance in a maze or the molecular structure of a protein.

Taking ourselves as the starting point in biology is not to be confused with Descartes' *cogito ergo sum*. For the former principle assumes a basic similarity between many of our faculties and those of animals. Descartes, on the other hand, denies that animals have sensations and emotions, considering them to be unconscious machines. If that were true, man's internal experience could give him no insight into animal behavior. Further, Descartes begins with the thinking self for skeptical reasons: because he considers his senses unreliable, he thinks the existence of the world is doubtful and so feels forced to withdraw into his own subjectivity. By contrast, acknowledging the utility of our internal experience for animal studies does not require us to doubt our senses or the world. Lastly, Descartes tries to deduce the world from his own ideas, whereas the observership principle uses our own experience as a tool and guide, not to deduce, but to investigate what takes place in animals.

Using internal experience as a guide, we can distinguish the various degrees of agency found in living things. Among natural creatures we humans enjoy the fullest sense of agency. We propose to ourselves a particular goal of action, knowing that we could substitute another if we wished, and we freely choose the appropriate means to the end. Before we act, we conceive in our minds various likely outcomes and then decide accordingly. Because of our ability to understand, we are fully aware of ourselves as agents, for understanding can reflect on its own acts and can understand itself. Our choosing power, the will, is the prime agent, setting other faculties into operation, since by choice a person sets his intellect to think of this or that; or directs his sense powers to this or that object; or moves his voluntary muscles. Our will can even override the emotions when necessary. But the will moves itself to choose.

Using ourselves as a standard yields a considerable advantage when we investigate animal behavior. We can distinguish intellect from sense and distinguish will from emotion because we have all four capacities ourselves. We have some idea what it is like for the animal to perceive without understanding intellectually, since we can experience in ourselves perceptual associations not based on reason. We have insight into the animal being inclined toward a thing or away from it by emotion, since we share emotions with the higher animals, although in them there is no intellect or will to override the feelings. We have a notion of what an animal's instinctive actions may be like when we respond to something impulsively without verbal thought or deliberation. Something in us corresponds to the animal's degree of agency, and operates autonomously if reason and will are suspended, as we say of a drunk or enraged person that he acts like an animal.

We experience this kind of nonverbal thinking ourselves when we search for the right piece in a jigsaw puzzle, or when without words we rearrange a room's furniture in our imagination. Such thinking employs percepts, not concepts; images, not definitions. We experience also the kind of nonrational association found in animals, when, for instance, the mere smell of pencil shavings evokes in us an unexpected swell of memories of grammar school. Involuntary memory associations such as these, though clearly limited to the perceptual plane, are capable of provoking emotions. A professional nurse sometimes will experience an unusual, incapacitating pity for a patient without realizing until later that the man with the disease is the same age and of the same general appearance as her father.[121] Such associations are not based on reason, though reason can reflect on them and discover the reason for them. Our own nonverbal thinking and involuntary memory associations give us some idea of what animal consciousness must be like.

Similarly, we can surmise that plants grow and metabolize without consciousness because in us these operations are unconscious. A child grows; his bruised arm heals itself; his cells divide and differentiate—none of these activities proceed under the child's direction or choice, nor does he perceive them from the inside by sensory awareness. They are all undeniably his activities, things his body does from within and not the result of external forces. But all the procedures and results are determined by nature and are aiming at a goal fixed by nature. This vegetative agency is in us as well as in the plants.

Lastly, we find in ourselves the kind of agency characteristic of matter. If pushed off a cliff, we fall, just like a rock. Both the motion and its limits are determined from without. A nonliving thing cannot move itself; it can only move something else. Billiard ball A cannot move itself, but striking billiard ball B sets it in motion. This is the only kind of agency available to nonliving things: one moves another totally from the outside.

Clearly matter exhibits the most imperfect kind of agency, since it lacks the higher kinds found in living things. Therefore, if matter is taken as the basis for understanding all nature, reductionism must necessarily result. And yet materialism uses the machine model for analyzing the agency of all natural beings; the plant, the animal, and man. Only a nonmechanical model—the observership principle— encompasses the full range of agency found in nature. For matter, growth, reproduction, sensation, emotion, intellect, and will are all found in man.

4

Cooperation

The paradigm of modern biology depicts nature as a ruthless struggle between opposing forces. In 1858 Charles Darwin set the tone when, in a paper delivered to the Linnean Society, he made public for the first time his theory of evolution. Darwin opens the paper with a stark image of nature: "All nature is at war, one organism with another, or with external nature. Seeing the contented face of nature, this may at first well be doubted; but reflection will inevitably prove it to be true."[1] The co-discoverer of natural selection, Alfred R. Wallace, in a paper presented simultaneously with Darwin's, employs the same imagery, describing animals and plants as locked in "a struggle for existence, in which the weakest and least perfectly organized must always succumb."[2] Biologist Thomas Huxley, Darwin's friend and defender, speaks in the same vein: "The animal world is on about the same level as a gladiator's show. The strongest, the swiftest and the cunningest live to fight another day...no quarter is given."[3] To describe this brutality Tennyson coined the now-famous phrase "Nature, red in tooth and claw with ravine [violence]."[4] In *The Origin of Species*, Darwin maintains that "all organic beings are exposed to severe competition" and to "the universal struggle for life." He argues that this conflict of living things follows inevitably from the tension between limited resources and unlimited population growth.[5]

This paradigm has dominated biology since Darwin's day. But paradoxically, it does not square with observation. Ruthless struggle between species can be induced artificially in the laboratory, but it is difficult to point out clear examples of mutual harm between natural species undisturbed by man. Many ecologists and others experienced in field studies of animals candidly admit that the theoretical expectations are not borne out by the observed facts. Daniel Simberloff writes: "It is rare to see two animals, particularly animals of different species, tugging at the same piece of meat. And even when competition is observed, it often appears inconsequential. Perhaps a fiddler crab scurries into a hole on a beach only to come running out again, expelled by the current inhabitant. But the crab simply moves off to find another hole. Competition between species—interspecific competition—thus appears to be little more than a minor, temporary inconvenience."[6]

After a three-year study of breeding bird communities in the North American plains and shrubsteppe, John Weins and John Rotenberry discovered that "variations in the population size of one species in an area are largely independent both of the presence or absence of other species and of variations in habitat features. Coexisting species appear to use resources more or less opportunistically. We find little evidence that they are currently much concerned about competition with one another or that competition in the past has led to an orderly community structure."[7] They conclude that "competition is not the ubiquitous force that many ecologists have believed" it to be.[8] Weins and Rotenberry began their observations with the conventional assumption that interspecific strife is the central factor in determining how the natural communities are put together. They confess that "as the research progressed, however, these expectations proved to be naive."[9]

Entomologist P. S. Messenger also writes that "Actual competition is difficult to see in nature."[10] Ecologist E. J. Kormondy asserts that competition in natural conditions is rare.[11] And biologists Allee, Emerson, Park, Park, and Schmidt in a collaboratively produced text declare, "Instances of direct mutual harm between species are not known to us."[12]

Because of this conflict between the accepted paradigm and what is actually observed in natural communities of species, discussion of competition in biology is fraught with confusion and contradiction. Evidence that undermines the premises of competitive struggle is presented as the *result* of competitive struggle. Some claim to see competition operating in the very mechanisms that enable animals to *avoid* competition. As ecologist Robert Ricklefs says, "Competition is perhaps the most elusive and controversial of all ecological phenomena."[13]

The Ways Nature Avoids Competition

A careful review of the many strategies nature employs to prevent competition* will bring light to this controversy and help to dispel some of the confusion. (Whether the cooperation present in nature now is the result of prior competition we will address in Chapter 6.)

The first and easiest way to prevent two species from harming each other is geographical isolation. Scattered across the globe are many species that could eradicate others in a short time, but this does not happen because they inhabit separate continents. In 1876, Wallace distinguished six biological land realms on the earth, each characterized by plants and animals unique to it and that naturally occur nowhere else (see Figure 4.1). Wallace's six realms, roughly corresponding to continental divisions, are still valid and recognized by biologists today. Hundreds of miles of ocean or vast deserts or huge mountain ranges like the Himalayas isolate the six realms from each other, effectively preventing competition and allowing the earth to support a much richer diversity of animals and plants than it did before the continents were separated from each other. This is why man's introduction of a species into a region where it does not naturally occur often brings ecological disaster and sometimes the extinction of native species.

But what about organisms in the *same* habitat? How can similar organisms avoid competing with each other if food and other resources are limited in supply? Similar species living together avoid competition by dividing the habitat into ecological niches. The habitat is where an organism lives; the niche is its profession. The presence of one species no more harms another species with a different livelihood than "the practice of a doctor harms the trade of a mechanic living in the same village," to use a comparison of Lorenz.[15] Niche means not only the physical space the plant or animal uses, but also how it fits into the community: whether it is a food producer, consumer, or decomposer; how it uses energy

*Colinvaux points out that "'Competition' is a word with a clear meaning, valid and hallowed in English usage. There is competition whenever two or more individuals or groups 'strive together' (the literal meaning of the Latin roots) for something in short supply. Men compete for prizes, and only one man, or one group of those competing, can win a prize."[14]

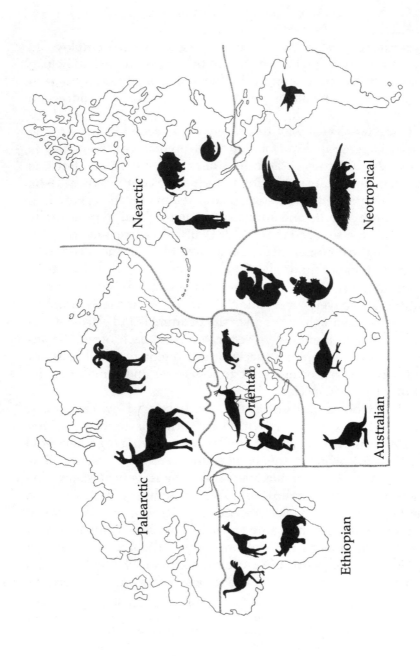

Figure 4.1. Wallace's six realms with a sample of the fauna unique to each. Natural geographical barriers prevent competition and allow the earth to support a rich diversity of plants and animals.

sources; what predators and prey it may have; its period of activity; and what changes it makes in the environment.[16]

Among the most thoroughly documented principles in the science of ecology is the dictum that two species never occupy the same niche. Thousands of examples are known where similar animal species coexist without competing because they eat different foods or are active at different times or otherwise occupy different niches. Each plant species also occupies a distinct niche: some specialize in sandy soil, others in rich humus; some prefer acid soil, others alkaline; still others require no soil, such as the lichens; some exploit the early growing season, others the late; some get by only because they are tiny, others only because they are huge. Experiments have shown, for instance, that two species of clover can flourish together in the same field. Of the two species investigated, "*Trifolium repens* grows faster and reaches a peak of leaf density sooner. However, *T. fragiferum* has longer petioles and higher leaves and is able to overtop the faster growing species, especially after *T. repens* has passed its peak, and thus avoids being shaded out."[17] Herbs and grasses have shallow roots to absorb moisture from light rains. Thus they do not compete with trees like oaks that have deep roots to tap more permanent sources deep in the soil water table. Also, in a deciduous forest many plants bloom and complete their yearly growth *before* trees have formed enough leaves to shade out the needed sunlight. Other plants require the shade and higher humidity that the forest canopy provides.

Plant physiologist Frits Went writes: "There is no violent struggle between plants, no warlike mutual killing, but a harmonious development on a share-and-share basis. The cooperative principle is stronger than the competitive one."[18] Went exemplifies this principle with the growth of seedlings. Even if several thousand per square yard spring up together they do not kill each other. They simply do not grow to full capacity while sharing the available water, nutrients, and sunlight. He points out that weeds sometimes crowd out desirable garden plants only because the latter have been planted out of season or in the wrong climate. The cooperative principle operates even in harsh environments: "In the desert, where want and hunger for water are the normal burden of all plants, we find no fierce competition for existence, with the strong crowding out the weak. On the contrary, the available possessions—space, light, water and food—are shared and shared alike by all. If there is not enough for all to grow tall and strong, then all remain smaller. This factual picture is very different from the time-honored notion that nature's way is cut-throat competition among individuals."[19] The same is true of the jungle: "The forest giants among the trees do not kill the small fry under them. They hold back their development, and they prevent further germination. In a mountain forest in Java it was observed that the small trees living in the shade of the forest giants had not grown after 40 years, but they were still alive."[20] Thus in garden, desert, and forest the paradigm for plants is not competition but peaceful coexistence.

Food specialization is one of the simplest ways that animal species avoid competition. Along the shore of Lake Mweru in Central Africa, three species of yellow weaver birds live side by side without struggle. They do not fight over food since one species eats only hard black seeds, another eats only soft green seeds, and the third only insects.[21] Many caterpillars will eat only one kind of plant. In some cases the plant's toxins render it inedible to all but one specialist herbivore, as with milkweed and the monarch butterfly larva. Twenty different insects feed on the North American white pine without competition because five species eat only foliage, three species concentrate on buds, three on twigs, two on wood, two on roots, one on bark, and four on the cambium.[22] Experiments show that newly hatched, inexperienced garter snakes pursue worm scent by preference over cricket scent. Baby green snakes that live in the same regions have just the opposite preference, though clearly both kinds of snake could eat both kinds of prey.[23]

Two species of cormorant found in Britain look very much alike, occupy the same areas of the shoreline, and feed and nest in similar ways. The competitive paradigm predicts that these animals must be locked in a ruthless struggle, each trying to supplant the other. Close investigation, however, reveals that one eats mostly sand eels and sprats, the other a mixed diet but no sand eels or sprats. One fishes out at sea, the other in shallow estuaries. One nests high on the cliffs or on broad ledges, the other low on the cliffs or on narrow ledges.[24] No struggle. No competition at all. The birds, in fact, occupy different niches.

Size of food is a major factor in determining food preferences. Carnivores, for example, must prey on animals small enough to overpower, but not so small as to be of negligible nourishment for the time and energy invested in the hunt. Man is the only animal not restricted to certain foods by size requirements. G. D. Carpenter, who studied the tsetse fly in the region of Lake Victoria, Africa, found it could suck the blood of mammals and birds whose blood cells vary from seven to eighteen microns in diameter but could not draw blood from the lungfish because its blood cells (forty-one microns wide) are too large to pass into the proboscis of the fly.[25]

Sometimes spatial division of the habitat is sufficient to prevent competition. Five species of cone-shelled, carnivorous snails live segregated from each other in five parallel strips along the shores of Hawaii, where within each strip each species attacks with poison darts a unique group of prey.[26] The niche of many fresh-water fish is circumscribed by their oxygen requirements. Catfish can inhabit the lower, slow-moving regions of a stream where there is little oxygen but brook trout, which require much more dissolved oxygen, can live only where the water is aerated by rapids and waterfalls. Figure 4.2 illustrates the differing tolerances for salinity in estuarine animals. Thus the clam does not compete with the mussel because it cannot live in the same places. The space that defines a niche need not be large or far away from others: three different species of mite occupy three different areas of the honey bee's body as their niches.[27]

Dividing the habitat according to time is another strategy nature uses to prevent competition. Most habitats support two ecological communities, the diurnal and the nocturnal. During the day, bees, butterflies, weasels, most lizards, and most birds are active. At dusk they retire and the night shift takes over, including cockroaches, moths, mice, bats, and owls. Moths feed on white or pale yellow flowers that open only at night, thereby avoiding competition with bees and butterflies. Ecologist Charles Elton describes the noncompetitive use of the habitat by diurnal and nocturnal animals: "Not only is one kind of animal replaced by another, but one kind of food-chain is replaced by another, and certain niches which are unused by any animal during the day become occupied at night. The weasel-bank vole industry is changed into a tawny owl–wood mouse industry. The woodpecker-ant connection has no equivalent at night, while the moth-nightjar or bat chain is almost unrepresented by day. In fact, one food-cycle is switched off and another starts up

% of Salt in Water

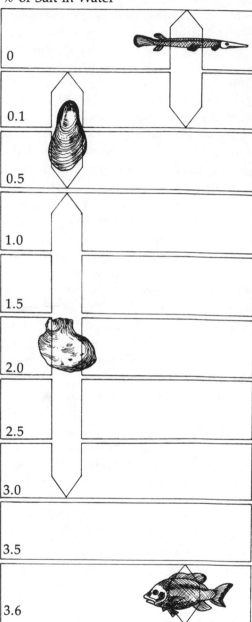

Figure 4.2. Differing degrees of saltiness establish invisible but rigid barriers between estuarine animals. The mussel, since it cannot tolerate more than 0.5 percent salinity, never competes with the oyster, which cannot live in water with less than 0.5 percent salt. For the same reason, the gar is incapable of trespassing into the snapper's niche, and vice versa. Spatial division of this sort is one way animals of similar species avoid competition.

to take its place. With the dawn the whole thing is switched back again."[28] Elton offers the unusual example of the gerbille that inhabits the South African veld. This rodent often shares the same underground tunnels with the carnivorous mongoose but is never attacked because "while the gerbilles come out exclusively at night, leaving their burrows after sunset and returning always before dawn, the mongoose ... feed only during the day, and retire to earth at night."[29]

Biologists Leyhausen and Wolf discovered that with "domestic cats living in free open country, several individuals could make use of the same hunting ground without ever coming into conflict, by using it according to a definite time-table.... An additional safe-guard against undesirable encounters is the scent marks which these animals...deposit at regular intervals wherever they go. These act like railway signals whose aim is to prevent collision between two trains. A cat finding another cat's signal on its hunting path assesses its age, and if it is very fresh it hesitates, or chooses another path; if it is a few hours old it proceeds calmly on its way."[30]

Similar species sometimes escape struggling with each other over resources by periodic migration. For example, the white storks and the black storks that winter in Africa spend the rest of the year in Europe. They "thus have avoided competition with their tropical relatives, not by radiating into unique food niches but by leaving the area," says zoologist M. Philip Kahl.[31] Other animals that migrate—some as far as twelve thousand miles—include caribou, bats, whales, birds, dragonflies, butterflies, fish, eels, and turtles.

The migration strategy is not open to plants, of course. Flowering plants avoid interspecific competition for pollinators by flowering sequentially, each species in its turn, as commonly occurs in the Arctic, the temperate zones, and in the tropics.[32] To these differences of timing correspond the active periods of pollinators such as bats, hummingbirds, and insects. Ricklefs points out that of the four species of honey bee that occur in England, *Bombus pratorum* coexists peacefully with *Bombus agrorum* because the former is active earlier in the season. The other two species do not fight over the same flowers because they restrict themselves to woods rather than open fields, and *B. hortorum* has a much longer tongue, so it feeds only at flowers with long corollas that the other three short-tongued species do not visit.[33] In a similar way, miconia trees of several species on the island of Trinidad fruit at different times, thereby avoiding competition for birds to eat the fruit and scatter the seeds.[34]

But how can different grass species living blade against blade in the same turf, using the same water and nutrients, avoid competition? There would seem to be no room for a division into different niches. The answer is the cropping principle, described by Darwin: "If turf which has long been mown, and the case would be the same with turf closely browsed by quadrupeds, be let to grow, the more vigorous plants gradually kill the less vigorous, though fully grown plants; thus out of twenty species growing on a little plot of mown turf (three feet by four) nine species perished, from the other species being allowed to grown up freely."[35] Stated the other way around, constant browsing allowed nine more species of grasses to thrive than would otherwise be possible. Here the browser eating the grasses prevents the competitive elimination of some species from the turf. Herbivores also have their preferences, and this leads to a kind of cooperation. In a mountain meadow goats will keep down the population of the plants they like best to eat. This gives other plants more chance to grow. These other species may be preferred by an elk or a big horn sheep, leading to a rich variety of plant species and food for all without competition. Part of the niche of a grass species in a meadow is being inedible or at least unpalatable to all but a particular herbivore; the plant accomplishes this by growing thorns or by producing special toxins such as nicotine, digitalis, or hypercin. As a general rule, the larger the mammal herbivore, the longer the list of plant species it eats, taking only a little of each one to minimize the effects of toxins and at the same time producing a balanced crop.

The herbivores also have special habits and equipment that preclude fighting over the same foods. Colinvaux explains how three browsers coexist on the African savanna: "Zebras take the long dry stems of grasses, an action for which their horsy incisor teeth are nicely suited. Wildebeest take the side-shoots of grasses, gathering with their tongues in the bovine way and tearing off the food against their single set of incisors. Thompson's gazelles graze where others have been before, picking out ground-hugging plants and other tidbits that the feeding methods of the others have both overlooked and left in view. Although these and other big game animals wander over the same patches of country, they clearly avoid competition by specializing in the kinds of food energy they take."[36]

The zebra, the wildebeest, and the gazelle in their turn are the common prey of five carnivores: the lion, the leopard, the cheetah, the hyena, and the wild dog. These predators can coexist because there are five different "ways which do not directly compete to make a living off three prey species," according to ethologist James Gould. He explains: "Carnivores avoid competition by hunting primarily in different places at different times, and by using different techniques to capture different segments of the prey population. Cheetahs are unique in their high-speed chase strategy, but as a consequence must specialize on small gazelle. Only the leopard uses an ambush strategy, which seems to play no favorites in the prey it chooses. Hyenas and wild dogs are similar, but hunt at different times. And the lion exploits the brute-force niche, depending alternately on short, powerful rushes and strong-arm robbery."[37] And these five predators are far from significantly reducing the three prey species. For there are in East Africa's Serengeti-Mara region alone approximately 170,000 zebras, 240,000 wildebeest, and 640,000 Thompson gazelles.[38]

The elimination of competition by division of the habitat into niches is so universal in the plant and animal kingdoms that it has become a principle of prediction and discovery for field studies. Colinvaux writes: "Whenever we find rather similar animals living together in the wild, we do not think of competition by tooth and claw, we ask ourselves, instead, how competition is avoided. When we find many animals apparently sharing a food supply, we do not talk of struggles for survival; we watch to see by what trick the animals manage to be peaceful in their coexistence."[39]

In a classic study, ecologist Robert MacArthur set out to learn how five species of warbler, similar in size, shape, and diet, could live together in the same coniferous forest of Maine. What factor was "preventing all but one from being exterminated by competition"? After months of painstaking observations, MacArthur discovered that each species had defined a subtle niche for itself based mainly on behavior: "The birds behave in such a way as to be exposed to different kinds of food. They feed in different positions, indulge in hawking and hovering to different extents, move in different directions through the trees, vary from active to sluggish, and probably have the greatest need for food at different times corresponding to the different nesting dates. All of these differences are statistical, however; any two species show some overlapping in

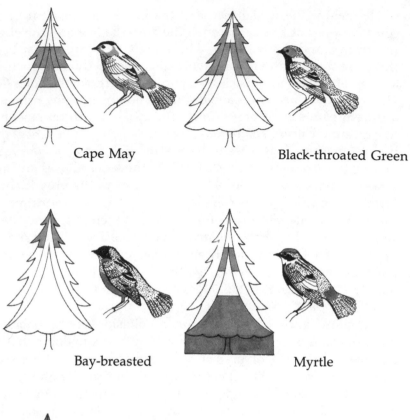

Cape May

Black-throated Green

Bay-breasted

Myrtle

Blackburnian

Figure 4.3. Derived from a classic study by ecologist Robert MacArthur, this diagram illustrates how five species of warbler, similar in size and shape, feed on bud worms in the same spruce trees. They avoid competition by occupying subtly different niches. The shaded areas indicate where each species spends more than half its time. The birds also use different methods of hunting. This pattern of noncompetition is typical of naturally coexisting species. (From MacArthur)

all of these activities."[40] (See Figure 4.3.) Colinvaux concludes that "Nature is arranged so that competitive struggles are avoided," and adds that "peaceful coexistence, not struggle, is the rule."[41]

Where food and other necessities are abundantly available many species may coexist in the same area without conflict. Herbert Ross found that six species of leafhopper in Illinois thrive side by side on the same trees without competition.[42] Such aggregations of similar species are called guilds. Hundreds of cases are known of large numbers of similar species coexisting without interference. An investigation of fourteen species of coexisting hummingbirds revealed that the birds feed differently according to flower density, height of flowers, and time of nectar renewal, with small overlap between species.[43] In the same forest log there are diverse niches for seven species of millipede.[44] Ricklefs reports that "The shallow waters of Florida's Gulf Coast can harbor up to eight species of large predatory snails.... Lake Malawi in Africa has more than 200 species of cichlid fish, which appear to have similar ecological characteristics."[45] Nature engages all her ingenuity in developing techniques to forestall strife among species. It is not surprising, then, that even careful and experienced investigators trying to document the paradigm of competition come up with disappointing results. Andrewartha and Birch comment on David Lack's paper "Competition for Food by Birds of Prey":[46] "We have discussed Lack's studies of birds in some detail because this work is so well documented. But we are forced to conclude that his interesting results do not in any way demonstrate that 'competition' between birds in nature is at all commonplace or usual. On the contrary, his results seem to show that it hardly ever occurs. Where he finds species together, there is evidence that their food is 'superabundant,' or else they live on different foods. When they are separated, there is no evidence that they do invade one another's territories."[47]

Because each species has its own niche and its own task, fights between animals of different species are exceedingly rare, if they occur at all. Lorenz after many years of studying fish remarks, "Never have I seen fish of two different species attacking each other, even if both are highly aggressive by nature."[48] Lions often steal the kills of cheetah, but there is never a struggle. The cheetah, much too wise to take on an opponent more than double its weight, abandons its prey without a fight.[49] The same prudent retreat occurs if a monarch eagle intrudes on a smaller eagle's meal of carrion, for instance. The smaller bird withdraws without protest and waits until the monarch eats its fill. As mentioned above, Allee and his collaborators did not know of any "direct mutual harm between species."[50] Colinvaux puts it succinctly: "A fit animal is not one that fights well, but one that avoids fighting altogether."[51]

Predation also is best understood not as a struggle but rather as a kind of balanced coexistence. In natural populations predators do not exterminate prey species. As a particular prey animal becomes more scarce, the predator turns to more abundant substitutes.

The wolf does not compete with the caribou but depends upon it. The caribou in its turn does not struggle with the lichens it consumes but depends on them for its livelihood. It is in the predator's interest that the prey thrive. Andrewartha and Birch state flatly, "There is no competition between the predator and its prey."[52] Odum notes that "where parasites and predators have long been associated with their respective hosts and prey, the effect is moderate, neutral, or even beneficial from the long term view."[53] Predation does not benefit the individual that is eaten but it can benefit the rest of the prey population in several ways. After a three-year study of the wolf population on Isle Royale, an island in Lake Superior, L. David Mech writes: "The wolves appear to have kept the moose herd within its food supply, culled out undesirable individuals, and stimulated reproduction. Wolves and moose probably will remain in dynamic equilibrium."[54] After a similar study of the wolves of Mount McKinley National Park in Alaska, Adolph Murie states of the Dall's sheep indigenous to the area: "Wolf predation probably has a salutary effect on the sheep as a species. At the present time it appears that the sheep and wolves may be in equilibrium."[55]

One benefit of predation is that in certain cases more diversity in prey species is allowed than would otherwise obtain because competitive exclusion is prevented. The addition of a single predator can *increase* the number of prey species that can live side by side in a given habitat. For example, biologist David Kirk writes: "One of the most important effects of predator-prey interactions is the reduction of competition between prey species that share a common predator. For example, the sea star *Pisaster* is a major predator on sedentary mollusks and barnacles of the intertidal zone. If the sea star is excluded from the community, one or two of the sedentary species soon crowd or starve out the other sedentary species because of their competitive advantage in feeding and reproduction. However, if the sea star is allowed access to the simplified community, it removes many individuals in these successful sedentary populations, leaving space for immigration of individuals of several other species. In other words, the addition of a single predator species can lead to an increase in the total number of prey species."[56] L. B. Slobodkin has obtained similar results with different species of hydra in laboratory cultures.[57] In the same way different insects preying on specific seeds and seedlings prevent or reduce tree competition.

The predator is not the enemy of its prey in the sense of hating it or being angry with it. Lorenz clarifies the relation: "The fight between predator and prey is not a fight in the real sense of the word: the stroke of the paw with which a lion kills his prey may resemble the movements that he makes when he strikes his rival, just as a shotgun and a rifle resemble each other outwardly; but the inner motives of the hunter are basically different from those of the fighter. The buffalo which the lion fells provokes his aggression as little as the appetizing turkey which I have just seen hanging in the larder provokes mine. The differences in these inner drives can clearly be seen in the expression movements of the animal: a dog about to catch a hunted rabbit has the same kind of excitedly happy expression as he has when he greets his master or awaits some longed-for treat. From many excellent photographs it can be seen that the lion, in the dramatic moment before he springs, is in no way angry."[58]

Even the unavoidable struggle is minimized. Mech reports that the fifty-one moose kills he examined were composed of the very young, the old, and the diseased. None of the animals killed by the wolves was in its prime.[59] A wolf pack sensibly seeks out prey that will offer the least fight. Murie found the same thing with wolf predation of Dall's sheep.[60] Finally, predators do not practice wanton killing, and even the pain seems to be minimized. Rodents attacked by snakes commonly go into shock before being killed and devoured. A wildebeest surrounded by attacking lions does not even resist but falls into shock.

The same principles hold regarding the parasites found universally among animals and plants. Authorities agree that parasitism is rarely harmful to the host. "It is the exceptional parasite that is deleterious," writes Thomas Cheng.[61] For example, "The Okapi, which lives in the tropical forests of central Africa, harbours at least five kinds of worms simultaneously and some of these may be present in numbers of several hundreds; the host does not seem any the worse for this and can feed itself as well as cater for the fauna it contains," according to parasitologist Jean G. Baer.[62]

Some parasites have intricate life cycles requiring one or more secondary hosts. The larvae of the brain worm that parasitizes the white-tailed deer live in slugs and snails that the deer inadvertently ingest when grazing. The larvae then penetrate the deer's stomach and enter the spinal column, eventually migrating to the spaces surrounding the brain. Here they mate and lay eggs that pass via the bloodstream to the deer's lungs where they are coughed up, swallowed, and passed out with fecal waste to reinfect another snail. But the damage to the host animal is minimal. Ecologist Robert L. Smith remarks, "As with most parasites and hosts, the deer and the brain worm have achieved a mutual tolerance, and the deer does not suffer greatly from the infection."[63]

The host's continued health and well-being are clearly in the interest of the parasite. This is why, as Cheng observes, "recent evaluations of the nature of the host-parasite relationship have intentionally avoided employing 'the infliction of harm' as a criterion in distinguishing parasitism from other categories of symbiosis."[64] Harm results only when parasites are present in excessive numbers. In fact, several controlled experiments have proven that certain parasites enhance the growth and vigor of the host, either by providing nutrients or by modifying the host's metabolism.[65]

Competition can be induced between species artificially in the laboratory. But the experiments of Gause[66] and others prove that such competition cannot persist with stability. Either the two species find subtly different niches and thereby avoid competition or one species replaces the other. This confirms the one species, one niche principle found in nature. Mathematical models, laboratory experiments, and field studies all show that competition between species cannot be sustained. The competition between paramecia in an aquarium, or between flour beetles in a jar is unnatural since migration, the natural means of avoiding competition, is prevented.

Furthermore, these laboratory experiments imply that if all nature were at war, one organism with another, then only one species would survive. If life is not to destroy itself, competition must be avoided. Thus competition is not the paradigm.

Cooperation between Species

A recognition of the peaceful coexistence among animals and plants is only half the story. The Darwinian images of struggle and war have led biologists to seek competition everywhere and to overlook or downplay cooperation. Biologist William Hamilton writes, "Cooperation per se has received comparatively little attention from biologists."[67] Zoologist Robert M. May notes that "mutualism has remained relatively neglected—in field, laboratory, theory and textbooks."[68] And Lynn Margulis writes, "Although they are often treated in the biological literature as exotic, symbiotic relationships abound; many of them affect entire ecosystems."[69] Nature's manner is not merely peaceful coexistence, but cooperation. Kirk declares: "It is doubtful whether there is an animal alive that does not have a symbiotic relationship with at least one other life form." [70] A few examples will give some idea of the magnitude of this mutual interdependence among living things.

One organism can be helpful to another in several ways: by providing food, protection from predators, a place to live, or transportation, or by ridding the other organism of pests, or by preparing some necessary condition for its life or welfare. The innumerable cooperative associations between different species constitute one of the most intriguing subject areas in all natural science. The variety and subtlety of interdependence is astounding.

The simplest service one organism can offer another is providing a place to stay. The sea worm *Urechis caupo* is nicknamed "the innkeeper" because it regularly harbors various fish, mollusks, arthropods, and annelids—up to thirteen species—in the U-shaped burrow it makes in California's coastal mudflats. Though able to live independently, the lodgers reside in the worm's tube for protection, some of them feeding on whatever *Urechis* brings in but does not consume.[71] Certain crabs live within the rectums of sea urchins, others within the shells of live oysters.[72] The horseshoe crab is also host to many guests. Clarke notes, "Anyone who has an opportunity to catch an elderly horseshoe crab (*Limulus polyphemus*) in the shallow waters off the New England coast is likely to find several species of mollusks, barnacles, and tube worms attached to the shell and a number of more motile commensals living in the 'book gills' or other anatomical nooks of this strange animal."[73] In fact, any sea animal with a shell or available space of any sort will serve as a home for other species. Farb adds that "the porous body of a sponge provides a home for a wide variety of sea creatures. One large specimen found growing off the Florida Keys served as a habitation of 13,500 other animals—some 12,000 of these were small shrimps, but the other 1,500 included 18 different species of worms, copepods and even a small fish."[74] Plants called epiphytes use other, established plants for a place to live. Tropical orchids, mosses, bromeliads, and vines grow along the horizontal branches of trees or hang down from them. These epiphytes are thus able to find a place in the sun and yet do not have to make the enormous investment in growing tall support structures.

It would be impossible to list all the animals that use plants for shelter and breeding. But some animals have formed close mutual relationships with certain plant species. Kirk writes of the *Acacia* of Central America: "Ants of the genus *Pseudomyrmex* live in the swollen thorns of the plant, gain their sugar from nectaries on the leaves, feed their larvae with modified leaflet tips that are rich in proteins and steroids, and have a nearly continuous food supply because these species of *Acacia* remain green during the dry season (in contrast to other *Acacia* species not associated with ants). The ants, in turn, drive away plant-eating insects and prune back vines and shrubbery that might crowd out the *Acacia*. This activity is of immediate benefit to the ants because it keeps the *Acacia* strong and healthy and ensures a more continuous and abundant food supply. The larger the ant colony, the more effective the continuous protection that it provides for the plant; thus, both ants and *Acacia* can maximize their growth through this close mutualism."[75] (See Figure 4.4.) Many other trees, shrubs, and plants carry on cooperative associations with ants. The aspen sunflower of the Rocky Mountain area secretes extrafloral nectar rich in sugar and containing eighteen different amino acids needed for ant nutrition. Ants feed on the nectar and protect the flower's seeds from devastating parasites.[76]

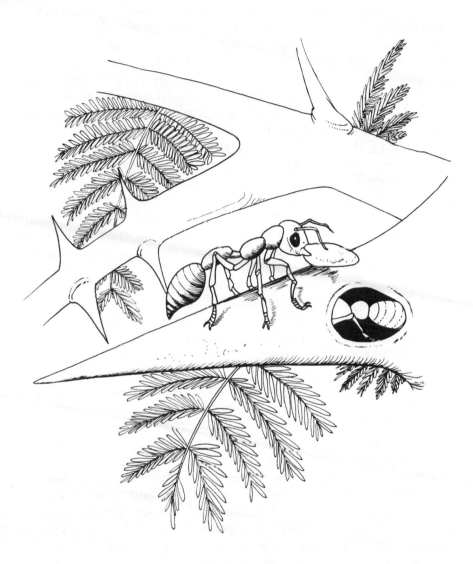

Figure 4.4. The cooperative arrangement between the *Acacia* of Central America and the ant *Pseudomyrmex*. The ant lives in the hollow thorns of the plant and feeds on its nectar. The ant, in turn, drives away plant-eating insects and prunes back vines that might crowd out the *Acacia*.

Other ants grow and maintain cultures of fungi for food. Still others nurture aphids to the same end. Wood-boring beetles live in association with wood-softening fungi. The female beetle carefully smears each egg she lays with fungus to guarantee that the partnership will continue in the next generation.

Many animals use the help of other species to obtain food. The blue jay can open acorns, but the bobwhite cannot. The blue jay is a sloppy eater, however, and leaves much meat uneaten in the opened shells. The bobwhite then feeds on a source it could not exploit itself. Eating the leavings of others is a widely exploited niche in every ecosystem. Hyenas frequently scavenge from lion kills that include animals the hyena could never kill by itself. The Arctic fox lives largely on the remains of kills made by polar bears.

Farb describes the amazing mutual assistance between a small African bird called the honeyguide and the badgerlike ratel: "Both the bird and the ratel seek the beehive—the ratel because of the honey and the larvae it contains, the bird because it is a wax eater. The honeyguide, however, cannot attack and break open a hive, so it needs a partner like the ratel, which is nearly impervious to stings because of its tough, furry skin that hangs loosely on its body. In return, the honeyguide aids the ratel in the forest, it attracts its attention by a loud chattering; the ratel follows it, issuing a series of grunts as if to reassure the bird that it is right behind it. Once the hive is located, the ratel tears it apart while the outraged bees furiously try to imbed their stingers; the bird waits on the sidelines and is content to eat the empty waxen combs after the ratel has finished with them."[77]

Another service one species can perform for another is to provide transport, either of the whole organism or of its seeds. To disperse themselves, stationary creatures often take advantage of mobile ones in remarkable ways. The mantle of one fresh-water mussel, Lampsilis ventricosa, is modified to look like a small fish. Clarke writes: "When a real fish, attracted by this mimic, swims over the mussel, casting a shadow, the mussel discharges its glochidial larvae. Some of these larvae reach the gills or fins of the fish to which they attach and live as parasites until they are ready to metamorphose into adults. Certain fishes thus parasitized wander upstream where the young mussels drop off and begin a new life as independent bottom animals. In this way these sessile forms are distributed against the current to the upper reaches of the stream."[78]

Barnacles attached to whales and anemones attached to crabs get free transport and an opportunity to obtain food otherwise unavailable. The anemones also provide the crabs with camouflage and probably prevent predation by octopus. There are hundreds of insects and worms that use other organisms for transportation and dispersal to more promising habitats. This practice of hitchhiking, called phoresis, has been going on for at least twenty-five million years, as is proven by amber fossils of various mites and nematodes clinging to beetles and wasps.[79]

Flowering plants use bees, moths, hummingbirds, and bats to achieve cross-fertilization, rewarding the workers with nutritious nectar. Many of these associations have developed into obligatory mutualism between plant and animal, so that they allow prediction. For example, when Darwin first examined *Angraecum sesquipedale*, a Madagascar orchid with a foot-long tubular nectary, he knew from experience that orchids usually have a single insect pollinator. But to reach the inch of nectar at the bottom of this orchid's whiplike nectary, the insect would need an incredibly long proboscis. Darwin made a bold prediction: there exists in Madagascar an insect with a proboscis twelve inches long![80] Entomologists scoffed at the idea of such an insect. But the scoffers were silenced when, several years later, *Xanthopan morgani praedicta*, a previously unknown Madagascar moth, flew into a collector's net, foot-long proboscis and all. Subsequently, this story repeated itself in reverse, when in South America a moth with a twelve-inch proboscis was first discovered; then, after a considerable time, a corresponding flower with a foot-long nectary was found.

Fruits are another way plants disperse their seeds with the aid of animals. The animal eats the fruit and, sometime later and some distance away, excretes the undigested seeds, which are thus provided with their own supply of rich fertilizer. Fruits commonly have a mild laxative effect just to ensure that the job is well done. For example, certain portions of *Amelanchier*, *Rosa*, and *Goultheria* seeds have been demonstrated to germinate after passing through the digestive tract of the black-tailed deer.[81] Certain seeds germinate better after being subjected to the forces of digestion. The *Calvaria* tree of Maritius Island in the Indian Ocean has not been able to germinate for over three hundred years—ever since the extinction of the dodo bird, which once inhabited the island. The dodo, in eating the *Calvaria* fruit, ground and abraded the hard shell of the pit in its powerful gizzard, such that when excreted, the seed was able to penetrate the shell and grow. Without the dodo's help the *Calvaria* seed could not break through its own shell. There are now on Mauritius only a few *Calvaria* trees, all dying, and all over three hundred years old.[82] (See Figure 4.5.)

Various algae form symbiotic partnerships with a wide range of animals: protozoa, snails and other mollusks, infusorians, coelenterates (including the hydra), rotifers, and many kinds of worms. Corals, for example, significantly increase their growth rate by forming cooperative associations with certain algae. The two partners make use of each other's waste products: the alga benefits from the carbon dioxide and nitrogenous wastes of the coral, and the coral benefits from the oxygen produced by the alga. The balance is so finely tuned that coral polyps with alga can live for two weeks in sealed glass containers filled with sea water.[83] Several species of ciliated protozoa, including the *Paramecium*, contain large numbers of small algal cells that live unharmed within the cell tissue, contributing the products of photosynthesis and enjoying a medium conducive to growth. A similar relationship is found in many species of flatworms; some even become green because of the many alga cells they harbor in their tissues.[84] The giant clam cultivates alga on the rim of its mantle. On the long, grooved hairs of the South American sloth, a green alga grows in such abundance that it gives the animal a greenish appearance, affording it a degree of camouflage while it sleeps in the treetops.[85]

Algae form intimate symbiotic relationships with many fungi, producing what amounts to a new organism, the lichen, that can grow under conditions where neither the alga nor the fungus alone could survive. Found all over the world, lichens represent a significant part of the earth's flora. Margulis states: "About one quarter of all fungal species enter lichen symbioses—some 25,000 species!...Lichens are remarkable examples of innovation emerging from partnership: they possess many morphological, chemical, and physiological attributes that are absent from either partner grown independently. The association is far more than the sum of its parts."[86]

Another plant-plant partnership is that of mycorrhizal fungi that live in association with the roots of most forest trees such as pines, oaks, hickories, and beeches, and many other plants also. Odum

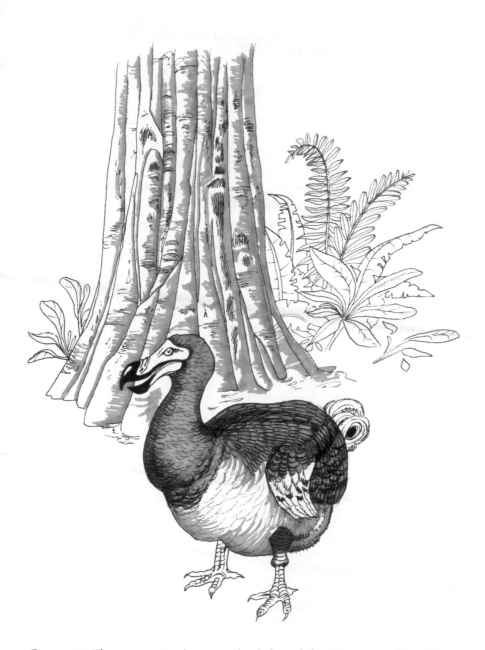

Figure 4.5. The cooperation between the dodo and the *Calvaria* tree. The *Calvaria* furnished the dodo with fruit, and in turn the bird ground and abraded the hard pit of the *Calvaria* seed so that it could germinate.

explains the relationship: "Many trees will not grow without mycorrhizae. Forest trees transplanted to prairie soil, or introduced into a different region, often fail to grow unless inoculated with fungal symbionts. Pine trees with healthy mycorrhizal associates grow vigorously in soil so poor by conventional agricultural standards that corn or wheat could not survive. The fungi are able to metabolize 'unavailable' phosphorus and other minerals."[87]

Another service is provided to certain plants by nitrogen-fixing bacteria. These microbes take up residence within the roots of legumes such as alfalfa, clover, and beans, and are able to fix atmospheric nitrogen to produce nitrates and nitrites, thus enriching the soil. Curtis gives an illustration: "A striking example of the capacity of the nitrogen-fixing bacteria to improve the fertility of the soil was seen in an experiment carried out by the U.S. Forest Service near Athens, Ohio. A planting of cedar trees was set out in an area of very poor soil. In one part of the area, a number of locust trees were set among the cedars. Locusts, which are legumes, carry nitrogen-fixing bacteria on their roots. Eleven years later, the cedar trees that had been planted alone averaged 30 inches high, while those planted among the locusts had grown to an average of 7 feet."[88] There are about 500 genera and 13,000 species of legumes that fix 100 million tons of nitrogen every year. Without this constant enrichment, the earth's soil would become too poor to sustain the quality and variety of plants, trees, and shrubs that we now witness.

Other bacteria and protozoans have developed a mutualism with hundreds of mammalian herbivore species, including elephants, cattle, sheep, goats, camels, giraffes, deer, and antelopes. Sometimes called ruminants, these animals are cud-chewers and have a complex three-stomach or four-stomach digestive system. The domestic cow, for example, does not have the enzymes necessary to digest cellulose, the main constituent of its diet. Special bacteria within the cow's first two stomachs digest the cellulose and convert it to fatty acids digestible by the cow. In the third and fourth stomachs, the bacteria, which die naturally after twenty hours, are digested, giving the cow necessary proteins. These bacteria would die in the presence of oxygen. They need an anaerobic environment and constant cellulose. Hence they thrive, warm, protected, and well fed, in the first two stomachs. Since the cow cannot digest its food without bacterial help, the existence of cattle in the world depends on the work of microbes. The action of the bacteria explains why vitamin B is found in a cow's milk but not in its feed. In human beings harmless intestinal bacteria similarly contribute vitamin B_{12} to the host.[89] Certain termites and cockroaches are able to digest wood only because of the help of flagellate protozoans that live in their digestive systems. The relation is mutually beneficial and obligatory. A termite without the protozoans in its gut will starve to death despite ingesting normal quantities of wood fiber.

A further service one organism renders another is protection. One strategy is to associate closely with a dangerous predator. Clown fish develop an immunity to the stings of a sea anemone and then live within its arms, acting as bait for other fish, and enjoying security from predators. The horse mackerel lives within the tentacles of the dangerous Portuguese man-of-war. Shrimp fish live among the spines of the sea urchin. Many birds build their nests near beehives. In Algeria a particular edible plant grows in close association with a thorny, inedible one. The former benefits, while the latter is unharmed.[90]

Many species take warning of danger from other species. Alarm calls in all prey birds are similar so that all species in an area are warned if one gives the alarm. Baboons frequently associate with gazelle and profit from their keen sense of smell, while the gazelles benefit from the superior vision of the baboons in detecting predators. Ostrich often herd with zebra for the same reasons.

Another service one animal can offer another is cleaning. This service is important for animals that are anatomically incapable of cleaning their own bodies. The arrangement is mutually beneficial since the client is rid of parasites and the cleaner gets fed. Among land animals the tickbird cleans the rhinoceros, egrets clean various cattle, and the Egyptian plover enters the mouth of the crocodile to feed on leeches and emerges unharmed. Biologist William Beebe observed red crabs removing ticks from the marine iguanas of the Galápagos Islands.[91] The existence of cleaning symbiosis among marine animals has come to light only since skin diving has allowed extensive observation of sea creatures. According to marine biologist Conrad Limbaugh, the cleaner-client association "represents one of the primary relationships in the community in the sea."[92] Known cleaners include some forty-two species of fish, six shrimps, and Beebe's crab. Cleaners establish fixed stations that are visited by countless species of fish. Limbaugh reports, "I saw up to 300 fish cleaned at one station in the Bahamas during one six-hour daylight period."[93] The client fish approaches the station and poses, allowing the cleaner to forage within its gills and even to enter its mouth without danger (see Figure 4.6). No one yet knows what prevents ordinarily voracious fish from eating the cleaners. Limbaugh found that the cleaners could prevent the spread of bacterial infections that would normally prove fatal to the client. He concludes, "The extent of cleaning behavior in the ocean emphasizes the role of cooperation in nature as opposed to the tooth-and-claw struggle for existence."[94]

An astounding example of cleaning is found in the bluebottle fly and the blowfly. These flies prefer to lay their eggs in the festering wounds of animals. At first thought this might appear to be one of nature's great cruelties. But when the larvae hatch, they feed on the pus and consume dead tissues. Even their excretions disinfect the wound! Far from being cruel, the fly larvae may be the animal's only chance to recover from a possibly lethal infection. Blowfly larvae were in fact used as wound cleaners in hospitals during the last century.[95]

Another mode of service occurs in ecological succession, the sequential replacement of a community's flora by other species. This is best understood as a kind of cooperation rather than as ruthless eradication by subsequent species. Succession occurs because the establishment of new species *modifies* the environment. The annual plants are like nomads. Their job is to prepare the soil, paving the way for the perennials, and then to move on. Permanence is not part of their niche: they are not equipped for it. The lichens are the most rugged pioneers of all. They do not *require* soil, they help *create* it, colonizing even bare rock, which they slowly break down into tiny amounts of humus, allowing mosses or other higher plants to gain a foothold. Succession continues until a stable climax stage is reached where new species can no longer change the community. In northern temperate forests, species such as hemlock, beech, and maple constitute the climax stage because only their seedlings can thrive in the shade of the mature trees. Cases of succession from bare ground to hickory climax within one hundred fifty years have been documented in North Carolina.[96] Ecological succession is

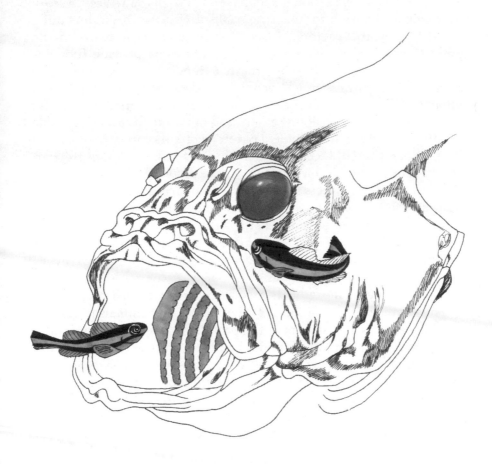

Figure 4.6. Two neon gobies cleaning a Nassau grouper. The cleaners forage within the client fish's gills and even enter its mouth without danger. Cleaning symbiosis is a common kind of cooperation.

merely nature's way of healing her scarred skin. Not all species are replaced in the succession: lichens grow on tree trunks, while the shady areas in dense forest are ideal for mosses and ferns.

In another form of interdependence, certain large animals support whole communities of species. A single hippopotamus, for example, is cleaned by twenty or so labeo fish and stirs up food for other fish, as it walks along under water. When it surfaces, a stork may ride on its back to hunt the snails it churns up. And its dung nourishes plants, bacteria, insect larvae, and crustaceans in the ponds and lakes it frequents. These organisms provide food for many species of fish, thereby greatly extending the food web. The aquatic life is always much richer in bodies of water that hippos inhabit.[97] The elephants of Sri Lanka are the foundation of a similar community. They are sloppy eaters and make much forage available to other browsers. In a single day ten elephants can deposit on the forest floor a ton of feces. None of that dung is wasted: butterflies and beetles feed on it; birds retrieve seeds from it; mushrooms and fungi thrive on it; insects lay eggs in it; and termites convert most of its cellulose into sugars. All these uses set up further food webs, including termite eaters such as the sloth bear and the pangolin. So what is a waste product for the elephant becomes an organic treasure for scores of other creatures.[98] In a community "every species . . . directly or indirectly, supplies essential materials or services to one or more of its associates," writes Dice.[99]

The exquisite cooperation between plants and animals in general is a marvel in itself. Each needs the products of the other. Plants use the carbon dioxide in the air and water from the soil to manufacture sugars, releasing oxygen as a by-product. Animals consume plant sugars and oxidize them to produce energy, breathing back carbon dioxide into the air and returning water to the soil as urine. The cycle is perfect and nothing is wasted. The following chart shows a simplified version of the chemistry involved.

PLANTS: $\quad 6CO_2 \quad + \quad 6H_2O \quad + \quad$ Energy $\quad \rightarrow \quad C_6H_{12}O_6 \quad + \quad 6O_2$
$\qquad\qquad$ from $\qquad\quad$ from $\qquad\qquad$ from $\qquad\qquad\quad$ sugar $\qquad\quad$ returned
$\qquad\qquad$ air $\qquad\qquad$ soil $\qquad\qquad\quad$ sun $\qquad\qquad\qquad\qquad\qquad\qquad$ to air

ANIMALS: $\quad C_6H_{12}O_6 \quad + \quad 6O_2 \quad \rightarrow \quad$ Energy $\quad + \quad 6CO_2 \quad + \quad 6H_2O$
$\qquad\qquad$ sugar eaten $\quad$ from $\qquad\qquad\qquad\qquad\qquad\quad$ expired $\qquad$ returned
$\qquad\qquad$ and absorbed $\;$ air $\qquad\qquad\qquad\qquad\qquad\quad$ through $\qquad$ to soil
$\qquad\qquad$ into tissues $\qquad\qquad\qquad\qquad\qquad\qquad\qquad$ lungs

Without this perfect cycle, life on the earth would have gone out of business long ago. Carbon dioxide is a rare gas on our planet. It constitutes only 35/1,000 of 1 percent of the atmosphere, less than argon. That amount of carbon dioxide, if not replenished, would support the present plant population of the world for only forty years.[100] Thus, respiration of animals and of certain bacteria is crucial for the continued life of plants. And without plants, no animals could live.

The same holds for nitrogen. Even though it constitutes almost 80 percent of the atmosphere, few plants can assimilate it directly. Plants must take nitrates from the soil to synthesize their proteins. So if plant and animal proteins were not recycled back into the soil, plants would have no source of nitrogen compounds and would eventually die out. Fortunately, various bacteria that specialize in decomposing organic matter routinely break proteins down to ammonia, while others change ammonia to nitrites, and others change nitrites to nitrates, making them available for plants. If there were no bacteria decomposers, all nitrogen would sooner or later get irretrievably locked into plant and animal bodies. Decomposition occurs only by the agency of specialized living beings, not by automatic chemical processes. Figure 4.7 summarizes the necessary interdependence of all living things for food.

"All organisms are dependent upon the varied activities of other organisms for the supplies of essential stuffs," writes Burkholder.[101] No single species could persist if it were alone on the planet. It would eventually exhaust all the available nutrients, and, having no way no convert its own waste products into food, it would die. Life is necessarily a cooperative venture. Lynn Margulis writes: "All organisms are dependent on others for the completion of their life cycles. Never, even in spaces as small as a cubic meter, is a living community of organisms restricted to members of only a single species. Diversity, both morphological and metabolic, is the rule. Most organisms depend directly on others for nutrients and gases. Only photo- and chemo-autotrophic bacteria produce all their organic requirements from inorganic constituents; even they require food, gases such as oxygen, carbon dioxide, and ammonia, which although inorganic, are end products of the metabolism of other organisms. Heterotrophic organisms require organic compounds as food; except in rare cases of cannibalism, this food comprises organisms of other species or their remains."[102]

The recognition of such universal, essential cooperation among animals and plants alters the conventional image of nature. Biologist Lewis Thomas writes: "One major question needing to be examined

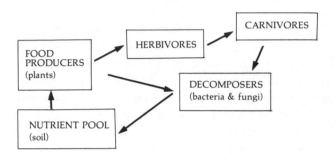

Figure 4.7. All living things necessarily depend on one another for food. Plants would eventually die out if decomposers did not make available to them a continuous supply of nitrogen compounds from decaying organic materials. Without plants, animals would die of starvation.

is the general attitude of nature. A century ago there was a consensus about this; nature was 'red in tooth and claw,' evolution was a record of open warfare among competing species, the fittest were the strongest aggressors, and so forth. Now it begins to look different.... The urge to form partnerships, to link up in collaborative arrangements, is perhaps the oldest, strongest, and most fundamental force in nature. There are no solitary, free-living creatures, every form of life is dependent on other forms."[103]

Cooperation within Species

Up to this point we have discussed only the relations between one species and another. Cooperation is also the ruling principle among members of the same species, despite Darwin's assertion that "The struggle will almost invariably be most severe between the individuals of the same species, for they frequent the same districts, require the same food, and are exposed to the same dangers."[104] How can members of the same species avoid competition if they all occupy the same niche? Nature is not at a loss for methods. One way is to have some technique to separate individuals from each other. This is accomplished in animals and plants by various dispersal techniques. Tinbergen explains: "These 'dispersion mechanisms' reduce competition to a minimum. Perhaps the simplest way to disperse is just to drift aimlessly about for a while, carried and scattered by the wind or water until the time for settling has arrived. The larvae of many marine animals, such as shellfish, starfish and crabs, do this; after a few days, weeks or even months of floating life they change their behavior, sink to the bottom and settle down. Many kinds of caterpillars would lose the effectiveness of their natural camouflage and become dangerously conspicuous if they stayed together in large groups. To prevent this, the moths of some species scatter their eggs when they lay them."[105]

Every living thing has a dispersal phase at some stage in its life cycle. Equal distribution prevents competition while maintaining a remarkable stability in populations. Curtis describes a striking example: "In one experiment, for example, a census of a particular species of butterfly was taken each year for eight years. Each fall, there were from 8,000 to 14,000 larvae of the species in a field in New England. In most years, about 30 larvae survived until spring; and most summers, there were about 20 butterflies. In autumn of the sixth year, the field was stocked with 20,000 additional larvae. Eighty spring larvae were present the following year, but by summer, there were only 22 butterflies in the field, about the usual number. That fall, only 400 autumn larvae could be found. Examination of the surrounding areas revealed that many more eggs than usual had been laid outside the field. In response to the overstocking of the field, the butterflies had emigrated, despite the fact that ample food was left for the larvae and ample space remained for the deposit of eggs."[106]

One way nature distributes members of a species evenly across the habitat is the territory principle. Animals that mark off and defend definite areas divide their niche into livable plots. Territories for mating or feeding, or both, are established by hundreds of species including limpets, lobsters, crabs, spiders, crickets, grasshoppers, many other insects, bony fishes, lizards, perching birds, raptors, oceanic birds, rodents, ruminants, and most other mammals. The power of territorial borders is surprising. Zoologist Hans Kruuk has seen hyenas break off the chase of a promising prey animal when they reach the border of neighboring hyena territory, even though no other predators are in sight. His field studies showed that "Fully 20 percent of unsuccessful wildebeest hunts could be attributed to hyena respect for one another's boundaries."[107] Kirk writes: "Territorial behavior leads to an optimum distribution of limited resources among a maximum number of individuals of a species."[108] For example, territory size appears to be regulated by innate factors. Song sparrows never establish territories greater than one acre, no matter how few are present. Nor do they defend territories below about half an acre, no matter how many other sparrows are present.[109] A study of four hundred coexisting howler monkeys in Central America revealed twenty-three different clans with definite territories.[110]

The defense of territory in all species is characterized not by battles to the death, but by highly stereotyped threats, aggressive displays, and appeasement gestures that rarely result in injury. Lorenz observes that these ritualized sign stimuli are as powerful as the impulses of hunger, sex, and fear in the animal.[111] (See Figure 4.8.) The encounter is more a ritualized contest than a real fight, with one animal eventually retreating unharmed. Territory boundaries tend to be respected. Kirk elaborates:

"Particularly when the territory is well established, the defender is usually successful in driving away an invader irrespective of differences in size, strength, development of specialized structures important in the aggressive display, and so forth. This is most clearly seen in the case of two individuals with adjacent territories. Here, each individual is usually successful in defending its own territory yet unsuccessful in attempts to encroach on its neighbor's domain. In every interaction each individual appears to be driven by opposing tendencies: fight and flight. The closer to the center of its own territory an individual is, the greater appears to be its motivation to fight. But the farther it is from the center of its home territory, the greater appears to be the tendency for flight."[112] This system can hardly be described as a brutal struggle or ruthless warfare if size and strength do not determine the outcome.

Figure 4.8. Intraspecies encounters between rival animals rarely result in injury because they are regulated by instinctual, stylized displays of aggression and by appeasement gestures. A wolf, for example, that feels it is no match for another wolf during an encounter avoids a fight simply by presenting its unprotected throat to the adversary. This stimulus never provokes attack by the other wolf. On the contrary, it causes the dominant animal to turn away, and the tension of the encounter is dissipated.

Zoologist Norman Owen-Smith notes: "Territoriality of the white rhinoceros may thus be described as a system for ordering specifically reproductive competition among males. Its primary function within the population seems to be to increase the reproductive efficiency of prime bulls by reducing the incidence of injury-inflicting combat. These statements can probably be broadened in scope to apply, with the exception of the Indian rhinoceros, to all other ungulates in which territoriality has been identified, and perhaps to any species in which territoriality is restricted to adult males."[113]

Some species maintain noncompetitive distribution without even encountering each other. Certain mammals accomplish this by leaving scent marks in their territory that other members of the same species then avoid. The male frogs of certain species distribute themselves evenly throughout the habitat by distancing themselves from the croaking of other males. Plants avoid competition with their own seeds by many dispersal techniques. A single crop spread over acres and acres of land is found only in man's artificial agriculture, never in nature.

Another means nature uses to prevent competition and fighting among gregarious animals is the dominance hierarchy, which minimizes aggression within the social group. First studied with pecking orders among birds, the dominance hierarchy prevents animals of the same group from wasting time and energy by constantly fighting over food and mates. Instead of fighting, the individual animal lower in the pecking order immediately concedes to the higher one, without any struggle. Kirk gives an illustration of what happens without this strategy: "For the group, dominance assures stability. Once the hierarchical order has been established, aggression over resources and mates is kept to a minimum. In one study, the investigator deliberately kept disrupting the dominance relationships in a flock of hens. The outcome was that the hens fought more, ate less, gained less weight, and suffered more serious injuries than the control flock in which the dominance relationship was stable."[114] Among Japanese macaques of Koshima Island, dominant males break up quarrels between females that have no dominance hierarchy of their own. Dominance hierarchies, found in many species of birds and mammals, show nature to be not only pacific but sensible. Why should a weaker individual fight a stronger one that would win anyway with probable injury to both?

On rare occasions injury results from territory defense or rival encounters, but the aim of aggression is never the extermination of fellow members of the same species. If it were, a species would destroy itself in a short time. Fights to the death and cannibalism do sometimes occur in unnatural circumstances, such as with birds in a cage, or fish in an aquarium where retreat is impossible. But such is not nature's way. Animals with the most dangerous weapons also have the strongest instincts to prevent their use against conspecifics. Male giraffes that can dispatch a lion with a single kick save their lethal hoofs for predators only, using their stubby, harmless horns for encounters with rival giraffes. Lorenz points out: "Those inhibitions which prevent animals from injuring or even killing fellow members of the species have to be strongest and most reliable, first in those species which being hunters of large prey possess weapons which could as easily kill a conspecific; and secondly, in those species which live gregariously."[115] After a study of dominance in bison herds, ethologist Dale F. Lott concludes: "Because fighting is dangerous and demands so much time and energy, substitutes have developed. In animals that establish—and defend—territories . . . fighting is often avoided because individuals are separated by distance. But species whose social life is organized by dominance depend heavily upon the ability to predict each other's behavior from such signals as postures and vocalizations."[116]

An ecological niche can also be divided by learned behavioral differences within a species. For example, one species of oyster catcher found along English shores is divided into two behavioral groups, the "stabbers" and the "hammerers," each of which mates only with its own kind. Stabbers feed on mussels and cockels that remain under water in tidal pools at low tide. Such mussels leave their shells partially open to continue filtering food from the sea water. The bird thrusts its beak into the shell, cuts the abductor muscle, and opens the shell to eat the contents. Hammerers feed on mussels and cockels that remain closed at low tide by persistently beating on a vulnerable spot on the shells until the beak can be inserted to pry the shell open. In this way two groups within the same species live in the same area and eat the same foods, but, because of their different hunting techniques, they do not compete.

Within a species, we take for granted the profound cooperation of the family, the herd, the colony, the flock, and the school. But these also are founded on strong natural instincts. Lorenz speaks of the powerful inhibitions in male wolves, lizards, hamsters, gold finches, and many other species against biting females.[117] He adds: "The fact that mothers of brood-tending species do not attack their young is thus in no way a self-evident law, but has to be ensured in every single species by a special inhibition. . . . Every livestock breeder knows that apparently slight disturbances can cause the failure of an inhibition mechanism of this kind. I know of a case where an airplane, flying low over a silver-fox farm, caused all the mother vixens to eat their young."[118]

There are many advantages of flocking together. Many eyes are better than a simple pair in looking for predators, and a circle of musk oxen is more formidable to a wolf pack than is a single animal. Moving in schools and flocks also makes it difficult for a predator to single out one individual when dozens of others cross its field of vision, as anyone knows who has ever tried to catch a single bird among many in a cage. A certain population density is necessary for many animals: muskrats, for example, do not breed successfully below a density of one pair per mile of stream or eighty-six acres of marshland.[119] Many sea birds hunt in flocks because it is more efficient. All social insects live by cooperation. The individuals in a termite colony depend on each other absolutely, some being unable to feed themselves and others being unable to reproduce. Parental care, feeding, protection, and training of young is simply too extensive to summarize. We may point out, however, that for those species that reproduce sexually, at least some kind of cooperation between the sexes is unavoidable. After years of studying group life among animals, Allee declares, "No free living animal is solitary through its life history."[120]

Darwin's Argument

Having reviewed the extent of cooperation between species and within a species, we can now reexamine Darwin's reason for proposing competition as the paradigm for living things. He maintains that "a struggle for existence inevitably follows from the high rate at which all organic beings tend to increase."[121] Darwin begins by assuming that each living thing is trying to produce an unlimited number of offspring: "Every single organic being may be said to be striving to the utmost to increase its numbers."[122] He adds, "There is no exception to the rule that every organic being naturally increases at so high a rate, that, if not destroyed, the earth would soon be covered by the progeny of a single pair."[123] He offers the example of the elephant to illustrate the point: "The elephant is reckoned the slowest breeder of all known animals, and I have taken some pains to estimate its probable minimum rate of natural increase; it will be safest to assume that it begins breeding when thirty years old, and goes on breeding till ninety years old, bringing forth six young in the interval, and surviving till one hundred years old; if this be so, after a period of from 740 to 750 years there would be nearly nineteen million elephants alive, descended from the first pair."[124] If, in fact, the earth is not swamped with elephants or any other species, there must be some check to their geometric growth rate. So he concludes: "Each species, even where it most abounds, is constantly suffering enormous destruction at some period of its life."[125] Darwin proposes four causes that check a species' natural tendency to increase without limit: predation, starvation, severities of climate, and disease.[126] In a word—death.

Lacking detailed field studies of natural populations—they were done one hundred years later—Darwin buttresses this argument based on "mere theoretical calculations"[127] with examples of domestic animals "run wild,"[128] in other words, from man's artificial introduction of a species into a habitat where it did not occur before. Recent field studies of native animals by ecologists have yielded conclusions quite different from Darwin's. Elton and Andrewartha and Birch argue that starvation rarely acts as a direct influence on numbers of species; Lack says the same of disease.[129] What, then, are the factors? Take Darwin's example of elephants. Biologist Richard M. Laws reports that a study from 1966 to 1968 of over three thousand elephants in Kenya and Tanzania showed that "the age of sexual maturity in elephants was very plastic and was deferred in unfavorable situations. . . . Individual animals were reaching maturity at from 8 to 30 years."[130] The same study showed that the females do not continue bearing young until ninety, as Darwin thought, but stop becoming pregnant around fifty-five years of age. Thus the elephant population is regulated not by predation, starvation, or death, but by adjustments in the onset of maturity in the females, which lowers the birth rate whenever overcrowding occurs. Nor are elephants unique in having an internal mechanism for regulating population growth. Evidence from other field studies indicate that the birth rate or the age of first reproduction depends on population density in many large mammals, including white-tailed deer, elk, bison, moose, bighorn sheep, Dall's sheep, ibex, wildebeest, Himalayan tahr, hippopotamus, lion, grizzly bear, dugong, harp seals, southern elephant seal, spotted porpoise, striped dolphin, blue whale, and sperm whale.[131] Increases in population density alter birth rates in small mammals also. Kirk observes: "In experiments with rats, mice, and voles, definite physiological changes accompanied increases in population density. An increase in the size of a population confined to a constant space led to an increase in the weight of adrenal glands and a decrease in the weight of thymus and reproductive glands. The degree of the effect was inversely related to social rank. Dominant individuals were affected little if at all; subordinate individuals were strongly affected. These changes were accompanied by decreases in reproduction."[132] Under crowded conditions, female mice ovulate more slowly or stop ovulation altogether. In some species of birds, failure to gain a territory prevents the onset of sexual maturity.

In many animals, then, population growth is regulated by benign internal causes without any need for the periodic devastations Darwin supposed. Another fault in Darwin's argument is the assumption that "amongst animals there are very few which do not annually pair."[133] On the contrary, a large nonbreeding portion of the adult population is the norm in many species. In a five-year study of nearly two hundred white rhinoceros in Zululand, South Africa, Norman Owen-Smith found that only two-thirds of the adult population maintain territories, allowing subordinate males to graze in their territory but not allowing them to breed.[134] Many bird species keep a reserve of nonbreeders in the population. This was discovered accidentally in a study of the spruce bud worm and its predators. Experimenters Robert Stewart and John Aldrich attempted to eliminate the birds from a forty-acre tract of land in Maine by shooting.[135] The number of territorial males before the shooting took place was 148. Stewart and Aldrich shot and collected 302 males from the area, however, in less than a month. They write: "For most species, over twice as many adult males were collected on the area as were present before the collecting started."[136] The explanation was a large, surplus population of unmated males that quickly filled in vacated territories. The replacement of removed birds does not demonstrate competition but is a safety device to regulate the population. In other experiments it was found impossible to reduce the numbers of juncos in a given area because of immediate replacement by immigrants from the surrounding area.[137]

We may infer from these experiments that predation would not significantly affect the population growth rate in such species. According to Ricklefs, "Detailed removal-replacement experiments have had similar results, indicating that territorial limitation of breeding population is quite general."[138] This includes field studies on blackbirds, red grouse, voles, dragonflies, and pomacentrid fish. Not taking these facts into account, any argument for geometric increase in natural populations is based on "mere theoretical calculation," which, though mathematically correct, are biologically irelevant.

And it is also erroneous to assume that those adults that do mate produce the same number of offspring each season. A wide range of animals vary their litter size and clutch size according to the amount of food available. Elton observes: "The short-eared owl (*Asio flammeus*) may have twice as many young in a brood and twice as many broods as usual, during a vole plague, when its food is extremely plentiful."[139] Lack points out that nutcrackers normally lay only three eggs but increase the clutch to four eggs when there is a bumper crop of hazelnuts. He also mentions that the arctic fox is known to produce much larger litters when lemmings are abundant, and that lions bear more or fewer cubs per litter according to the availability of food.[140] By contrast, in lean years many species do not breed at all.

In some cases the herbivore population is controlled by the plant. For example, in years following a drought, sagebrush develops high concentrations of phytoestrogens that mimic reproductive hormones in the California quail. These hormones inhibit ovulation in the quail that consume the sagebrush, causing a sharp drop in the size of the quail population. When rainfall becomes more plentiful, the sagebrush has little or no estrogen mimics, and quail populations return to normal. Here the herb imposes birth control on the herbivore. Studies show also that ovarian activity is shut down in mountain voles in the late summer because of phytoestrogen buildup in the grasses they consume.[141]

Also false is the assumption that animals and plants produce as many eggs and seeds as physiologically possible. All bird species have a normal clutch size, but if eggs are removed, the female can be induced to lay many more. The domestic fowl, if left all its eggs, produces a clutch of about twelve, but if the eggs are removed daily, it can lay up to 360 per year.

The normal number of eggs varies greatly from one species to the next. Flamingos lay one egg, ostriches twelve to fifteen. Ecologist Y. Ito records that "Among the frogs an egg mass of *Rana nigromaculata* contains about 1,000 eggs but the number of eggs laid by *Flectonotus pygmaeus* ranges from four to seven, which is smaller than the clutch size of many birds or the litter size of rats."[142] The general rule is that the number of eggs is inversely proportional to parental care and protection. The female mackerel, which offers no care to its young, lays two to three million eggs, 99.9996 percent of which are eaten by predators within seventy days, leaving only two or three individuals that reach adulthood.[143] The sea catfish, on the other hand, lays only thirty eggs per season; almost all survive because the male protects them in his mouth. Producing enormous numbers of offspring is not proof of ruthless competition but rather of cooperation since the excess of eggs and seeds supports thousands of predators that could not otherwise subsist. If all species used the high-care, low-fecundity strategy, the vast numbers and varieties of animals we see in nature would not be possible. And this is not accomplished at the price of annihilating the prey species. There are still millions of mackerel in the sea every year.

No species strives to increase without limit, any more than an individual tends to grow to infinity. And animal populations are limited not by struggle, starvation, and death, but by restricting the number of breeders in various ways and by varying the number of offspring produced at a time by each female. Biologist V. C. Wynne-Edwards comments on Darwin's assumption that every living thing strives to increase its numbers geometrically:

"This intuitive assumption of a universal resurgent pressure from within held down by hostile forces from without has dominated the thinking of biologists on matters of population regulation, and on the nature of the struggle for existence, right down to the present day.

"Setting all preconceptions aside, however, and returning to a detached assessment of the facts revealed by modern observation and experiment, it becomes almost immediately evident that a very large part of the regulation of numbers depends not on Darwin's hostile forces but on the initiative taken by the animals themselves; that is to say, to an important extent it is an intrinsic phenomenon."[144]

That populations are self-regulating fits well with the notion of life as directed self-movement. Nature is not at war, one organism with another. Nature is an alliance founded on cooperation.

5

Harmony

Darwin considered animals and plants to be at war not only with each other but also with the elements: "There must be in every case a struggle for existence, either one individual with another of the same species, or with the individuals of distinct species, or *with the physical conditions of life*."[1] In the preceding chapter we examined the claims that hostility exists between organisms. In the present chapter we shall consider the alleged antagonism between living beings and the environment. Darwin offers an example: "A plant on the edge of a desert is said to struggle for life against the drought."[2] Sometimes called "environmental resistance," this notion is commonly assumed in textbooks, in monographs, and in journal articles. For example, one textbook of plant ecology states that "properly speaking, the struggle for existence in the plant world is between each plant and its habitat."[3]

Examples of apparent friction between life and the forces of inanimate nature spring readily to the imagination. Gravity weighs down birds and land animals and must be overcome. Aquatic animals must fight the overwhelming pressures of the deep ocean waters. Plants and animals must struggle to maintain body temperatures at which metabolism and life functions can occur despite the harsh fluctuations of climate. In some areas dryness threatens all organisms; in others excessive rains wash all nutrients from the soil. One imagines that living things are in continuous conflict with their environment and must expend a maximum effort simply to survive in an inhospitable universe.

We shall begin by looking at how today's animals and plants are related to the environment and take up questions of origin in the next chapter. Logically one must start with the way nature behaves right now before trying to explain how things got that way.

Any struggle of organisms against the environment should be most obvious in extreme habitats. The Arctic is a good test case.

How are animals able to maintain sufficient body heat in such frigid surroundings? Is it by struggle and the expenditure of maximal energy? The arctic fox, smaller than the average dog, ranges within twenty-five miles of the North Pole and yet easily withstands the severities of the arctic winter. "They survive in a place that would be unendurable for most mammals. Apparently, they even find it comfortable," writes naturalist Larry Underwood.[4] But how? Underwood explains: "They are covered in winter with a thick layer of soft, luxuriant fur. Although thick fur does not actually warm an animal, it creates a barrier to heat loss, slowing down the rate at which heat passes out of the body. As with most mammals, the fox's blood flow is pulled away from its body's periphery in cold weather, decreasing heat loss and sequestering heat in the body core. Mammals piloerect their fur—that is, stand the hair up—thickening the fur layer and trapping more air among the hairs to provide added insulation. They also pull their legs closer to their trunk and minimize the amount of surface exposed to the cold."[5]

By these means the fox can tolerate wind chill temperatures of -60°F at resting metabolism. If the temperature drops below this, the fox makes a den in the snow and simply waits out the storm, sustaining itself on body fat. And in extreme circumstances the fox keeps warm by shivering to increase its metabolism. Since shivering muscles do no external work, all the energy used to contract the muscles must eventually appear as heat inside the fox's body. In this way it can withstand temperatures down to -95°F while increasing its metabolism by little more than a third.[6] Thus, shivering does not imply suffering or struggle but is merely a natural means to keep warm. The arctic fox is so well equipped by nature with special insulation, appropriate behavioral instincts, and metabolic capacities that it does not have to struggle against such harsh surroundings. In fact, the fox is so well insulated that it would soon become overheated (even in winter) when running or being otherwise active unless it had some way to dissipate excess heat. Its thinly insulated feet and muzzle serve this purpose. (See Figure 5.1.) The fox, the Eskimo dog, and the caribou also use panting as a means of evaporative cooling when necessary.[7]

Nature does not insulate and equip all mammals in the same way as the arctic fox, however, but only those that need it. The tropical coati mundi, for example, must increase its metabolism when the air

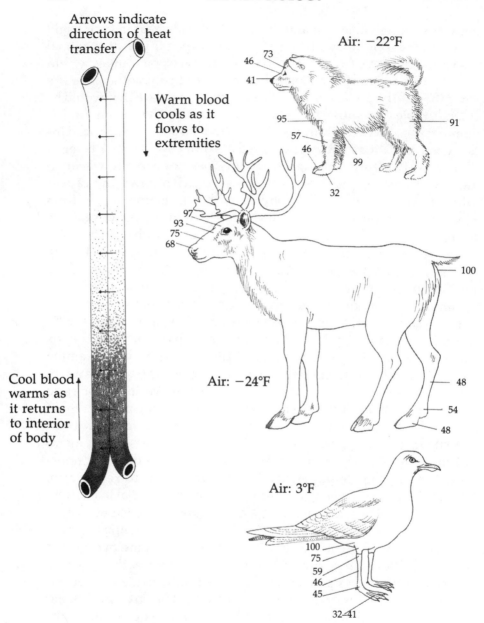

Arrows indicate
direction of heat
transfer

Warm blood
cools as it
flows to
extremities

Cool blood
warms as
it returns
to interior
of body

Air: −22°F

46 73
41
95
57
46
99
32
91

97
93
75
68
100

Air: −24°F
48
54
48

Air: 3°F
100
75
59
46
45
32–41

Figure 5.1. The differential heating of extremities found in all mammals
and birds that live in cold regions greatly reduces the loss of body heat to
the environment. The countercurrent exchange system enables animals
to maintain extremities at a lower temperature than the rest of the body
without losing heat.

temperature dips below 68°F.[8] And not all animals deal with cold in the same way. Some migrate before the cold season begins, while others hibernate. Bears are the champions of hibernation. In Minnesota, black bears sleep for seven months without taking food or drink, and without urinating or defecating. They live on stored-up body fat and are able to cut their metabolism in half: their heart rate drops from fifty beats per minute to as few as eight, and the bear's basal temperature declines from a normal of 100°F to 88°F, turning down the thermostat as it were. Zoologist Lynn Rogers explains: "Bears that are living off their fat have cholesterol levels more than twice as high as their summer levels and more than twice as high as the cholesterol levels of most humans. Yet bears have no known problem with hardening of the arteries or with the formation of cholesterol gallstones. Medical studies have shown that bears in winter produce a bile juice, ursodeoxycholic acid, that may help them to avoid problems with gallstones. When given to people, this acid dissolves gallstones, eliminating the need for surgery. Black bears also greatly reduce their kidney function in winter. They do not urinate for months but still do not poison their bodies with waste products such as urea. The urea is somehow broken down and the nitrogen from it reused to build protein. This ability to build protein while fasting allows the bears to maintain their muscle and organ tissue throughout the winter. They only use up fat."[9] So the bear does not struggle against the severities of winter; its unique metabolism allows it to sleep through the whole thing.

But how do aquatic mammals like whales keep warm in the freezing waters of the Arctic (especially since water carries away heat much faster than air does)? Insulation is only part of the answer. The whale's body is amply insulated with blubber, but its flippers are not. Since the flippers must be constantly supplied with blood, how does the whale avoid losing all its body heat to the ocean water? First of all, the whale's flippers are maintained at a temperature much lower than its interior body temperature. The same differential heating of extremities is found in all mammals and birds that live in cold regions. But how can such animals send warm blood to their extremities without losing all their body heat? The answer is a countercurrent exchange system, a marvel of engineering efficiency and simplicity, put to many uses by nature and by industry. (See Figure 5.1.) By this means, the heat is removed from the blood before it reaches the extremity and then the blood is slowly rewarmed before it enters the body mass. This system allows the whale's flippers a continuous blood supply without heat loss. The whales are comfortable even in subzero seas.

What about cold-blooded animals? How do antarctic fish keep from freezing when the water temperature is below the freezing point of their blood plasma? Antifreeze! Physiologist Knut Schmidt-Nielsen reports that "the blood of the antarctic fish *Trematomus borchgrevinki* contains a glycoprotein which acts as an antifreeze substance. This permits this fish to swim in sea water at a temperature of -1.8°C, although the osmotic pressure of its blood, in the absence of the antifreeze, is insufficient to prevent ice formation at this temperature."[10] Antarctic fish are clearly not at odds with their habitat.

Staying warm is more of a challenge for small animals because their surface-to-volume ratio is high. Nonmigrating birds employ a host of strategies, not to fight against the cold, but rather to circumvent it. These include special insulation, metabolic flexibility, and prudent behavior. One striking example is the insulation of Alaska's willow ptarmigan. This bird's plumage "varies seasonally not only in color—from brown in summer to white in winter—but also in insulative value. Because of the difference in insulation, the heat production required for the ptarmigan to maintain a high body temperature is the same at 32°F in the summer as it is at -13°F in winter."[11] No sign of struggle here. By shivering, birds can elevate their metabolism rate by five times the normal. Shivering also enables bumblebees to forage at freezing temperatures when all other insects are immobilized.[12] Birds that winter over find roosts in vegetation and crevices that protect them from the cold, saving up to 30 percent of the energy that would be required if they roosted in unprotected places. There is evidence that Alaskan chickadees forage for shorter periods during cold spells, a sensible procedure. And studies have shown that the chickadee is able to reduce its basal temperature by about twenty degrees at night, returning spontaneously to its normal temperature the next morning. This temporary hypothermia saves the bird up to 23 percent of its energy requirements each winter night.[13] The chickadee wins against the cold, then, not by brute force but by ingenuity.

Corresponding strategies occur in hot, dry habitats. How do

animals that lack internal temperature controls maintain sufficient warmth without overheating? Lizards, for instance, through special behavior, exploit the desert heat but avoid being over come by it. They bask in the morning, broadside to the sun, until their bodies reach a temperature sufficient for activity. During the hottest part of the day lizards like the chuckwalla seek shelter, or turn their bodies parallel to the sun's rays to expose a minimum surface to the heat, or resort to panting for evaporative cooling. With these techniques spiny lizards control their temperatures to within 4.5°F all during their active period. The Texas horned lizard can even make its skin color darker or lighter in order to absorb heat faster or more slowly.[14] Imagine clothing that changed color according to the heat requirements of the wearer!

One tactic to circumvent lack of water is estivation. The African lungfish, when faced with a pond drying up, buries itself in the mud, forms a cocoon, and remains there on reduced metabolism until the next rain. At such times the fish does not urinate and its blood can tolerate an extraordinary 4 percent level of urea without harm.[15] Again no struggle.

In hot environments, mammals face a more acute challenge than cold-blooded animals because mammals' bodies constantly produce internal heat, which cannot be turned off. Nevertheless, even California's hot, arid Mojave Desert supports two species of ground squirrel, each well adjusted to its surroundings. The antelope ground squirrel can comfortably tolerate a higher body tempera- ture—up to 110°F—than any other nonsweating mammal. It can store heat and then dump it off by crawling into its burrow and flattening itself against the cool earth. This squirrel can drink water 1.4 times saltier than the sea without ill effect. No other mammal can live on such saline water.[16] With such extraordinary capacities, the antelope squirrel does not have to struggle against the heat or dryness.

But the kangaroo rat takes the prize for going without water. This animal "thrives in the driest regions, even in the bare sand dunes of Death Valley. Water to drink, even dew, is rarely available in its natural habitat," the Schmidt-Nielsens write.[17] The kangaroo rat never drinks, lives on a diet so dry as to kill other rodents from thirst, almost never eats juicy vegetation, and flourishes indefinitely in captivity without water, subsisting on dry barley seeds alone.

This apparently waterless life was long a puzzle to biologists. Experiments revealed that the kangaroo rat balances its water budget by producing metabolic water as a by-product of oxidizing its food. Other special equipment and behavior help this rodent to keep its water losses to a minimum: it is nocturnal, it loses less water through evaporation than other rodents, and it loses minimal water through excretion because of its extremely efficient kidneys.[18]

The antelope squirrel and the kangaroo rat, then, get along quite well without strain or struggle in some of the most inhospitable regions of the earth. The solution to the water problem for many other animals in those areas is simple: find and eat juicy plants. Thus the pack rat eats cactus pulp, which is 90 percent water. But this pushes the question back one step—in areas that average less than two inches of rainfall per year, where do the plants get the water in the first place? The techniques desert plants use to obtain and preserve water are almost as diverse as the number of species. To reduce water loss, the barrel cactus has thick skin and spines instead of leaves. Also the accordionlike folds on its surface allow it to expand and fill with water during a rain. When fully stored with water, the barrel cactus can live comfortably for a year or more. A different strategy is to tap special water resources. The mesquite bush, for instance, grows roots up to one hundred feet long that reach underground water unavailable to other plants.

Another unusual technique is controlled dessication. Various species of resurrection plants can survive almost complete dehydration, during which they exhibit no measurable metabolism. These plants "have the highest tolerance to dessication in the plant kingdom."[19] Drying up causes them some limited damage but it is not lethal, and with the first rain the plants unfurl, repair injuries, and resume full photosynthesis within twenty-four hours.

Other desert plants succeed by sheer opportunism, germinating, flowering, and setting seed only when it rains. Frits Went comments on the annual flowers that carpet Death Valley every ten years or so: "Probably their most remarkable feature is that they are perfectly normal plants, with no special adaptations to withstand drought. Yet they are not found outside the desert areas. The reason lies in the peculiar cautiousness of their seeds. In dry years the seeds lie dormant. This itself is not at all amazing; what is remarkable is that they refuse to germinate even after a rain unless the rainfall is at least half an inch, and preferably an inch or two."[20]

Certain shrubs grow only in desert washes (dry rivers). The seeds of the smoke tree, paloverde, and ironwood, for example, germinate only if abraded and cracked by sand and gravel driven along by a rainstorm. Thus seedlings of these shrubs sprout only after an adequate rain and become established between 150 to 300 feet downstream from the parent plant (any longer distance pulverizes the seed; any shorter distance fails to cause germination). It is an elegant system to guarantee both adequate moisture and good spacing for the new plant.[21]

But what if there is no rainfall at all? Not even this banishes all vegetation. Tributsch describes a remarkable case: "The Atacama Desert of northern Chile is one of the driest desert regions on earth. In some areas it has not rained within the memory of man; in others it rains only once every few years. On the average, no more than 2 centimeters of water per year reach the bone-dry desert soil. In spite of this acute lack of water, the hills of mountain ranges near the coast harbor some vegetation. It is not very dense, but it includes many large cacti and the stately tamorugo tree. These desert plants do not find a trace of moisture in the soil. They extract whatever moisture they get from the fog that frequently forms when the moist air cools."[22] In the same way the American pygmy cedar and the caper plant of the Sahara need no ground water. They live on the water vapor absorbed from the humid night air of the desert.[23] These plants are no less amazing than the kangaroo rat.

All these examples of desert plants and animals illustrate the same principle: organisms do not fight the environment; they work with it or around it. Some evade the drought, other provision for it. But none confronts it head on; none is foolish or inefficient or wasteful in its life plan. Neither do organisms waste energy struggling against the wind. If a tree is subjected to winds coming consistently from a single direction, its trunk puts on more wood parallel to the wind than at right angles to it, gradually producing an elliptical shape with the long axis parallel to the wind. The elliptical shape is aerodynamic and minimizes the wind's force against the tree. Many trees begin to grow spirally in response to heavier pressure from wind or snow.[24] Other trees, especially in the tundra, become dwarfs or grow horizontally to avoid the brunt of wind. The same species that takes on these unusual shapes under pressure will grow tall and spindly in a crowded forest, but spreads wide when grown alone in a park. None of this argues struggle on the tree's part, merely flexibility and adaptability. (See Figure 5.2.)

Another natural element thought to be destructive to life without qualification is fire. But together with weather, soil, topography, and animal life, naturally occurring fires are part of the forest's ecology and help to determine the kind of trees that will grow in a given area. Many species of fast-growing but short-lived trees specialize in pioneering newly cut or recently burned areas. One example is the quaking aspen, the most widely distributed tree in North America.[25] The cones of the jack pine open only after being heated by a forest fire, giving its seeds an advantage on open areas of fertile ash and mineral soil following a burn. Forester Charles F. Cooper points out that "Prescribed fire has become an accepted management tool in the southeastern longleaf pine forests."[26] He explains that periodic small fires eliminate the build up of forest debris, thus preventing huge conflagrations that would destroy whole stands of trees. Fire also thins out young trees. Limited fires are essential in establishing the Douglas fir and the ponderosa pine.[27]

Extremes of heat, cold, aridity, fire—life thrives in the most improbable habitats imaginable. Certain microbes flourish in sulfuric acid; some algae live in 140°F water, others at -76°F. But never do we witness an organism struggling against its environment. Nature does not solve the problems of life by brute force—which would be unnecessary and foolish—but by ingenious structure, metabolism, and behavior. The accurate image is not the animal battling the elements. Recall the bear that sleeps instead of battling the winter. Recall the tree that grows *with* rather than *against* the wind. Recall the finch that simply turns down its thermostat rather than waste energy fighting against the cold. Nature's motto is "Work smarter, not harder."

Nature's Efficiency and Economy

No organism, then, contradicts its habitat; on the contrary, every living thing is beautifully attuned to its environment. Effort is not maximal but minimal because each animal and plant is so well designed. The perfection of organic form is seen in its use of the least material to produce structures to accomplish what is needed with the least work.

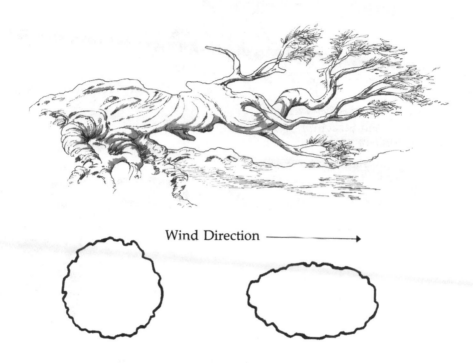

Wind Direction ⟶

Figure 5.2. Life works with the environment, not against it. If a tree, for example, is subject to continuous wind from one direction, it puts on more wood parallel to the wind, resulting in an elliptical trunk (shown in cross-section at *right*) that reduces wind pressure on the tree. The cross-section (*left*) shows what the growth pattern would be without wind pressure. Where winds are fierce and constant, trees do not struggle against them but simply hug the ground and grow horizontally (*top*)

The rule of least material is seen in the hollow bones of animals. Here nature exploits the principle of physics and engineering that says hollow support columns are just as sturdy as solid ones. The same principle is found in the hollow stems of plants. A hollow tube like a straw can withstand great vertical stress without collapsing but relatively little stress against its sides before it bends. In fact, solid support columns would be weaker because they would have to support their own extra added weight. (See Figure 5.3.) Certain

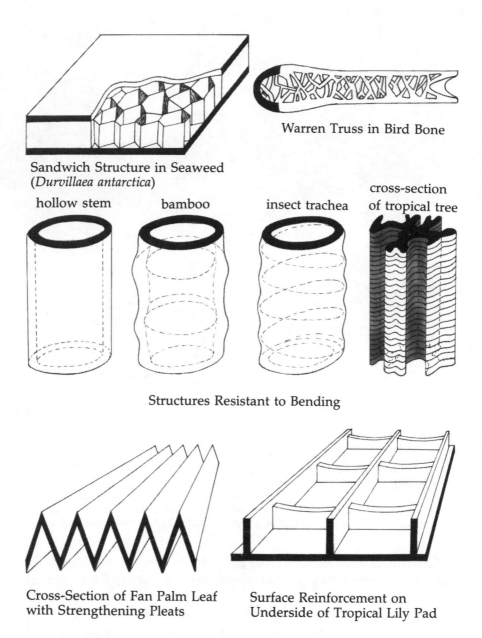

Sandwich Structure in Seaweed
(*Durvillaea antarctica*)

Warren Truss in Bird Bone

hollow stem   bamboo   insect trachea   cross-section of tropical tree

Structures Resistant to Bending

Cross-Section of Fan Palm Leaf
with Strengthening Pleats

Surface Reinforcement on
Underside of Tropical Lily Pad

Figure 5.3. All the engineering principles for strengthening structures are found in nature. The application of these principles produces living structures that have a maximum of sturdiness but require a minimum of material. (From Tributsch)

mammals have hollow hairs to trap more air for superior insulation. Whenever less gets the job done, nature economizes on materials.

The hexagonal shape of the honeycomb's cells is another familiar example of nature's economical use of material. Tributsch comments on the cells: "Their hexagonal shape provides a maximum of inner space for the brood with a minimum of material and no unnecessary interspaces. One could imagine them having been formed by the pressing together of cylindrical cells and the adjustment of the six contact areas to identical thickness. It is notable that the geometric formation is equally ideal at the base, where two layers of honeycombs are put together to form a double comb. Here, too, material is used economically. The result is a honeycomb floor consisting of three rhombic planes. Each of these planes represents a common wall between the two combs, so that the pattern of cells is shifted one against the other.

"The honeycombs of bees can of course not be expected to be mathematically exact, but their precision is quite amazing: The cell walls are built to a thickness of 0.073 millimeter, with deviations of not more than 2 percent. The diameter of the honeycomb is 5.5 millimeters, with 5 percent tolerance. The cells are inclined at a 13° angle against the horizontal plane. Humans would need rather fine measuring instruments for such precision. Bees achieve it with their antennae."[28]

It is mathematically demonstrable that the hexagon is the two-dimensional figure with the greatest area that can be fit together with itself in a continuous pattern. This makes the hexagonal prism the most efficient choice for honeycomb cells, yielding maximum volume for least amount of wax (and consequently least labor). Mathematics can explain why the hexagon is the most efficient shape but mathematics cannot explain why the most efficient shape *occurs in nature*. We must add to what mathematics tells us the postulate that nature, especially in living things, aims at the most efficient form.

Where no particularly efficient material for some special purpose exists in nonliving nature, life invents one. Every time a bone is subjected to stretching from one side, it simultaneously is compressed on the other side. The material of which bone is composed answers this challenge perfectly: unlike man-made materials, its capacity for stretching equals its capacity for compression. That great student of morphology and anatomy, D'Arcy Thompson, remarks, "From the engineer's point of view, bone may seem weak indeed; but it has the great advantage that it is very nearly as good for a tie as for a strut, nearly as strong to withstand rupture, or tearing asunder, as to resist crushing." He adds, "There is great economy, then, in any material which is, as nearly as possible, equally strong in both ways; and so we see that, from the engineer's or contractor's point of view, bone is a good and suitable material for purposes of construction."[29]

Another example of a material with remarkable properties is spider's silk. It must be thin enough not to be seen by a flying insect until too late, yet strong enough to hold the insect once caught. The tenacity of spider's silk (7.8 gm/denier) is more than double that of steel, while its elasticity is 9 percent greater than that of nylon.[30] So if a material of suitable efficiency is not available in the inorganic world, living things manufacture a new substance often superior to man-made materials.

Living things are composed of exceptional materials that assume remarkably efficient structures. This guarantees that the minimum energy will be required to produce the living body, to maintain it, and to make it function. This is the principle of least work. It is found at all levels beginning with the cell, which is its own toolmaker, troubleshooter, and construction company. How efficient is the cell's metabolism? For example, how efficiently do the cells of our body extract energy from sugar molecules? A calculation based on measuring the energy released by oxidation during ATP hydrolysis in intact red blood cells yields an efficiency of 72 percent, which far surpasses the 25 to 30 percent efficiency of internal combustion engines.[31] Further, Tributsch notes that "With an almost 100 percent quantum yield, the process of photosynthesis is optimally efficient. This could only be achieved by a sophisticated structural organization of matter."[32] Though it exploits only 2 percent of the sun's available radiant energy, photosynthesis makes the most of that 2 percent. Molecular biologist George Wald points out that chlorophyll "possesses a triple combination of capacities: a high receptivity to light, an inertness of structure permitting it to store the energy and relay it to other molecules, and a reactive site equipping it to transfer hydrogen."[33] This makes chlorophyll an unparalleled agent, the most effective photosynthetic molecule anyone could invent. Enzymes, the cell's tailor-made catalysts, are far more efficient than inorganic catalysts. Catalase, for example, causes hydrogen peroxide to decompose one trillion times faster than when no catalyst is present, while iron speeds up the decomposition only one-hundredfold. "Without enzymes, most of the rapidly occurring reactions in cells would not occur, to any perceptible degree, within a human lifetime."[34]

Nature's law of efficiency is illustrated everywhere in the living world. Animals, because of their special design and habits, move with the least energy expended. Birds, for instance, from the hummingbird to the albatross, cruise at the minimum speed necessary to maintain flight.[35] Special devices also reduce the work needed to fly. The sparrow hawk's wing bears a special feather on its leading edge that serves to reduce air turbulence during slow-speed flight. Modern aircraft use a similar device. (See Figure 5.4.) The hollow bones of birds make them much lighter for flying. A frigate bird's bones weigh less than its feathers. Birds eliminate all excess baggage: "To keep their weight low and feathers dry they forgo the luxury of sweat glands," writes zoologist Carl Welty. "They have even reduced their reproductive organs to a minimum. The female has only one ovary, and during the nonbreeding season the sex organs of both males and females atrophy. T. H. Bissonette, the well-known investigator of birds and photoperiodicity, found that in starlings the organs weigh 1,500 times as much during the breeding season as during the rest of the year."[36] Sea birds, predatory birds, and migrating birds make use of rising air currents to lift themselves high into the sky with a minimal expenditure of energy. Geese and other migrators fly in a V-formation, allowing all individuals except the leader to take advantage of the slight updraft behind the bird immediately in front. Lissaman and Shollenberger: "Formation flight of birds improves aerodynamic efficiency. Theoretically, 25 birds could have a range increase of about 70 percent as compared with a lone bird. . . . And, contrary to other statements, the lead bird does not necessarily have the most strenuous position."[37] Birds waste no energy.

Other animals have similar advantages built right into their bodies. Aerodynamicist Mohamed Gad-el-Hak states that "some insects have envelops [flight structures] that are better than anything we know as far as aircraft are concerned."[38] By application

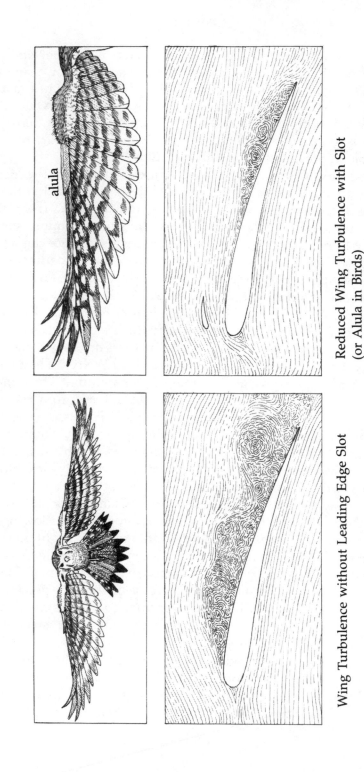

alula

Wing Turbulence without Leading Edge Slot

Reduced Wing Turbulence with Slot
(or Alula in Birds)

Figure 5.4. A special appendage called an alula on the sparrow hawk's wing reduces air turbulence over the wing to a minimum. This prevents the bird from stalling during slow flight. Commercial airplanes use slots on the forward edge of the wing to achieve the same efficiency. (After McMahon and Bonner)

of simple hydrodynamic principles, Egbert G. Leigh of the Smith-sonian Tropical Research Institute demonstrated that sponges have a maximally efficient shape for feeding.[39] When a horse's fetlock joint bends upon meeting the ground, an elastic ligament is stretched. As soon as the foot leaves the ground, the ligament snaps the joint back straight and gives the foot an upward lift. This is all accomplished by ligament elasticity with no need for muscle work. The same occurs in other hoofed runners. Different animals even exhibit different gear ratios in the way their muscles are joined to their bones. Zoologist Milton Hildebrand: "Cursorial animals not only have longer legs; their actuating muscles are also attached to the bone closer to the pivot of motion. Their high-gear muscles, in other words, have short lever-arms, and this increases the gear ratio still further. In comparison, the anatomy of walking animals gives them considerably lower gear-ratios; digging and swimming animals have still lower gear-ratios."[40] Some animals have the ability to move in different gears according to need. Just as with automobiles and other machines, the ability to shift gears economizes on fuel.

The efficiency of nature is often astounding. Welty offers the example of the golden plover's high mileage per unit of fuel: "In the fall the plover fattens itself on bayberries in Labrador and then strikes off across the open ocean on a nonstop flight of 2,400 miles to South America. It arrives there weighing some two ounces less than it did on its departure. This is the equivalent of flying a 1,000-pound airplane 20 miles on a pint of gasoline rather than the usual gallon. Man still has far to go to approach such efficiency."[41]

Water normally contains only about .05 percent dissolved oxygen. This means a fish's gills must be singularly efficient. Thanks to the countercurrent exchange principle, a fish's gills can extract up to 90 percent of the oxygen in the water they process.[42]

Nature has adjusted the necessary equipment of animals and plants so precisely that little can be improved without compromising something else. Geneticist Richard Lewontin points out that longer legs would not necessarily improve a zebra: "A longer bone might break more easily, or require greater developmental resources and metabolic energy to produce and maintain, or change the efficiency of the contraction of the attached muscles."[43]

A sign of nature's efficiency is that often a maximally efficient form discovered in mathematics or engineering is subsequently found in animals or plants. For instance, topology demonstrates that the most efficient pattern of arranging veins and arteries for maximal surface transfer is either a checkerboard of squares or a pattern of hexagons with triangles at the open corners. And the microscope reveals precisely these two patterns in the swim bladders of deep-sea fishes.[44]

Nature's economy and efficiency are principles for the biologist whenever he examines a mechanism. Thompson declares: "That this mechanism is the best possible under all the circumstances of the case, that its work is done with a maximum of efficiency and at a minimum of cost, may not always lie within our range of quantitative demonstration, but to believe it to be so is part of our common faith in the perfection of Nature's handiwork. All the experience and the very instinct of the physiologist tells him it is true; he comes to use it as a postulate, or *methodus inveniendi* [method of discovering], and it does not lead him astray."[45] Efficiency, as Thompson implies, must be defined in terms of the requirements and life of the organism. For nature to give a structure more efficient than the plant or animal needs would be wasteful. Thus mammals do not have the extraordinary lungs of birds because they do not need them.

In any event, nature can certainly set man to school. For example, the largest seagoing vessel of the 1850s was the *Great Eastern*, a huge iron ocean liner. Despite paddle wheels, a screw propeller, and auxiliary sails, it could not be operated at a profit because it traveled too slowly. Its hull, designed largely by guesswork, caused it to move too much water as it traveled so that it could never run efficiently. As a result of this engineering error and subsequent experiments, the physical laws governing wave resistance, drag, and turbulence caused by various shapes moving through fluids were discovered.[46] Only then did man appreciate how fish always conform to the rules of most efficient shape. (See Figure 5.5.) One does not find among living things fiascos such as the *Great Eastern*.

Another testimony to the perfection of organic form comes from prosthetic medicine. Biophysicist Keith Copeland remarks: "At best, attempts to replace, simulate, or supplement normal body functions by artificial devices are crude and incomplete. No man-made system has ever captured and faithfully reproduced the elegant freedom of the toss of a head, a flick of the wrist, the subtleties of a smile, or the

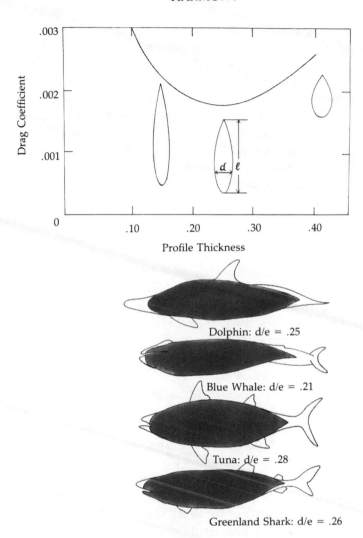

Figure 5.5. Laboratory tests proved that a body with a thickness profile of 0.25 moves through water with minimal work. Anything shorter, and thus relatively blunter, wastes energy by generating too much turbulence; anything longer and slimmer must overcome too much surface friction with the water. The profiles of fast-swimming fish and mammals are very close to 0.25, as can be seen from their silhouettes. The efficiency of their design thus requires not struggle but minimal effort for them to move through their environment. (After McMahon and Bonner)

versatility of the human voice. Even with the most advanced micro-miniaturised electronic techniques we cannot imitate with comparable compactness those body actions that may be absent because of congenital defect, or lost through traumatic injury, illness, disease, or even old age."[47] The prototype artificial heart, for example, after twenty-five years and seven million dollars' research, is run by a 375-pound air compressor. Even future models costing perhaps $20,000 each and still requiring a separate power supply will be bulky and awkward compared with natural equipment and will not be able to adjust to the body's ever-changing blood needs as the natural heart does.

Nature's Beauty

We could multiply examples without limit, but it should already be clear that nature is a wise and thrifty builder, a master engineer. But organic form incorporates more than efficiency. There is also great beauty in living things. But because of their almost exclusive emphasis on competition and struggle, some biologists tend to consider beauty scientifically insignificant. In this they are out of step with modern physics. Werner Heisenberg declares that beauty "in exact science, no less than in the arts... is the most important source of illumination and clarity."[48] And all the most eminent physicists of the twentieth century agree that beauty is the primary standard for scientific truth.* This holds as much for biology as for physics. James Watson mentions in his book *The Double Helix* that beauty guided the discovery of DNA's physical structure.[49] Speaking of his work in genetics, Matthew Scott says, "What keeps us going is it's a nice feeling to work on something that at its fundamental level is very beautiful."[50]

The living world incorporates many different kinds of beauty: not only elegant forms and dazzling colors to please the eye, but also intricate harmony and order to please the mind. As physicist David Bohm notes, "Almost anything to be found in nature exhibits some kind of beauty both in immediate perception and in intellectual analysis."[51] The flight of a bird not only has grace perceptible to the

---

*See *The New Story of Science*, chap. 3.

eye but also has intellectual beauty in the analyses of the biophysicist and anatomist. For instance, D'Arcy Thompson exclaims, "In all
the mechanical side of anatomy nothing can be more beautiful than
the construction of a vulture's metacarpal bone. . . . The engineer
sees in it a perfect Warren's truss, just such a one as is often used for
a main rib in an aeroplane. Not only so, but the bone is better than
the truss; for the engineer has to be content to set his V-shaped
struts all in one plane, while in the bone they are put, with obvious
but inimitable advantage, in a three-dimensional configuration."[52]
And nineteenth century ornithologist Elliott Coues called the
beautifully designed avian skull a "poem in bone."[53]

The beauty of living things cannot be accounted for by Darwin's
hypothesis of sexual selection, especially if, as Kirk reports, the
defender of territory "is usually successful in driving away an
invader irrespective of differences in size, strength, [and] development of specialized structures important in aggressive display."[54]
Biologist John M. Smith comments that Darwin's hypothesis of
sexual selection has been generally abandoned as indemonstrable.[55]

Not all organisms show the same kind of beauty. Some show
simple charm, while others are elaborately decorated; some please
the eye by a stark plainness, others overwhelm it with a gorgeous-
ness of color. At the turn of the century, when the first specimen of
an unusually magnificent bird of paradise was shown to Dr.
Bowdler Sharpe, keeper of the birds in the British Museum, "he
refused to believe it was not a human artifact!"[56] Often the young
and the adult of the same animal species are beautiful in different
ways; the former charm us with their cuteness, the latter awe us
with their noble grandeur. Naturalist Joseph Krutch observes that
insects can hardly be considered of Homeric stature, but lions and
elks certainly can.[57] Naturalist John Muir writes this tribute to the
Rocky Mountain bighorn sheep: "Possessed of keen sight and scent,
and strong limbs, he dwells secure amid the loftiest summits,
leaping unscathed from crag to crag, up and down the fronts of
giddy precipices, crossing foaming torrents and slopes of frozen
snow, exposed to the wildest storms, yet maintaining a brave, warm
beauty."[58]

The beauty of the organic world is evident to all, including the
nonspecialist. Tree lover Hugh Johnson begins a book on trees with
this admonition: "You can walk past seventy feet of the greatest

beauty every morning for years without noticing it. I did. Or you can open your eyes, and begin to follow the patterns of branches, and discover the causes and origins, and find an infinity of sensuous detail to enjoy, in every tree in every street." And he adds, "I am not a botanist, nor a forester, nor even (except in my own garden) a gardener, but a writer who has found in trees a new point of contact with creation, a source of wonder and satisfaction."[59]

The specialist, too, is moved by nature's beauty. Sinnott does not consider it trivial or accidental: "Beauty's variety and profusion in sound and form and colour . . . are far greater in the products of life than elsewhere. Beauty is of life's very essence. It is one of the permanent and indestructible parts of nature."[60]

Zoologist Adolf Portmann, who studied extensively the ornamental and aesthetic morphology of animals, shows that nature troubles herself as much with the coach work of an animal as with its internal mechanisms. A mammal's fur coat is a joy to behold, a feast for the eye, he says, and then argues that this beauty cannot be explained away or reduced to survival value: "We cannot adequately understand the structure of such objects as feathers and fur in all their finest details unless we assume that this outward appearance has been designed for something more than those functions which we know are necessary to preserve life (such as protection from cold, from mechanical injury, the checking of evaporation, sensory functions). We must assume that they have also been designed in a very special way to meet the eye of the beholder." Only the visible feathers of birds carry the characteristic pattern or shimmering colors of the species, he points out, not the hidden interior feathers. By contrast, the shapes of the internal organs of related animals are "all most monotonous" and extremely difficult to distinguish: "Lion and tiger—what a contrast in spite of their close relationship! Anyone who as a child has seen those two feline species at the zoo will never in all his life again confuse them. But how embarrassed he would be if he had to judge merely from the stomach or the liver, for these carry no incontestably characteristic features. Not even the skeleton reveals such. Naturally, specific differences do also exist inside the body. But a great deal of trouble and knowledge is required to grasp these deviations in proportion and shape—and even far more effort is required to impress such differences firmly on one's memory."[61]

Darwin held that beauty is a subjective feeling: "The sense of beauty obviously depends on the nature of the mind, irrespective of any real quality in the admired object."[62] If this were true, beauty could hardly be the beacon it is for physicists. In a real sense beauty is the main reason that the best mathematicians do mathematics, and physicists, physics. Poincaré writes, "The scientist does not study nature because it is useful to do so. He studies it because he takes pleasure in it; and he takes pleasure in it because it is beautiful. If nature were not beautiful, it would not be worth knowing and life would not be worth living."[63] But Darwin was too great a scientist not to recognize this in practice if not in theory. Listen to his journal's description of his first day in a tropical jungle:

"The day has passed delightfully. Delight itself, however, is a weak term to express the feelings of a naturalist who for the first time has wandered by himself in a Brazilian forest. The elegance of the grasses, the novelty of the parasitical plants, the beauty of the flowers, the glossy green of the foliage, but above all the general luxuriance of the vegetation, filled me with admiration. A most paradoxical mixture of sound and silence pervades the shady parts of the wood. The noise from the insects is so loud that it may be heard even in a vessel anchored several hundred yards from the shore; yet within the recesses of the forest a universal silence appears to reign. To a person fond of natural history such a day as this brings with it a deeper pleasure than he can ever hope to experience again."[64] Beauty not only delights but motivates men and women to do science in the first place, and then guides them in selecting the theories most likely to correspond with nature.

Prolific variety is part of the beauty of living things. The diversity of life is bewildering. The drawings in Figures 5.6, 5.7, and 5.8 give some idea of the astounding diversity in organisms. The fourteen species of fish illustrated represent only 1/1500 of the variety of fish species. And there are over thirteen times more species of plants than fish. "How many species of organisms are there on Earth? We do not know, not even to the nearest order of magnitude," writes E. O. Wilson.[65] After intensive sampling in a tropical rain forest in 1982, entomologist Terry Erwin estimates there are probably 30 million species of insects alone.[66] Untold millions of species of plants and animals grace our planet, each with its own form, its own niche, and its own life story. This represents more variety of kinds than is

Figure 5.6. The variety of animal and plant sizes illustrates nature's astounding diversity. Shown here is a sampling of the largest organisms in various categories. A hundred-foot larch is shown superimposed on the silhouette of a giant sequoia, the largest organism. All organisms are drawn to scale. (After Wells, Huxley, and Wells)

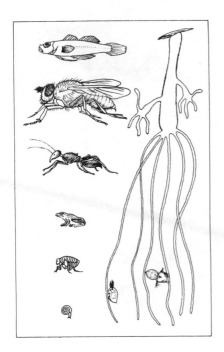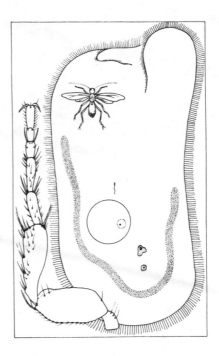

Figure 5.7. Nature exhibits surprising variety on the small scale also. Shown at *left* is an adult tropical frog, which is smaller than a housefly. A hydra with water fleas in its tentacles is also shown. The fly's leg is reproduced at *right*, where, superimposed on the largest ciliate protozoan, is seen the smallest flying insect. It approximates the size of the human ovum shown below a human sperm. (After Wells, Huxley, and Wells)

found in all the rest of the nonliving universe put together. Of these unknown myriads of living creatures, only about 1.7 million have been identified and named. "New species are being found and named at the rate of some 10,000 yearly!"[67] Most of the unnamed species are insects and bacteria, but expeditions regularly turn up new animals of other phyla. In March 1985 a team of more than 120 American, British, and Venezuelan botanists and zoologists brought

Figure 5.8. These fourteen fish species represent less than 1/1500 of the diversity of the kinds of fish in the world: 21,000 species. Multiply this diversity by ten and you approximate the number of different kinds of flowering plants (210,000). And there are at least four times more known species of insects on our planet (900,000+) than flowering plants.

back dozens of previously unknown species of plants, reptiles, and amphibians from Cerro de la Neblina, a mountain in southern Venezuela so isolated that it went undiscovered until 1953.[68] Even more dramatic was the discovery by geologists in 1977 of a rich variety of sea creatures living along heat vents in the Pacific Ocean floor without dependence on the sun. The warm water allows sulfur-processing bacteria to thrive. These are the foundation food for several communities of previously unknown species: giant blood-red tube worms, white brachyuran crabs of a brand-new family, mussels and clams with bizarre red flesh because of high concentrations of hemoglobin, a new siphonophore named the dandelion by its discoverers, and new limpets, whelks, barnacles, and leeches. "To marine biologists, vent communities are as strange as a lost valley of prehistoric dinosaurs," write expedition members Robert Ballard and J. Frederick Grassle.[69]

If we include extinct species, a conservative estimate is that two billion different kinds of organisms have at one time or other inhabited the earth. In producing such a profusion of kinds, nature acts like an artist who creates beautiful variations on a theme. Both for nature and the artist, a basic form sets the limits within which great variety is possible. Nature, then, is not only a superb engineer, she is also a master artist. Tributsch notes that nature's architecture is not only sound and economical, but also beautiful.[70] And Bohm observes, "Nature is more like an artist than an engineer. . . . Therefore it requires a basically artistic attitude to understand it."[71]

6

Origins

The modern synthetic theory of evolution, developed in the 1930s and 1940s chiefly by biologist Julian Huxley, paleontologist George Simpson, systematist Ernst Mayr, and geneticist Theodosius Dobzhansky, is essentially a form of neo-Darwinism. It incorporates modern discoveries in genetics and other areas but retains the core of Darwin's theory, especially natural selection. The genius of Darwin was to elaborate for evolutionary change a mechanism consistent with Newtonian physics. Thus Wallace rightly characterized Darwin as the Newton of biology.

The limitations of Newtonian physics and of mechanistic explanations in general have been amply demonstrated with the discoveries of relativity theory and quantum physics. The physics that Darwin took as a model for his science has undergone a profound transformation. This does not automatically invalidate Darwin or neo-Darwinism, but it does suggest that evolutionary theory ought to be reexamined in the light of the new physics.

Evolutionary theory is currently being seriously rethought and is the occasion of some controversy and turmoil within biology. The debate is not whether evolution has occurred but whether Darwin's mechanisms, namely natural selection and gradualism, adequately account for evolution. On one side are the critics of neo-Darwinism. Among them, Stephen Jay Gould declares, "The synthetic theory . . . as a general proposition, is effectively dead, despite its persistence as textbook orthodoxy."[1] Colin Patterson, senior paleontologist at the British Museum of Natural History, also reflects skepticism and disillusion with conventional evolutionary theory: "For over twenty years I had thought I was working on evolution in some way. One morning I woke up . . . and it struck me that I had been working on this stuff for more than twenty years, and there was not one thing I knew about it. It's quite a shock to learn that one can be misled for so long."[2]

On the other side, defenders of neo-Darwinism maintain that critics have overstated their case and that everything known about evolution can be assimilated within the general framework of Darwin's natural selection. Thus G. Ledyard Stebbins and Francisco J. Ayala look for a compromise solution: "With modifications both to the traditional views and to the competing theories most of the challenges can be accommodated within the encompassing vision of the synthetic theory."[3] In a similar way biologist Richard Dawkins sees no menace of upheaval in Stephen Gould's and Niles Eldredge's theory of punctuated equilibria that challenges Darwinian gradualism: "The debate about this interesting little theory is a technical, parochial affair if ever there was one. It lies firmly *within* the neo-Darwinian synthesis. It is no more revolutionary than many another argument that has enriched the synthetic theory."[4]

In general it is better to keep what we have with minor changes, if possible, unless it proves completely unworkable. But what do we have? The essence of natural selection is succinctly expressed by Darwin himself: "If under changing conditions of life organic beings present individual differences in almost every part of their structure, and this cannot be disputed; if there be, owing to their geometrical rate of increase, a severe struggle for life at some age, season, or year, and this certainly cannot be disputed; then, considering the infinite complexity of the relations of all organic beings to each other and to their conditions of life, causing an infinite diversity in structure, constitution, and habits, to be advantageous to them, it would be a most extraordinary fact if no variations had ever occurred useful to each being's own welfare, in the same manner as so many variations have occurred useful to man. But if variations useful to any organic being ever do occur, assuredly individuals thus characterised will have the best chance of being preserved in the struggle for life; and from the strong principle of inheritance, they will tend to produce offspring similarly characterised. This principle of preservation, or the survival of the fittest, I have called Natural Selection."[5]

Darwin's argument is clear. He considered that the study of variation in domestic animals and cultivated plants "afforded the best and safest clue" to understanding evolution.[6] Recognizing that man's skillful crossbreeding and artificial selection have improved nearly every domestic animal and farm crop, Darwin made the plausible extension to animals and plants in the wild. It seemed likely that nature could by crossbreeding and selection of traits produce new species. But what mechanism in nature would correspond to the selecting hand of man? Here Darwin answers with a brilliant syllogism: (1) on the principle of geometrical increase more individuals of each species are produced than can possibly survive; (2) a struggle for existence ensues, one organism competing with another; and, (3) owing to this struggle for existence, slight variations, if in any degree advantageous will accumulate and produce a new species. Darwin calls the elimination of the disadvantaged and promotion of the advantaged "natural selection," by analogy to animal breeder's artificial selection of traits.

Critique of Natural Selection

How could natural selection be controversial? It seems so cogent and plausible. One of its appeals has always been its intrinsic logic. Critics do not question Darwin's logic, however, but the truth of his premises. All the key assumptions, those about population growth, competition, and accumulation of slight differences, conflict with the results of modern ecological studies and genetic research. First, field studies show that animal populations are limited not by predation, starvation, severities of climate, and disease that Darwin postulated, but by various natural restraints on the number of breeders and by adjustments in the number of offspring produced by each female (see Chapter 4).

Second, no ongoing competition is observable in nature between species or between individuals of the same species. Similar animal species coexist without competing because they eat different foods or are active at different times or otherwise occupy different niches. Dispersion mechanisms reduce competition between individuals of the same species to a minimum. (See Chapter 4.) Niles Eldredge points to the many "ecologists skeptical of the very concept of competition between species...who claim they simply cannot see any evidence for such raw battling going on nowadays in nature."[7] Evolutionary biologist William D. Hamilton indicates the inconsistency: "The theory of evolution is based on the struggle for life and the survival of the fittest. Yet cooperation is common between members of the same species and even between members of different species."[8] The renowned Japanese biologist Kinji Imanishi has developed a theory of evolution based on the opposite of Darwin's starting point. He writes: "I regard the biological nature we see not as the scene of survival competition, but as the scene of peaceful coexistence among specia."[9]

And third, Darwin's gradualism assumes that "varieties are species in the process of formation, or are, as I have called them, incipient species," and that "the lesser difference between varieties become[s] augmented into the greater difference between species."[10] This requires unlimited plasticity within each species. But the results of animal and plant breeding and of genetic experiments with artificially induced mutations contradict Darwin's assumption that organisms are moldable in any direction without restraint. The natural limits of artificial selection were soon discovered by plant breeders. For example, between 1800 and 1878, crossbreeding increased the sugar content of sugar beets from 6 percent to 17 percent. But fifty years of subsequent experiments produced no further increases.[11]

All experienced breeders recognize the constraints. Luther Burbank: "I know from my experience that I can develop a plum half an inch long or one two and a half inches long, with every possible length in between, but I am willing to admit that it is hopeless to try to get a plum the size of a small pea, or one as big as a grapefruit. I have daisies on my farms little larger than my fingernail and some that measure six inches across, but I have none as big as a sunflower, and never expect to have. I have roses that bloom pretty steadily for six months in the year, but I have none that will bloom twelve, and I will not have. In short, there are limits to the developments possible."[12] Burbank also concluded that no one has ever been able to grow blue roses or genuinely black tulips because the necessary genetic material was lacking in these species.[13] What is more, the accumulation of traits by crossbreeding never exceeds the confines of the species. After 14,000 years of breeding dogs, man has produced scores of varieties but not a single new species. All races of dog are interfertile, though some are prevented from mating by disparity of size.[14] After a certain limit is reached, crossbred organisms frustrate further attempts at improvement by becoming sterile or by reverting to type.

These results are corroborated by experiments with artificially

induced mutations. Since the early part of this century, in continuous genetic experiments, fruit flies, subjected to x-rays and other
treatments to increase their mutation rate up to 150 times the
normal, have been bred for thousands of generations and closely
monitored. These experiments have produced offspring with fringed
wings, vestigial wings, no wings at all, and other variations, but all
were clearly fruit flies.[15] No beetles, no mantids, no butterflies. Not
even a new species of fly.* The work revealed much about genetics,
but it contradicted Darwin's assumption that the accumulation of
varietal characteristics can produce organisms differing in species,
and eventually differing in genus, order, class, and phylum.

Thus all Darwin's premises are defective: there is no unlimited
population growth in natural populations, no competition between
individuals, and no new species producible by selecting for varietal
differences. And if Darwin's premises are faulty, then his conclusion
does not follow. This, of itself, does not mean that natural selection
is false. It simply means that we cannot use Darwin's argument,
brilliant though it was, to establish natural selection as a means of
explaining the origin of species.

The way nature acts right now does not agree with Darwin's
premises, but does the *history* of life, perhaps? Darwin himself
recognized that the fossil record does not support gradualism. But
instead of changing his theory, he argued that the geological record
was incomplete and unrepresentative.[16] Paleontologist Eldredge
puts it bluntly: Darwin's discussion of the "imperfections of the
geological record is one long *ad hoc,* special-pleading argument
designed to rationalize, to flat-out explain away, the differences
between what he saw as logical predictions derived from his theory
and the facts of the fossil record."[17] Darwin had no reason
independent of his theory for claiming the fossil evidence to be
unrepresentative.

Today, more than one hundred years later, the fossil record,
much more complete and much better understood, still contradicts
gradualism. It shows virtually none of the intermediary species
between major groups required by natural selection. Paleontologist
David Raup: "Different species usually appear and disappear from

*The production of new plant species by chromosome doubling will be discussed
below.

the [fossil] record without showing the transitions that Darwin postulated."[18] Paleontologist Steven Stanley agrees: "The known fossil record is not, and never has been in accord with gradualism."[19] And Heribert Nilsson of Lund University, Sweden, after forty years' experience, writes, "It is not even possible to make a caricature of evolution [Darwinian gradualism] out of paleobiological facts. The fossil material is now so complete that... the lack of transitional series cannot be explained by the scarcity of the material. The deficiencies are real, they will never be filled."[20]

This is not to say that gradualism never occurs among fossils. It does. But the changes are trivial, often reverse themselves, and even when added up over millions of years, do not produce new species. "Gradual change... never seems to *get* anywhere.... The change amounts to a *within-species* historical trend," writes Eldredge.[21]

Nor does the fossil record support Darwin's assumption of competition. He thought that through natural selection "new varieties continually take the place of and supplant their parent-forms."[22] He conceived of one species driving out another as one wedge might force out another by occupying the same space.[23] But the fossils say otherwise. New species typically appear suddenly in the fossil record and persist alongside the progenitor, often for several million years.[24] There is no gradual change of one into the other, no replacement. This hardly argues competition. It suggests rather the peaceful coexistence discussed in Chapter 4.

The Second Line of Defense

Thus natural selection accords neither with the evidence of the present nor with the evidence of the past. Aware of these criticisms, contemporary defenders of neo-Darwinism, however, offer a rebuttal that we shall refer to as the *second line of defense*.

First, many neo-Darwinians concede that nature is not competitive now but attempt to explain present cooperation as the result of prior competition and the elimination of unviable strategies. Apart from the implausibility of trying to derive a thing from its contrary, their procedure posits an unevidenced state of nature in the remote and unobservable past.

How do defenders of neo-Darwinism answer the charge that no gradualism is found in the fossil record? Stebbins and Ayala argue that "the 'geological instants' during which speciation and morphological shifts occur may involve intervals of the order of 50,000 years. There is little doubt that the gradual accumulation of small-effect mutations may yield sizable morphological changes during periods of that length."[25] Paleontologists agree that even in the best fossil beds the smallest amount of reliably known time between strata is 50,000 years. So neo-Darwinism maintains that gradualism occurs in periods too short for us to observe in the fossil record. No reason is given as to why the gradualism takes place only when we cannot see it. Again the theory takes refuge in the unobservable. Mayr insists that "speciation is a slow historical process, it can never be directly observed by an individual observer."[26]

The same pattern recurs when it comes to measuring "differential reproduction" between individuals of the same population, a key notion in neo-Darwinian gradualism. Patterson explains: "Natural selection theory says that very small selection coefficients, of the order of 1 per cent or less, are effective in causing evolutionary change, yet the demonstration of such small differences in fitness is simply not possible in experiments. It has been calculated that a 1 per cent difference in fertility between two genotypes could be shown with 95 per cent confidence only if the fertility of 130,000 females of each type were measured. If the fertility of 380 females of each type were measured, the investigator has only an even chance of detecting a much larger difference in fertility, of 10 per cent. So selection theory is trapped in its own sophistication: it asserts that small differences in fitness are effective agents of evolutionary change, yet differences of that order are not detectable in practice."[27]

The untestable and unobservable appear in many other forms in natural selection theory. Stabilizing selection is invoked to account for the long periods where species go unchanged in fossil history. Apparently some unknown factor prevents natural selection from operating during these times. Natural selection, when combined with the notion of genetic drift (unselected, random mixing in the gene population), is untestable and beyond criticism in principle. Patterson writes: "No matter how many cases fail to yield to a natural selection analysis, the theory is not threatened, for it can always be said that these failures of selection theory are explained by genetic drift. And no matter how many supposed examples of genetic drift are shown to be due, after all, to natural selection, the neutral theory is not threatened, for it never pretended to explain all evolution."[28]

The defenders of natural selection have insulated it from criticism by pushing it away from the facts into the realm of the unobservable. Biologist Søren Løvtrup points out that the use of ad hoc arguments permits the adherents of the second line of defense "to reject any kind of refuting evidence."[29] This second line of defense results in an unverifiable, unfalsifiable theory. Sir Karl Popper's long-standing critique of evolution applies to this second line of defense, not to natural selection as such, which *is* subject to falsification if one allows it to be.

There are two ways to adjust a theory with respect to observations that contradict it. One is to change something in the substance of the theory, to modify it to fit the new facts, to change a basic assumption to its opposite, or, if necessary, to abandon the theory for a completely fresh approach. All these changes are made so that the resulting theory will predict new testable results. This leads to further discoveries, to eventual confirmation or invalidation, in a word to the advancement of knowledge.

Another way to modify a theory in the face of observations that contradict it is to make no change in the substance of the theory but rather to place the theory's claims beyond the limits of our capacities of observation. Recast the theory so that it will have no testable results in the area of the contradicting observations. This makes it impossible to compare the theory with the facts. True, this maneuver puts the theory beyond all attack but at the price of stripping it of all explanatory value. It loses its purpose as a theory: it cannot help us understand anything and it becomes an unquestionable presupposition. This is not the direction of good science but of stagnation and obscurantism. Maintaining a theory at all costs in face of contrary evidence does not serve the cause of truth. It is questionable whether a theory in no way open to refutation by sense experience even pertains to natural science.

The history of the ether hypothesis offers a clear example of this second way of modifying a theory. Physicists of the nineteenth century postulated that the phenomena of light required a material substratum, which came to be called the luminiferous ether. This substance, assumed to permeate all bodies and all space, was considered weightless, invisible, frictionless, and undetectable by ordinary chemical and physical means—an unobservable if there ever was one. Even when experiment demonstrated that the supposed ether would have to have contradictory properties, many physicists clung to the theory and tried to circumvent the obvious consequences of the experiments with auxiliary assumptions that were ad hoc and gratuitous. Physicist Leopold Infeld comments: "Scientific prejudices die hard. The desire to invent a medium for the propagation of electromagnetic waves was so strong that even after it was proved that ether neither rests nor moves, attempts were made to hold on to the concept of ether by introducing new assumptions, which made the structure of theoretical physics more complicated, more artificial, and less convincing."[30] Physics was finally liberated from this dead end when Einstein proposed relativity theory in 1905.

The part of evolutionary theory analogous to ether is the hypothetical past when natural populations increased geometrically, nature was ruled by competition, and new species arose by the gradual accumulation of small variations. These features are not observed in present-day nature, nor are they documented or suggested by the fossil record. So this hypothetical past is unobservable.

Evolutionary theory today, like physics in the nineteenth century, stands at a crossroad. One alternative is to maintain the second line of defense, to insist on natural selection and hold that present-day nature must be understood in terms of a hypothetical past whose features are derived from the theory of natural selection, not from present-day observations nor from the actual historical record. But that choice would require us to affirm an unobservable mechanism, and a theory that is not verifiable, not a research program, and not even science. Ironically, these are the very criticisms that evolutionists make of creationism. Stanley contends, "The 'Will of Allah' viewpoint is untestable, or irrefutable, and therefore unscientific."[31] Evolutionist James Valentine uses the same middle term: "Falsification of the creation hypothesis, or creationism, is impossible, therefore the whole idea lies beyond the purview of science."[32]

The alternative is to make a fresh beginning, to examine all the evidence without partisanship, and to determine what is known about the history of life, with the realization that this may require us to modify or abandon some of the conventional assumptions of neo-Darwinism. Not only is this alternative reasonable in itself, it also agrees with the whole spirit of Darwin's own work: "I have steadily endeavoured to keep my mind free, so as to give up any hypothesis, however much beloved (and I cannot resist forming one on every subject), as soon as facts are shown to be opposed to it."[33]

The Fossil Record

We must begin again, then, taking the chief issues back to first principles, carefully separating the known from the unknown, the certain from the doubtful, and the more probable from the less probable. Since the questions of adaptation and the causes of extinction are posterior to the question of evolution, they will be taken up in the next chapter.

A very general principle to be clear about at the outset is that the present is more known than the past. As paleontologist David Kitts puts it, "Extant plants and animals will always take precedence over fossil organisms in the testing of biological theories."[34] To claim that nothing in biology makes sense without reference to evolution is a foolhardy exaggeration. It would be more accurate to say that nothing in evolution makes sense without the rest of biology. Ecology, ethology, anatomy, physiology, and molecular biology are not only intelligible independently of evolution, they must provide the patterns necessary to understand the past, which is less certain. Ecologists Birch and Ehrlich point out that there are two questions in biology that must not be confused: "When an ecologist investigates a species he may ask: given the existing characteristics of the species, as for example its temperature tolerances, birth rates, death rates, capacity for dispersal and so on, what determines the distribution and numbers of the species in the world? In order to answer that question we do not need to know how the species evolved its particular characteristics. The phylogenetic question is interesting in itself but it is not relevant to the investigation of the question of distribution and abundance. How the species acquired its present adaptive characteristics is a second and independent question."[35] One inquiry is "What are the properties of living things right now?" Quite another is "How did they come to be that way?" The first question would be ample material for a full-fledged science even if we could never obtain information about the second. To argue otherwise would be like saying you cannot understand anything about a saw unless you know precisely how saws are manufactured. We must not expect evolutionary theory to correct ecology, physiology, and the other life sciences. On the contrary, evolutionary theory must be judged and interpreted in the light of these disciplines. All fossilized organisms must be understood and interpreted by analogy with living organisms. The rule is simple: know living things first.

Darwin respected this principle when he based natural selection on the experience of contemporary animal breeders and on ecological claims (geometric increase of natural populations and competition). For a summary of the way nature acts now, see Chapters 4 and 5. We may add merely that nature is assumed by many biologists to be competitive only because of neo-Darwinian preconceptions, which modern ecology has undermined.

Next we must outline what is known about the past, beginning with the fossil record. Without fossils there would be no reason to think that prehistoric animals and plants were any different from today's species. Without fossil evidence we would naturally assume that all species are fixed and eternal, except the ones man himself has driven to extinction, such as the dodo. Fossils document the existence of ancient species and provide evidence for the sequence of evolution, its course, and its time scale. In a word: no fossils, no evolution. And yet Stanley writes, "Fossils played only a minor role in Darwin's conception of an evolutionary process, and their study added little to evolutionary theory during the century that followed Darwin's revolutionary publication of 1859."[36] The reason for this neglect is that the paleontological data do not agree with the predictions of Darwin's theory.

What can be known on the basis of the fossil record? Even without a method to date fossils, extinction can be proven. This was first accomplished by Georges Cuvier, the father of paleontology, in 1786, with regard to certain large land animals. Soon after Cuvier, geologists reasoned that lower strata of rock must be older than the layers on top of them. This gave a rough means of relative dating. Not until the twentieth century did techniques of absolute dating become possible. Patterson explains the methods used most frequently: "During the twentieth century, reliable methods of estimating the age of rock samples became available with the discovery of radioactivity. Radioactive elements are unstable, and decay at a rate which is constant for each type of atom. If a newly formed mineral containing a radioactive element is embedded in rock, the products of radioactive decay will also be trapped, and the proportions of the element and its decay products will give an approximate age for the rock. The elements commonly used are uranium and thorium, decaying to produce lead and helium, radioactive potassium producing argon, rubidium producing strontium, and, in comparatively recent rocks (up to about 50,000 years old), radioactive carbon.

"Real ages of particular rocks, calculated from radioactive assays, can be combined with the traditional geological time scale, derived from the fact that strata can be correlated by the fossils they contain, and that younger strata lie on top of older strata, to give a time-scale of earth history."[37] (See Figure 6.1.)

We can use these techniques of dating rock strata to discover the first appearance of the various phyla, classes, and families of organisms in the earth's history. Each kind of organism has a definite origin and a history. (See Figure 8.1 in Chapter 8.) Taxonomists group similar but distinct species within a single genus that has basic characteristics common to all. In the same way genera are grouped into families, families into orders, orders into classes, and classes into phyla. For example, the pink glowworm, species *Microphotus angustus*, falls within the genus *Microphotus*, which includes all glowworms. This genus in turn comes under the family *Lampyridae*, which includes nocturnal beetles, often with phosphorescent organs. This family falls under the order *Coleoptera*, the order of all beetles, which in turn falls under the class of insects, which in turn falls under the phylum of arthropods, segmented animals with external skeletons and jointed legs.

The pattern of fossil evidence over the whole of geological history shows a long-term decrease in the number of phyla and other higher categories despite an overall increase in the number of different species. The result is a greater intensity of diversification within progressively smaller confines. Gould offers the example of marine animals: "Our modern seas are dominated by just a few groups—primarily clams, snails, crabs, fishes, and echinoids—each with far more species than any Paleozoic phylum ever attained (with the

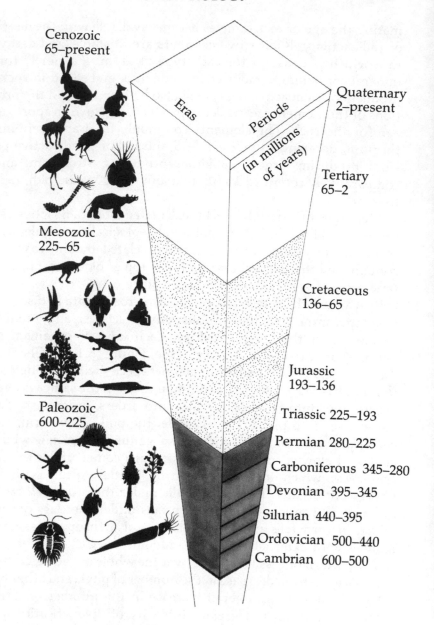

Figure 6.1. The geological column is composed of layered strata distinguished into eras and periods reflecting the history of life and of the earth. Some of the life forms characteristic of each era are depicted at the left. (After Lambert et al.)

possible exception of trilobites in the Ordovician and crinoids in the Carboniferous). Paleozoic seas may have contained only half the species that grace our modern oceans, but they were distributed over a vastly expanded range of basic body plans. And this steady decrease in kinds of organic design—all in the face of a strong increase in numbers of species—may represent the most outstanding trend of our fossil record."[38]

Zoologist James Brough of the University of Wales sees "evolution as a decelerating process."[39] He points out that the phyla of today's animals have existed since the Cambrian age, 500 million years ago. No new phyla have developed since then, and in fact some of the early phyla have become extinct. In the same way, new classes within phyla stopped emerging during the lower Paleozoic era, about 400 million years ago. All today's classes existed at the time as well as others that did not persist to the present. New orders stopped emerging at the end of the Mesozoic era, about 60 million years ago. Brough, noting also a decrease in the production of new families, comments on this general trend: "Evolution seems to have worked in a series of more and more restricted fields with large-scale effects steadily decreasing...as to the future, evolution may go on working in smaller and smaller fields until it ceases altogether."[40] This trend argues that evolution is not a perpetual or unlimited force, but rather is subject to constraints and plays itself out in a large but finite time. The second law of thermodynamics says that the universe as a whole is running down. The fossil record says the same for the process of evolution.

This "pattern of shift from few species in many groups to many species in fewer groups"[41] flatly contradicts Darwinian gradualism; for if evolution proceeded by species accumulating small variations, we should see over long periods new orders, classes, and phyla emerging with increasing frequency. But just the opposite occurs in the fossils. Darwin's model is backward.

Another unmistakable feature of the fossil record is the remarkable stability of new species once they become established. Stanley reports: "Evolution is not quite what nearly all of us thought it to be a decade or two ago. This evidence comes largely from the record of fossils—a record that until recently was not well scaled against absolute time. The record now reveals that species typically survive for a hundred thousand generations, or even a million or more, without evolving very much.... After their origins, most species undergo little evolution before becoming extinct."[42] This stability is easily seen by comparing fossil species to their living counterparts. G. R. Coope of the University of Birmingham has shown that all beetle fossils from the most recent Ice Age are identical with living species.[43] This means that beetles have not changed significantly in two million years. Stanley points to the bowfin fish, which has a superb fossil record extending back to the Cretaceous period: "What has happened to the bowfin fishes during their long history of more than one hundred million years? Next to nothing! During the latter part of the Cretaceous, bowfins became slightly more elongated, but during the entire sixty-five million years of the Cenozoic era, they evolved in only trivial ways. Two new species are recognized, but these differ from their Late Cretaceous ancestors only in subtle features that represent no basic shift of adaptation. The bowfins of seventy or eighty million years ago must have lived very much as their lake-dwelling descendants do today."[44] (See Figure 6.2.)

The lungfish has an even more impressive record: it has undergone no substantive change in over 300 million years. The same pattern of long-term stability without change is found in a wide variety of animals including sturgeon, garpikes, snapping turtles, alligators, tapirs, aardvarks, ants, various mollusks, and echinoderms (see Figure 6.3). And even species known to be extinct have typically long histories in the fossil record without change. For example, among snails and bivalves, species endure an average of 10 million years; among foraminifera, 30 million years.[45] The pattern in other species is similar. Geneticist Gabriel Dover of Cambridge University considers long-term species stability "the single most important feature of macro-evolution."[46]

Again, these unavoidable paleontological facts cannot be accounted for by Darwinian theory. Natural selection predicts just the opposite—all species are expected to undergo continual change, especially if, as Darwin writes, "Natural selection is daily and hourly scrutinising, throughout the world, the slightest variations; rejecting those that are bad, preserving and adding up all that are good; silently and insensibly working, *whenever and wherever opportunity offers,* at the improvement of each organic being in relation to its organic and inorganic conditions of life."[47] As Darwin conceives the mechanism of competition sifting varieties in the population, there

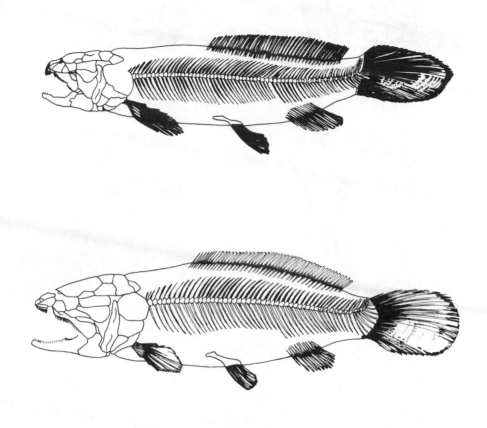

Figure 6.2. The living species of bowfin fish (*above*) is only slightly different from its 65-million-year-old ancestor (*below*), illustrating the absence of the gradualistic evolution of new species predicted by Darwin. Long-term stability is typical of virtually all species in the fossil record. (After Boreske)

is no way to turn off the process. Stanley concludes: "Living fossils have represented a thorny puzzle in the traditional, gradualistic scheme of evolution. If natural selection is constantly reshaping species in significant ways, why have some species been almost immune to the process? Darwin, who seems to have coined the phrase 'living fossils' in the first edition of the *Origin* (p. 107), suggested that 'they have endured to the present day, from having inhabited a confined area, and from having thus been exposed to less

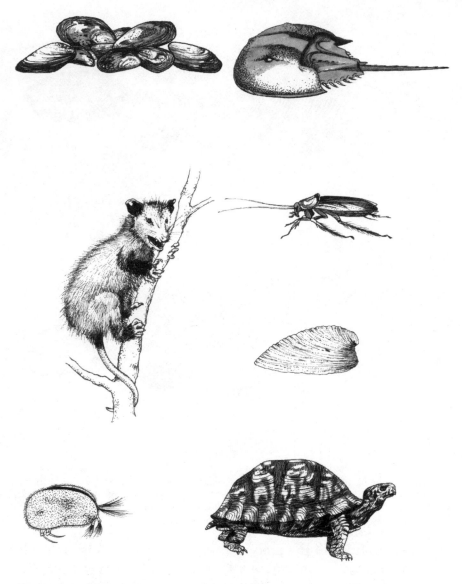

Figure 6.3. Species, once established, exhibit remarkable stability. These living animals, for example, have undergone no substantive change since their first appearance in the fossil record. The mussel (*upper left*) first occurs in the Devonian period over 345 million years ago; the opossum in the Cretaceous 63 million years ago; the ostracode *Bairdia* (*lower left*) in the Ordovician 425 million years ago; the cockroach in the Pennsylvanian 280 million years ago; the mollusk *Neoplina* in the Cambrian; and the turtle in the late Triassic 180 million years ago.

severe competition.' On the contrary, we can now see that many species of living fossils are not narrowly distributed."[48]

Eldredge points out that long-term species stability, or *stasis*, "was known to paleontologists before Darwin (all the paleontological critics of the *Origin* mentioned stasis in their reviews!)—though stasis had become something of a professional embarrassment to be politely ignored, so alien did it seem to what evolution ought to look like in the fossil record."[49]

Another significant feature of the fossil record is the rapidity of divergence. Whole new orders appear suddenly and simultaneously, with no evidence of intermediate stages. These sudden bursts of new flora and fauna, so typical of the fossil data, are called radiations since the ancestral stock develops at one time many new body plans and diversifies in several directions at once. Mammals are a fine example. During the early Cenozoic era some 50 million years ago, mammals suddenly diverged into about twenty-four different orders ranging from bats to whales, kangaroos to elephants, and rodents to rhinoceroses (see Figure 6.4). This pattern is not peculiar to mammals. Rapid "radiation has accounted for most of the large-scale evolutionary changes in the history of life," writes Stanley.[50] Invertebrates, widely varied and abundant, appear suddenly and fully formed in the Cambrian period. Fish rich in kinds and in abundance occur in the Ordovician period with no evidence of prior intermediary types. Flowering plants appear abruptly in the Creta-ceous period without any hint of origin from other pre-existing forms. And they are, even in the oldest fossil forms, already amazingly varied in kind.

The pattern, then, is great clusters of diversified organisms appearing like Athena, full-blown from the head of Zeus. This typical pattern of radiation dramatically contradicts Darwinian gradualism. Darwin himself recognized this and called the sudden appearance and early diversity of flowering plants "an abominable mystery."[51] He also conceded that the apparently immediate diver-sity of invertebrate life in the Cambrian period was inexplicable according to his theory.[52] Stanley constructs a telling argument taken from mammal radiation: "Let us suppose that we wish, hypothetically, to form a bat or a whale without invoking change by rapid branching. In other words, we want to see what happens when we restrict evolution to the process of gradual transformation of

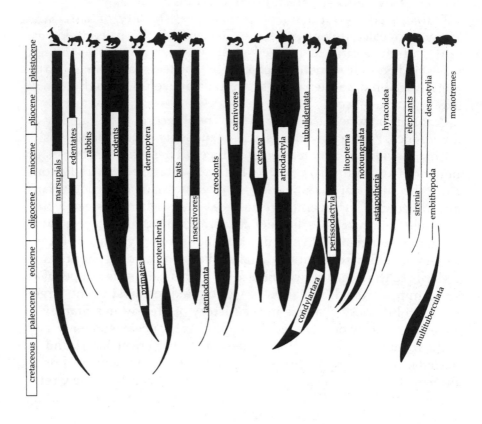

Figure 6.4. Rapid radiation of mammals in the early Cenozoic era approximately 50 million years ago. Width of line represents number of genera within an order. The enormous changes that ushered in the Age of the Mammals were achieved in less than 12 million years. Darwinian gradualism fails to account for the appearance of so many different kinds of animals so suddenly.

established species. If an average chronospecies—a segment of lineage judged to encompass little enough evolution that individuals within it can be assigned a single species name—lasts nearly a million years, or even longer, and we have at our disposal only ten million years, then we have only ten or fifteen chronospecies to align, end-to-end, to form a continuous lineage connecting our primitive little mammal with a bat or a whale. This is clearly preposterous. Chronospecies, by definition, grade into each other, and each one encompasses very little change. A chain of ten or fifteen of these might move us from one small rodent-like form to a slightly different one, perhaps representing a new genus, but not to a bat or a whale."[53] If we insist on gradualism, evolution of new orders would require far greater time than the age of the earth.[54]

In summary, gradualism and natural selection cannot explain the decreasing number of phyla and other larger classifications over time, nor the long-term stability species exhibit, nor rapid radiation of new kinds. Most of the best-documented features of the fossil record contradict the premises and corollaries of Darwin's theory. Evolution is not a slow and even process as Darwin thought. Stanley complains that "Since the time of Darwin, paleontologists have found themselves confronted with evidence that conflicts with gradualism, yet the message of the fossil record has been ignored. This strange circumstance constitutes a remarkable chapter in the history of science, and one that gives students of the fossil record cause for concern."[55] Raup concurs: "We are now about 120 years after Darwin and the knowledge of the fossil record has been greatly expanded ... but the situation hasn't changed much. ... The record of evolution is still surprisingly jerky and ... we still have a record which *does* show change but one that can hardly be looked upon as the most reasonable consequence of natural selection."[56] Eldredge agrees that a reassessment in paleontology is long overdue: "We have a theory that ... is out of phase with the actual patterns of events that typically occur as species histories unfold. ... Yet on the other hand, the certainty so characteristic of evolutionary ranks since the late 1940s, the utter assurance not only that natural selection operates in nature, but that we know precisely how it works, has led paleontologists to keep their own counsel. ... We have proffered a collective tacit acceptance of the story of gradual adaptive change, a story that strengthened and became even more entrenched as the synthesis took hold. We paleontologists have said that the history of life supports that interpretation, all the while really knowing that it does not."[57] Something is gravely wrong with a theory that forces us to deny or ignore the data of an entire science.

We have seen that the experience of modern ecology and genetics undermines the assumptions of natural selection, that gradualism cannot account for macroevolution, and that the predictions of natural selection are contradicted by the fossil record. These difficulties are not light or negligible, but attack the essence of the theory in its premises and in its consequences. It is evident at this point that minor revisions cannot save the theory of natural selection.

Unfortunately the critics of Darwinism have not offered a unified alternative. The theory of punctuated equilibria by Gould and Eldredge, for example, grafts a new mode of speciation (jumps) onto Darwinism, thereby destroying the tight logic of natural selection. The result is two unrelated theories and no theoretical understanding of why speciation should occur in jumps. Thus neither the critics nor the defenders of neo-Darwinism offer a satisfactory evolutionary theory. The need for a new synthesis is evident.

A New Evolutionary Synthesis

Darwin took his model for evolution from animal breeding. This choice, though reasonable in itself, suffers from one serious defect: no breeding experiment has ever produced a new species of animal. Thus Darwin's extrapolation of gradualism to all evolutionary change was based on an uncertain mechanism. Much better would be a model that has successfully produced new species. Fortunately, such a model exists, not in animals but in plants. Chromosomal doubling, a process well understood for over forty years, is known to be responsible for scores of new plant species both natural and artificially bred. Stebbins points out that this phenomenon is rapid and widespread: "In a single generation or two an old species or pair of species suddenly gives rise to a brand-new plant, strikingly different from its parents and capable of breeding true to type in its new form. The occurrence of this cataclysmic type of evolution is by no means uncommon: it was responsible for the origin of cultivated wheat, oats, cotton, tobacco, sugar cane, and probably, in the remote past, of apples, pears, lilacs, willows and many other plants."[58] Patterson adds that chromosomal doubling or "polyploidy is uncommon in animals, but it has been of great importance in plant evolution: almost half the known species of flowering plants are polyploids."[59]

In 1937 it was discovered that weak concentrations of colchicine would induce chromosomal doubling artificially in plant cells undergoing division. This not only gave rise to the development of new species of plants useful to man, but also allowed experimental verification of plant genealogies where chromosomal doubling was suspected to be the cause of speciation.[60] (See Figure 6.5.)

This model suggests that we construct a syllogism similar to Darwin's but with opposite premises and an opposite conclusion. Darwin argued that since species are competitive, slight variations having any advantage will be gradually selected and favored. This wasteful trial-and-error system requires that nature do almost everything the wrong way first. Darwin's model is epitomized by three concepts: competition, inefficiency, and gradualism. But nature is not wasteful and inefficient. The noncompetitive relation between species observed in nature follows from the more universal principle that nature operates in the most efficient, economical way. This general premise is empirically supported by every natural science. For instance, in physics, the simplicity and economy of nature are well known. The principle of least work states that inanimate systems change with the least expenditure of energy. Water flows downhill. Soap bubbles are spherical. The shape of a virus, like all molecular structures, is determined by minimal energy. In living things, materials and energy are also employed in the most economical way (see Chapter 5). These reflections lead us to argue in the following way:

1. Nature operates in the most efficient, economical way.
2. The relation between species in nature is noncompetitive.*
3. The most efficient way to produce a new species such that it will not compete with its progenitor is by an immediate jump. Therefore, we should expect nature to produce new species by jumps.

In this way the new organism is similar enough to its ancestor to make sense as a living thing, yet different enough to avoid competition. The essence here is noncompetition, efficiency, and saltationism.

* In biology these first two principles are inductively as certain as the laws of thermodynamics in physics.

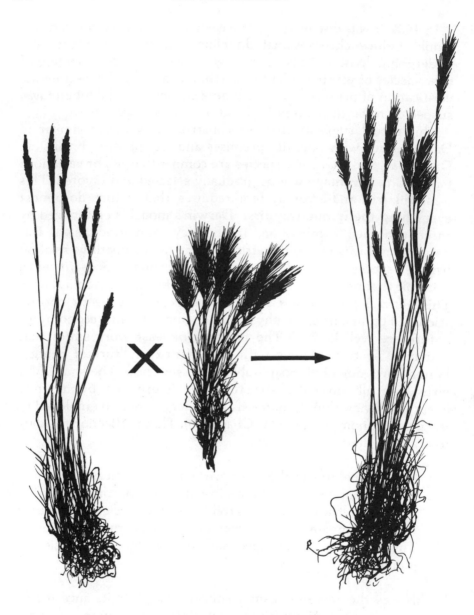

Figure 6.5. Two species of grass, blue wild rye (*left*) and squirrel-tail grass (*center*), were crossed, producing a hybrid species (*right*). Though initially sterile, the hybrid became fertile when its chromosomes were artificially doubled by means of a colchicine treatment. The result was a new, true-breeding species in two generations. Natural chromosome doubling, or polyploidy, has produced almost half the known species of flowering plants. (From Stebbins, 1951)

Once produced, a new species has the capacity to adjust to a changing environment. Polymorphism, or variation in color, shape, or metabolism, gives flexibility to a species, so that an environmental change need not mean its extinction. An example of this is the familiar case of industrial melanism. Early in the last century, the dark form of the common peppered moth was rare, but with industrialization the dark form became increasing common, until now it makes up nearly 100 percent of the population in some areas. The reason for this is that in industrial areas pollution has darkened the trees, so the white form stands out and is easily found by predators.[61] Polymorphism, then, is not a mechanism of evolutionary novelty; it is a mechanism of stability that helps to maintain a species once it is established.

In plant polyploidy we have a model that fits all the facts but accounts for only part of the evolution in plants. Animal polyploidy is rare with only a few occurrences in frogs and lizards. What similar internal mechanism could have operated to produce the majority of plants and animals? We can eliminate point mutations (random changes in single DNA bases) at the outset because their rate of occurrence is roughly the same in all species, yet certain families have evolved much faster than others. Allan Wilson makes this argument clear:

"Although the investigation of point mutations has increased understanding of evolutionary processes, it has failed to describe completely the link between molecular and organismal evolution. The sharp difference in the rates of organismal evolution for two groups of species, frogs and mammals (such as cats, bats, whales, and human), for instance, does not reflect the similarity in the rates at which point mutations accumulate for both groups. Frogs are an ancient group of animals consisting of thousands of species. Yet they share so many anatomical similarities that zoologists classify all frogs in one order. Indeed, during the period that saw the rise of cats, bats, whales, and humans from a common ancestor, one type of frog evolved so slowly that both fossils 90 million years old and the present-day representatives of its lineage are classified in the same genus, Xenopus. Placental mammals, on the other hand, even though they represent a younger group, differ so much from one another that zoologists classify them in 16 orders.

"Facts such as these indicate that the pace of organismal change in mammals has been much faster than it has been in frogs. Yet point mutations accumulate in the DNA of mammals at the same rate as they do in frogs. Similar contrasts between the rate at which point mutations accumulate and the rate of organismal evolution characterize many other groups."[62]

Thus the mechanism responsible for the origin of new species, genera, orders, classes, and phyla must be more profound than the random mutations of single DNA bases. The evidence points in the direction of regulatory genes. Britten and Davidson argue that "major events in evolution require significant changes in patterns of gene regulation. These changes most likely consist of additions of novel patterns of regulations or the reorganization of pre-existing patterns."[63] Their reasoning is compelling: the differentiation and coordination of tissues and organs in higher organisms are produced by cell growth, which in turn results from genetic regulatory programs. Therefore, major events in evolution require the origin of novel programs of gene regulation.[64] Every cell of an organism carries all the genetic information for how to build *every* part of the body. But obviously, most of this information is suppressed when the cell develops into a blood cell, a muscle cell, a nerve cell, or a cell of some other specific type. The suppression of the unneeded instructions is accomplished by regulatory genes. Unlike structural genes that code for the production of single proteins, regulatory genes exercise control over whole repertoires of other gene sequences, activating them or suppressing them whenever appropriate. Organisms of different species compared on the basis of their structural genes are very similar. For example, many of the metabolic pathways and over 90 percent of the enzymes are identical in bacteria and in mammals. Since the materials and molecular tools of all organisms are much the same, the major differences between living things must be the programs according to which these same materials and tools are used.[65] Wilson, Maxson, and Sarich agree that "anatomical evolution is due chiefly to regulatory system changes."[66]

This molecular approach is revolutionizing evolutionary biology because it offers the possibility of experimental verification and causal explanations. Microbiologist Bernard Davis of Harvard Medical School comments: "Molecular genetics is not just strengthening evolutionary biology. It is also providing a new foundation. We are at the beginning of a grand new synthesis in evolutionary biology."[67]

The molecular approach has already generated many exciting breakthroughs. Regarding growth and development, for example, Walter Gehring reports the isolation of a gene sequence called the homeobox that is responsible for certain unit structures in fruit flies, annelid worms, and mammals.[68] Another application of this method is DNA sequencing. Present molecular techniques allow specialists to compare not just a few morphological features of two species, but the entire DNA of each species. Implementing this method ornithologists Charles Sibley and Jon Ahlquist of Yale have developed an evolutionary tree for all birds. Their work has solved certain long-standing, intractable problems of classification and ancestry.[69] Similar investigations have shown that the giant panda is more closely related to bears than to raccoons.[70] All these fruits and discoveries establish the credentials of the molecular approach to evolution.

At this point neo-Darwinism raises an objection. If evolution proceeds by jumps, without gradualism or intermediaries, then whom does the new organism mate with? If it is the only member of a new species and is by definition sterile with respect to its progenitor, then how can it reproduce itself? Plants can solve this problem by self-fertilization, but what about animals?

Here neo-Darwinism is making two key assumptions:

1. All the genetic material of a species is expressed, if not in the individual, at least in the population as a whole.
2. Natural selection decides which variations in the population will continue and which will be eliminated.

Both of these assumptions are challenged by modern molecular genetics. First, it has been recently discovered that only a tiny percentage of the DNA in plant and animal cells is necessary for building the organism, the rest being composed of superfluous sequences repeated over and over again, hundreds even thousands of times, sometimes joined together, sometimes appearing on separate chromosomes.[71] It is possible that within this superfluous DNA some process develops new regulatory gene patterns that eventually produce new body plans and hence new species.[72] The

DNA being discussed here is superfluous: it does not normally express itself in the individual or in the population. Therefore, it would be immune to natural selection. As a consequence, nothing would prevent the superfluous DNA of a whole population from becoming quickly homogenous. This could answer the difficulty of finding a mate for the new species. If this theory of superfluous DNA slowly organizing itself by means of an internal, autonomous process is correct, then many individuals of the new species might be produced simultaneously.

With this new theory, the long stasis of fossil species is easily understood. *A species does not itself change into another species.* Rather it harbors superfluous genetic material (the "seed" of a new species, as it were) that slowly develops an unexpressed new body plan. During this long developmental period, no morphological change occurs in individuals of the parent species. When a new species finally appears, suddenly and fully formed, its progenitor continues without change. Evolution occurs only in a species' superfluous and unexpressed DNA without changing the individual organism or the extant population. Hence, stasis.

Resolving evolution to an internal, genetic mechanism allows us to explain the *origin* of new kinds of living things and in the simplest way possible. We know that every organism grows and differentiates its tissues according to a preprogrammed, chemically coded set of genetic instructions. Major changes in these internal algorithms for building an organism will necessarily produce new kinds of plants and animals, differing in species, order, class, or phyla, according to the level of change in the algorithm. Britten and Davidson point out that "Evolutionary changes in the developmental process could certainly come about by alterations of individual genes expressed at given stages of development. It is clear, however, that alterations in the genes which determine the regulative programs could cause enormous changes in the developmental process and that this would be a much more potent source of evolutionary change. We feel that to explain the magnitude of the functional and structural change which has occurred in evolution it is necessary to postulate changes in the regulatory apparatus."[73]

Explaining evolution by means of changes in regulatory genes also accounts for the saltational character of speciation found in the fossil record. For a single regulatory gene either switches on or switches off whole sequences of structural genes. There is no middle ground. Such a mechanism necessarily proceeds by jumps, not by gradualism. Stasis (explained above) and jumps (explained here) constitute the essence of punctuated equilibria. Thus the new synthesis incorporates the theory of punctuated equilibria as a corollary.

It is useful to imagine the elaborate genetic instructions coded in the chromosomes as a master computer program which has two major parts: one for building the organism and another, independent part that gradually develops on its own a new master program. In a recent article in *The Sciences*, Peter Oppenheimer describes a computer program he developed that generates visual images of natural-looking trees. More than just a visual simulation, Oppenheimer's program models the growth process by mimicking the logic of an organism's genetics.[74] Slight adjustments in the program change a scrawny pine into a gnarled apple tree. Other changes produce the delicate branching of a fern. These programs for three-dimensional models illustrate the principle that dramatically different results can arise from small key changes.[75]

The analogy with a computer program also helps us to see how life became more intensely diversified throughout geological history. The internal genetic mechanism operating with superfluous DNA began by making all the biggest decisions first. Thus the greatest differences of phyla involving the widest divergence of body plans occur early in the fossil record. Once an organism has developed the possibilities of a theme in one direction, however, there is no turning back. The decision is locked in. Thus evolution does not reverse itself. Instead the genetic material begins to diversify at a lower taxonomic level and develops whatever themes are available there, and so on until the smallest categories are reached. We may call this process of diversifying, locking in, and then diversifying again at a lower level, *systematic differentiation*, since it methodically generates the possible variations at each level. This is the pattern observed in the fossil record of progressively more intense diversity within progressively fewer categories.

For example, Valentine and Campbell have proposed that the reprogramming of the regulatory genes of a primitive coelomate worm gave rise to various phyla of coelomates.[76] Then each new phylum radiated in turn into a variety of classes and orders; each of these new branches involved a further reprogramming of regulatory genes.

That evolution is not perpetual but subject to constraints and eventually plays itself out also follows from systematic differentiation. Pere Alberch of Harvard University observes that monsters "are a very good example of the internal rules of morphology." Two-headed monsters, for instance, occur (if rarely) in many species; if variation were random, three-headed ones should be as likely, says Alberch, but "you never see them." From the absence of three-headed monsters, he concludes there are constraints on the types of possible animal patterns. Thomas and Reif estimated the number of possible animal patterns by investigating the effects of constraints upon such structural variables as internal or external skeleton and rigid or flexible materials. Once they eliminated nonsensical combinations, the number of designs was reduced to fewer than one thousand. Of those, more than half are abundantly represented in nature and fewer than one-third are rare. This suggests, Thomas says, that "the number of shapes is not only finite, but has been nearly fully exploited."[77]

Methodical diversification from within would account for the frequent parallelism found in plant and animal evolution, for example, the striking similarity in body plans between many Australian marsupials and their placental counterparts on other continents (see Figure 6.6).[78] If these animals shared a common ancestor whose genetic potential differentiated according to a fixed procedure, we should expect the descendants to follow roughly the same morphological paths even in different environments. Hence, parallelism.

This process of systematic differentiation has much to recommend it as a new mechanism for evolution. It works in a manner consonant with all the facts. First, it is an internal cause of change, arising from potentialities within the organism itself. This fits the theme that life is *self*-directing in its activities. Second, it operates by jumps, producing new species immediately. Third, it does not depend on competition, but rather on a cooperative effort of the whole population. Fourth, it is a natural, orderly process that plays out the possible variations on a theme, nature here acting like a creative artist. Fifth, it is economical and simple, proceeding with a

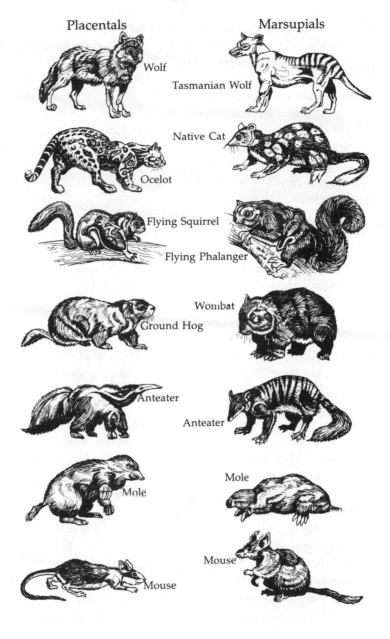

Placentals   Marsupials

Wolf
        Tasmanian Wolf

Native Cat
Ocelot

Flying Squirrel
Flying Phalanger

Wombat
Ground Hog

Anteater
        Anteater

Mole
        Mole

Mouse
Mouse

Figure 6.6. Systematic differentiation from within would account for the striking similarity in body plans between many Australian marsupials and their placental counterparts on other continents. (After Dobzhansky et al.)

minimum energy, minimum material, and minimum waste. And sixth, systematic differentiation really produces new species, and *in a way that can be duplicated and verified in the laboratory*. By contrast, natural selection assigns the environment as the filtering principle selecting out certain advantaged organisms. It also requires gradualism and competition. It operates essentially through chance and would be most wasteful, in essence producing many changes at random and throwing away the ones that make no sense. Furthermore, natural selection is incapable of accounting for the origin of new species and higher taxa. And finally, the *second line of defense*, which alone prevents natural selection from being abandoned, is itself nonverifiable in the laboratory and unobservable in nature.

The foregoing outline of an alternative to Darwinian natural selection has necessarily been imperfect because much research remains to be done. But with this outline we can proceed with a consistent model that truly illuminates the facts.

The Fact of Evolution

Nothing of what we have said so far in this chapter constitutes a proof that evolution has occurred, something we have been assuming all along. The fossil record shows that all living species did not come into existence simultaneously. Fossils also establish the order of appearance, the historical steps from bacteria and alga to large invertebrates, fishes, amphibians, reptiles, birds, mammals, and finally man. The generic theory of evolution asserts that these various historical steps are linked together by inheritance. Darwin further adds to generic evolution that the steps are linked by gradual changes under the operation of natural selection. To reject natural selection, therefore, is not to reject evolution as such, but only one mechanism proposed to account for how it occurs. As for proof of generic evolution, that is, proof of hereditary descent with change, the arguments proceed mainly by pointing to certain phenomena in living things which can be explained only or most easily by assuming a common ancestry among all organisms.* One such phenomenon is

---

* Evolution's historical character is not unique, nor does it require a different kind of proof than is usual in science. The Big Bang is also tied to history and is verified by arguments from effect to cause.

the universality of the genetic code. If living things have not descended from a common ancestor, it is difficult to see why they would all share essentially the same code for genetic information, especially since there is no chemical necessity for this. Other evidence can be drawn from similarity of metabolic pathways. Dobzhansky writes: "All living bodies are astonishingly similar in chemical composition. Not only do they contain atoms of the same elements, but often in similar proportions. The same classes of compounds, particularly nucleic acids and proteins, are found everywhere. Proteins are composed of the same 20 amino acids, and the amino acids, with rare exceptions, are represented only by left optical isomers. Energy carriers (such as adenosine triphosphate, ATP) and enzymes with identical functions (such as cytochrome c) are present in most diverse organisms. To an evolutionist, these chemical similarities are meaningful; they affirm that man is kin to all that lives."[79] The identical chirality (handedness) of biomolecules is another example of something most easily understood as caused by common origin.[80]

The evolutionary development of life fits the larger pattern of the universe itself, which has a history traceable back to the Big Bang. The chemical elements themselves are not immutable but were generated by thermonuclear processes in the cores of stars over millions of years. If so, it should not surprise us if species, orders, classes, and phyla of animals and plants have origins and histories also.

Independent of these arguments drawn from modern discoveries are the observations of taxonomy that all organisms, living and extinct, fall into an orderly series of successively larger and larger groups subordinated to each other on the basis of similarity (for example, the series lions, felines, carnivores, mammals, vertebrates). This argument was known to Darwin, as Eldredge explains:[81] "This hierarchy of life—the pattern of interested resemblances interlinking all organisms—was perhaps Darwin's best argument of all that life has in fact evolved. After all, *if* life has evolved, we would predict that some sort of features of that primordial ancestral form would be passed along to all its descendants—all forms of life around today. That's what we do see: RNA, and to a slightly lesser extent, DNA, are precisely that: biochemical inheritance common to all life. Later evolutionary inventions,

novelties introduced into the genealogical tree after some separation of genealogical lines had already occurred, were passed on only
to descendants of one particular species. All mammal species have
hair, bequeathed from the original species with hair. Hairlike
structures abound in other nooks and crannies of the plant and
animal worlds, but true hair is found only in mammals."[82]

Other arguments taken from nature's simplicity could also be
made, but the most convincing evidence will have to come from
molecular genetics. When the secrets of regulatory genes are
unraveled, we will be able to understand how nature produces new
body plans and how she varies them. The much simpler process of
chromosomal doubling in polyploid plants is already well understood, although how this alters gene regulation is not.

The Origin of Life

But what about the origin of the first living thing? How did life get
started in the first place? The common opinion holds that Darwin
rid biology of the need for God once and for all. Eldredge says,
Darwin "taught us that we can understand life's history in purely
naturalistic terms, without recourse to the supernatural or divine."[83] Julian Huxley has said: "Darwinism removed the whole idea
of God as a creator of organisms from the sphere of rational
discussion."[84] Jacob writes: "The idea that each species was separately designed by a Creator, was demolished by Darwin."[85] And
Simpson writes of the origin of the first organism: "There is, at any
rate, no reason to postulate a miracle. Nor is it necessary to suppose
that the origin of the new processes of reproduction and mutation
was anything but materialistic."[86]

But, as we have seen, Darwin's natural selection fails as a
biological theory. So we must reconsider whether materialism is
sufficient to account for the origin of life.

Matter has many capacities but also definite limitations. We can
distinguish two categories of forms that matter is able to assume.
One kind of form is produced by an agency within matter itself
according to recognized laws of physics and chemistry. This kind of
form includes all chemical compounds, the elements themselves,
and even mixtures, though these do not have the same degree of
unity as the others. We discussed this kind of form briefly in Chapter 2.

Another category of form is that which does not originate from any agency within the matter itself. For example, a block of ice is carved into a statue of Poseidon. The ice receives this form in a purely passive way, having no natural inclination to it. The ice is open to an infinity of forms of this kind and is perfectly indifferent to all them. Thus the determination to this particular form Poseidon must come from an outside cause—the artist in this case. All human artifacts are examples of this kind of form imposed on matter from without.

Into which of these two categories does organic form belong? Where shall we place the form of the adult horse or the mature oak tree? The forms of the elements or compounds arise by physical or chemical necessity. For example, hydrogen and oxygen have a natural inclination to form water (see Chapter 2). Organic forms are not produced in this way but are built according to genetic instructions. Matter has of itself no innate inclination to produce a horse or an oak tree, any more than it has an innate inclination to produce a chair or a microchip. It must be told how to produce a horse or an oak tree cell by cell, protein by protein, through chemically coded instructions. Matter can be shaped into an unlimited number of organic forms and is indifferent to all them. Therefore, organic forms are not the product of physical or chemical necessity like the forms of compounds and elements.

The genetic code itself is not a product of physical or chemical necessity either. Unlike the periodic table of elements which is determined by the necessities of atomic structure, the genetic code is conventional. There is no natural or necessary connection between the proteins manufactured by the cell and their equivalents in the DNA code. This is clearly seen if we consider that more than one code form is used for every amino acid. Leucine has six interchangeable code forms, for example. And there are three different ways that DNA can code for "Stop building." This would not be possible if there were any natural or necessary connection between the triplet code of nucleotides of the DNA and the proteins that are produced in the cell. They are related only by conventions established in organisms themselves, just as neither nature nor necessity connects the words of any human language to the things they represent. Even onomatopoeic words differ from one language to the next. Languages and codes are conventional.

Another proof that the genetic code is conventional is that the whole cell and the mitochondria within it have slightly different codes even for the same protein. Yet no confusion occurs. If the genetic information were not stored in a chemically arbitrary manner, it would not be correct to call DNA a code. Codes correlate mutually unrelated systems: the dots and dashes of Morse code have no necessary connection with the letters of the alphabet they represent.

Thus the organism has something in common with artistic forms. Both organic forms and artistic forms have variety and infinity; also, matter is indifferent to both kinds of forms. The major difference is that artistic forms have an external cause while organic forms have an internal cause. There is, therefore, in each living thing something analogous to human art.

This explains why in nature only living things produce organic molecules. "Proteins are chemical compounds which are produced only by living organisms," writes Patterson.[87] In experiments, some (not all) of the amino acids necessary for protein synthesis have been produced spontaneously by sparking a mixture of methane (CH_4), ammonia (NH_3), water vapor, and hydrogen.[88] But none of these experiments or their variants has generated nucleic acids, fats, starches, or proteins spontaneously.[89] Each cell in a human body contains about 10,000 different kinds of protein—all self-built and all coded for in the DNA. Biochemist Robert Shapiro comments on the minimal results of spontaneous generation experiments:

"The important construction materials used in a bacterium (or us, if we set aside special equipment such as bones and teeth) are proteins, nucleic acids, polysaccharides, and lipids. Together they make up perhaps 90 percent of the dry weight of a bacterial cell. These large molecules contain from hundreds to billions of atoms. None have been detected, in any amount, in a Miller-Urey experiment." The amino acids spontaneously produced were simple chemical compounds composed of only a few atoms each. Shapiro thus dismisses the building-block claim that life could be spontaneously generated: "A mixture of simple chemicals, even one enriched in a few amino acids, no more resembles a bacterium than a small pile of real and nonsense words, each written on an individual scrap of paper, resembles the complete works of Shakespeare."[90]

Matter does not need special instructions to manufacture snowflakes or sodium chloride. These forms are within its power. Not so with organic forms. Thus living forms transcend all other natural forms, not merely because of their unique activities (see Chapter 2) but also because the laws of physics and chemistry alone cannot produce them.

What does produce them? What cause is responsible for the origin of the genetic code and directs it to produce animal and plant species? It cannot be matter because of itself matter has no inclination to these forms, any more than it has to the form Poseidon or to the form of a microchip or any other artifact. There must be a cause apart from matter that is able to shape and direct matter. Is there anything in our experience like this? Yes, there is: our own minds. The statue's form originates in the mind of the artist, who then subsequently shapes matter, in the appropriate way. The artist's mind is the ultimate cause of that form existing in matter, even if he or she invents a machine to manufacture the statues. For the same reasons there must be a mind that directs and shapes matter into organic forms. Even if it does so by creating chemical mechanisms to carry out the task with autonomy, this artist will be the ultimate cause of those forms existing in matter. This artist is God, and nature is God's handiwork.* Divine art—that is, nature—is more profound and more powerful than any human art because it constitutes the very essence of things.

---

* There is ample additional scientific evidence for a mind behind this universe of ours. In Chapter 4 of *The New Story of Science* we offer arguments drawn from the Big Bang, the Anthropic Principle, and the beauty of nature. The present argument is independent evidence taken from the uniqueness of organic form.

7

Purpose

Adaptation

Darwin maintained that evolution was driven exclusively by external causes. In 1862 he upbraided Hooker for speaking of "an inherent tendency to vary wholly independent of physical conditions," himself claiming that "all variability is due to change in the conditions of life."[1] On Darwin's view, the environment pushes or pulls the inert and passive organism in various directions. This Newtonian image places all causes of organic change *outside* the living thing. All change, then, is adaptive change. Dover remarks that beginning with Darwin, "The processes of adaptation and speciation became irretrievably confounded."[2] In a neo-Darwinian context, extinction is often given as proof that an organism was ill-adapted to its environment.

But if what we saw in Chapter 6 is correct, that evolution is a process of systematic differentiation, resulting from autonomous changes in superfluous DNA, then Darwin's approach is backwards. The whole cause of evolution is *within* the organism. This is borne out by morphological studies. The environment is too generic to be the cause of the 100,000 different species of butterflies and moths that exist. H. Frederick Nijhout writes: "Few things in nature match the beauty and the variety of patterns on the wings of butterflies and moths. This order of insects—the Lepidoptera—consists of some 100,000 species, and virtually every one of them can be distinguished from the rest solely by the color pattern of its wings. The phenomenon is even more remarkable when one examines how patterns are formed, as I have done over a period of years, and finds that the answer is essentially rather simple.... The development of color patterns can be achieved, at least in principle, by the same kinds of processes that guide the development of morphological features, because all development is ultimately the outcome of progressive changes in the expression of genes."[3] Nijhout resolves the 100,000 patterns to variations on about a half-dozen basic plans. This fits well with the expectations of evolution through systematic differentiation.

At this point neo-Darwinism raises a difficulty: if natural selection and gradualism are not operative in evolutionary change, how does a new species manage to fit into a niche? Lewontin answers this question by pointing out the organism's agency in modifying the environment and in creating its own niche: "Organisms do not experience environments passively: they create and define the environment in which they live. Trees remake the soil in which they grow by dropping leaves and putting down roots. Grazing animals change the species composition of herbs on which they feed by cropping, by dropping manure and by physically disturbing the ground.... Finally, organisms themselves determine which external factors will be part of their niche by their own activities. By building a nest the phoebe makes the availability of dried grass an important part of its niche, at the same time making the nest itself a component of the niche."[4] Any animal or plant sensibly designed will find a place in nature and create a niche for itself.

Nor does extinction prove that nature produces organisms at random and then allows the ill-fit to die off. For a major feature of the fossil record is repeated *mass* extinction. Evolutionist Norman Newell writes: "Widespread extinctions and consequent revolutionary changes in the course of animal life occurred roughly at the end of the Cambrian, Ordovician, Devonian, Permian, Triassic and Cretaceous periods. Hundreds of minor episodes of extinction occurred on a more limited scale at the level of species and genera throughout geologic time."[5] There is disagreement whether these extinctions occur with exact periodicity or not, but no one disputes their existence. In fact, they define the several geological periods. Gould observes: "Geologists have known for nearly two centuries that extensive extinctions, affecting life in a wide range of environments, have occurred sporadically and rapidly many times during the past 600 million years. Our geological time scale depends upon these events of mass extinction since they set the boundaries of major divisions."[6]

Gould states that 90 percent of all species perished at the end of the Permian period.[7] And there are five other great extinctions in the fossil record. It is evident that such large-scale indiscriminate destruction had nothing to do with competition or differences in adaptation, especially since "it is striking that times of widespread extinction generally affected many quite unrelated groups in separate habitats."[8] Thus extinction is no proof that a species was ill-adapted to its environment, especially if the extinction is preceded by the species's presence in the fossil record for millions of years.

We should not consider adaptation as an evolutionary mechanism, since every organism today is already beautifully adapted to its environment (see Chapter 5), and, as far as can be determined, the same holds for every organism in the past. Raup states that "it is not always clear, in fact it's rarely clear, that the descendants were actually better adapted than their predecessors. In other words, biological improvement is hard to find."[9] Adaptationism has lent itself to wide abuse. Tinbergen comments on the exaggerated trend of the post-Darwinian era: "Some men went so far in supporting improbable theories about the survival value of organs, color patterns and behavior that they gradually discredited this whole line of research. One well-known and respected naturalist seriously claimed that the bright-pink coloration of the roseate spoon bill served to camouflage this bird at sunrise and sunset—without trying to consider how this bird managed the rest of the time."[10] Some evolutionists decry the unfounded speculation and outright storytelling that pass for science merely because the vocabulary of natural selection and adaptationism is employed. For example, Gould and Lewontin write: "We would not object so strenuously to the adaptationist programme if its invocation, in any particular case, could lead in principle to its rejection for want of evidence. . . . if it could be dismissed after failing some explicit test, then alternatives would get their chance. Unfortunately, a common procedure among evolutionists does not allow such definable rejection for two reasons. First, the rejection of one adaptive story usually leads to its replacement by another, rather than to a suspicion that a different kind of explanation might be required. Since the range of adaptive stories is as wide as our minds are fertile, new stories can always be postulated. And if a story is not immediately available, one can always plead temporary ignorance and trust that it will be forth-coming. . . . Secondly, the criteria for acceptance of a story are so loose that many pass without proper confirmation. Often, evolutionists use *consistency* with natural selection as the sole criterion and consider their work done when they concoct a plausible story. But plausible stories can always be told. The key to historical research lies in devising criteria to identify proper explanations among the substantial set of plausible pathways to any modern result."[11]

What Darwin took for a source of evolutionary change in a species is, in fact, a source of stability. An individual plant, for example, may assume rather different forms according to soil conditions, winds, altitude, and other external conditions.[12] This adaptability helps it to make the best of many different habitats, but it does not carry the plant beyond the bounds of its genotype. In a similar way, individual variation or polymorphism does not take a population of organisms beyond the bounds of the species. Polymorphism does, however, give flexibility to a species so that a small environmental change need not bring extinction. Having several different forms benefits a snail population, for instance, since many bird predators employ a search image, looking for prey of the same kind after a successful capture. The many forms reduce the likelihood that all snails in a certain region will be eaten. Polymorphism allows a population to adjust to external factors, not by evolving or by extinction, but simply by changing the proportion of various forms within the population. The familiar examples of insect populations "developing" immunities to insecticides are actually cases of reapportioning the ratio of immune variants already present in the population. No evolution is required.

Variation, then, is not the source of evolutionary change that Darwin thought it was. Its function is to allow a species to adjust ecologically without extinction or evolution. An even simpler way species avoid extinction when the environment changes is by relocating, or "tracking the environment" as Eldredge calls it.[13] During the periods of glaciation in northern Europe, for example, certain species of beetles and presumably the entire ecosystem simply moved south.[14] Polymorphism and relocation, then, are not mechanisms of evolutionary novelty; they are mechanisms of stability that help maintain a species once it is established. (The mass extinctions that punctuate the fossil record were apparently caused by changes so sudden and so violent that these means of stability were insufficient to preserve many species.)

Purpose in Living Things

If evolution is not the product of random mutations and survival of the fittest, then the production of new species is not a matter of chance. The genetic material systematically develops the possibilities of new themes: in each case it is heading toward a predetermined goal, just as in the growth of the individual organism. This suggests purpose.

Since the time of Darwin, purpose has been a source of confusion in biology. Some biologists deny purpose outright. Alex Novikoff, for example, claims that "Only when purpose was excluded from descriptions of all biological activity . . . could biological problems be properly formulated and analyzed."[15]

Other biologists hold that purpose is essential. Oparin declares that "The universal 'purposiveness' of the organisation of living beings is an objective and self-evident fact which cannot be ignored by any thoughtful student of nature."[16] And Ayala agrees: "Teleological explanations cannot be dispensed with in biology, and are therefore distinctive of biology as a natural science."[17]

Still others attempt to compromise both viewpoints, denying the reality of purpose but admitting the appearance. Julian Huxley writes, for example, "At first sight the biological sector seems full of purpose. Organisms are built as if purposefully designed, and work as if in purposeful pursuit of a conscious aim. But the truth lies in those two words 'as if.' As the genius of Darwin showed, the purpose is only an apparent one."[18]

Luria reflects the same conviction: "The whole system of chemical catalysis and its regulation is so precise that it almost suggests purpose, and indeed a special term, *teleonomy*, has been coined to denote the pseudo-purposeful functioning of biochemical mechanisms. Again, the agency at work is natural selection."[19]

T. H. Huxley thought that "teleology . . . received its death blow at Mr. Darwin's hands."[20] But as we saw in Chapter 6, natural selection is not the cause of evolution; and, as we have just seen in this chapter, adaptation is an ecological adjustment, not the source of new organs, species, or body plans. If natural selection is removed, there is no reason for the "as if," and "apparent purpose" becomes purpose. What is seen in nature no longer needs to be explained away. Thus the role of purpose in biology demands reconsideration.

Purpose, of course, is most known to us in our own actions. We freely select the ends we wish to pursue; we deliberate about those ends, and then we execute our plans. At the other extreme in nature, nonliving things do not direct their own activities. They are determined by external conditions. Animals and plants stand between the two extremes of man and nonliving things. They do direct their own activities to some extent, but not to an end they choose.

The executor of a purpose need not have knowledge or consciousness. A washing machine washes clothes, rinses them, and spins them dry without knowing what it is doing. The purpose is built right into the mechanism. Plants execute purposes in a similar way, without consciousness but clearly from an intrinsic cause. We have already seen in Chapter 6 that in every living thing there is something analogous to human art. Animals share in purpose in a higher way since they direct themselves by sense perception, though not by intellectual understanding (see Chapter 3).

The testimony of eminent biologists about purpose is clear and emphatic. Medawar writes: "Purposiveness is one of the distinguishing characteristics of living things. *Of course* birds build nests in order to house their young and, equally obviously, the enlargement of a second kidney when the first is removed comes about to allow one kidney to do the work formerly done by two." And he adds the example of the "body-wide monitoring system that exists in order to spy out and eradicate malignant variants of the body cells (immunological surveillance)."[21]

Monod compares natural organs to man-made instruments: "How arbitrary and pointless it would be to deny that the natural organ, the eye, represents the materialization of a 'purpose'—that of picking up images—while this is indisputably also the origin of the camera. It would be the more absurd to deny it since, the purpose which 'explains' the camera can only be the same as the one to which the eye owes its structure.... One of the fundamental characteristics common to all living beings without exception is that of being *objects endowed with a purpose or project*.... Rather than reject this idea (as certain biologists have tried to do) it is indispensable to recognize that it is essential to the very definition of living beings."[22]

Sinnott holds that "Life is not aimless, nor are its actions at random. They are regulatory and either maintain a goal already achieved or move toward one which is yet to be realized." He says that every living thing exhibits "activity which tends toward the realization of a developmental pattern or goal.... Such teleology, far from being unscientific, is implicit in the very nature of the organism."[23]

Jacob states: "There is a definite purpose in the fact that a haemoglobin molecule changes shape according to oxygen pressure; in the production of cortisone by a cell of the suprarenal gland; in the registration by a frog's eye of the forms moving in front of it; in the mouse fleeing from the cat; in the male bird parading in front of the female." He contends that purpose is part of the essence of the organism: "The very idea of organization, hereafter implicit in the definition of a living organism, is inconceivable without the postulate of a goal identified with life: a goal no longer imposed from without, but which has its origin in the organization itself. It is the notion of organization, of wholeness, which makes finality necessary, to the degree that structure is inseparable from its purpose."[24]

Dobzhansky writes: "A living body...is a work of art. Its beauty resides in its internal teleology. The beauty of human artistic creations is imposed by their makers; it is external teleology."[25]

Thorpe points out that purpose opens a line of inquiry unique to the life sciences: "We can ask of the structures in a living organism, just as we can ask of the structures in a man-made machine, what is this for? We can often give fairly exact and plausible answers. It has been argued, I think convincingly, that we cannot sensibly ask that kind of question of natural nonliving systems. It is surely nonsense to ask of a solar system or its parts, or of a nebula or an atomic structure, or of the parts of a mineral, 'What is this for?'"[26]

Simpson continues the same idea, arguing that purpose cannot be reduced to physical or chemical considerations: "'How?' is the typical question in the physical or chemical sciences. There it is often the only meaningful or allowable one. It must also always be asked in biology, and the answers can often be put in terms of the physical sciences. That is one kind of scientific explanation, a reductionist one as applied to biological problems: 'How is heredity transmitted?' 'How do muscles contract?' and so on through the whole enormous gamut of modern biophysics and biochemistry. But biology can and must go on from there. Here, 'What for?'—the dreadful teleological question—not only is legitimate but also must eventually be asked about every vital phenomenon.... Heredity and muscle contraction do serve functions that are *useful* to organisms. They are not explained, in this aspect, by such answers to 'How?' as that heredity is transmitted by DNA or that energy is released in the Krebs cycle."[27]

The attempt to drive purpose from biology was partially inspired by an overzealous desire to imitate the methods of physics. This desire was misguided because purpose is one of the features that *distinguishes* the life sciences from physics. Niels Bohr: "A description of the internal functions of an organism and its reaction to external stimuli often requires the word purposeful, which is foreign to physics and chemistry."[28] Tinbergen echoes the same sentiment: "Whereas the physicist or the chemist is not intent on studying the purpose of the phenomena he studies, the biologist has to consider it."[29]

Nor can the purposes found in living things be dismissed as mere anthropomorphic impositions of the observer. First, the experts cited above insist that purpose is not an invention of the observer but is in the organisms themselves. They use such phrases as "essential to the very definition of living beings" and "implicit in the very nature of the organism." And second, no one denies the appearance of purpose in every aspect of living things, or that the language of purpose is unavoidable in biology. If purpose were a projection of the human mind, we would find it in every science. But we do not. No one feels compelled to use the language of purpose in mathematics. Mathematicians do not strive to discover what prime numbers are *for*, or to discover what purpose the legs of a triangle serve. Mathematics is not plagued by an all-pervasive teleology. The same holds for physics and chemistry. Therefore, the inevitability of purpose in biology must come from the subject matter and not from the human observer. Life incorporates genuine goals and purposes.

In biology we do not understand a structure if we do not know what it is for. Ricklefs illustrates the point: "The leaves of most kinds of trees exhibit a consistent pattern, that of flatness. How does this flatness arise? We could determine how cell growth organizes the leafbud into a structure that we recognize as the leaf, but we would merely have described its development. Would a knowledge of the chemical constituents of leaves allow us to predict the shape of the leaf? Does anything about the organism, the tree itself, imply that a particular pattern, that of flatness, should be imparted to its leaves?

Why should deciduous trees not have needles, or for that matter, a big blob of leaf tissue at the end of each twig? Why should there be leaves at all? The only meaningful answer to these questions is that the flat shape of the leaf must serve some purpose. Flatness makes the leaf an ideal organ to intercept light, the source of energy for the photosynthetic process of the tree, and for gas and heat exchange with the air. A flat object has a large surface and requires relatively little material for its construction."[30]

The pear shape of guillemot eggs cannot be understood without reference to purpose. Because of this shape the eggs are incapable of rolling any distance in a straight line. Thus they do not roll off the flat cliff ledges on which the guillemot lays them without a nest.[31] The best explanation *begins* with purpose (assuming it is known). For example, the first thing a student should learn about lungs is that they are organs for breathing, that is, for assimilating oxygen and expelling carbon dioxide. Only then should the lungs' anatomy and physiology be studied, right down to the microstructures, respiratory pigments, and all the details of the necessary chemistry. None of these details make sense, however, except in view of the purpose of lungs: respiration. Understanding the goal of respiration, we can understand *why* the structures exist and *why* they are necessary.

A striking subordination to an end is found in the temporary structures of many organisms. Tinbergen speaks of the neck muscle in chicks, specially designed to help them hatch: "The chick's initial act in entering the world consists of pushing off the egg's 'lid' through a series of forceful stretching movements of the neck. The special muscle used for this shrinks after it has done its duty."[32] Ricklefs observes that reproductive capacity is delayed in many species until the individual animal has developed sufficient experience and hunting skills.[33] Reproduction itself is also beautifully timed. The female moose, for example, mates in the fall and carries the young for eight months. These two facts of observation are illuminated by purpose, since the result is that the young moose is born in the spring when food is more abundant and the mild weather is just beginning. Even more amazing synchronizations are found in other mammals. Ethologist John Crook describes how the Stellar sea lion and the northern fur seal coordinate conception, implantation, and birth for the benefit of their young: "The animals roam the oceans for most of the year, then congregate in early summer. Mating occurs soon after the cows have 'hauled out' from their year's wanderings and given birth. This is convenient, since otherwise the males and females would have to seek each other over the trackless sea. But only eight months are needed for development of the embryo, and this would mean that births would occur at an unsuitable time [midwinter]. Seal cows 'solve' the problem by carrying the fertilized egg within their bodies in a kind of suspended animation. Attachment of the egg to the uterus—implantation—is delayed until eight months before the ideal time."[34]

Another striking coordination is found among molting birds. Ornithologist Georg Rüppell notes that "species that need not depend entirely on flying to escape from their enemies—water birds like auks, loons, grebes, or geese as well as cranes and birds on secluded nests...cast off all the primary feathers at once and for a time cannot fly; when danger threatens they find hiding places or simply dive out of reach." He then adds that among species that must "remain capable of flight during molting, the primaries are replaced one after another, in a specific sequence[!]"[35] Among plants, many woodland seeds have mechanisms that require the seed "to be chilled for a long time (occasionally *two* cycles of chill and thaw)....Were it not for these mechanisms, a seed might sprout in the warm days of Indian summer or during a February thaw, only to be killed by the return of winter."[36] In all these examples, nature's elegant subordination of means to end is evident.

Purpose is also illustrated in countless instances where man discovers on his own the best way to do something, only later to find that nature has been exploiting the same principle all along. This is particularly frequent in military inventions. Sonar was developed as a means of locating submarines years before ethologist Donald Griffin discovered that bats direct themselves at night by a similar echolocation system. Helicopter pilots found that if they flew at the proper angle behind another helicopter, they could exploit the updraft caused by the other vehicle and get a more efficient ride. Only subsequently was it recognized that migrating birds have taken advantage of this principle for million of years by flying in V formation. Again, after camouflage experiments during World War I, the United States Navy found the most concealing color to be omega gray, which has the same optical properties, wavelength, absorption, and reflection as the color of an Antarctic bird, the petrel.[37] This implies that human ingenuity could not have given the petrel a better color for camouflage than it received from nature.

Acknowledging end or purpose in no way excludes the need to consider other causes. On the contrary, purpose works only in and through material, structural, and mechanical causes. Bohr comments: "The attitudes termed mechanistic and finalistic are not contradictory points of view, but rather exhibit a complementary relationship."[38] Lorenz says the same: "The fact that life processes are directed at aims or goals, and the realization of the other fact that they are, at the same time, determined by causality, not only do not preclude each other but they only make sense in combination."[39] In human actions this is obvious. The goal of the art of medicine is to produce health in the patient. Everything the doctor does is directed to this end. But this orientation to a purpose does not encourage the doctor to ignore the mechanics of health and disease. On the contrary, the more thoroughly he understands these, the more efficacious will be his treatment. With respect to the end, all other causes are means. It is the same in nature. An animal's desire for food would be futile if it did not set into motion activities in the animal that were likely to procure food. The desire is clearly a cause of the activities.

Moreover, we do not expect purpose to explain *everything* even in human actions. The curly shavings on the floor of the carpentry shop serve no purpose. They are waste, a by-product of some purposeful action such as planing a board. Likewise, in nature fecal matter and urine serve no purpose as far as the individual animal is concerned.* They are excreted as waste, being by-products of the purposeful actions of digestion. In the same way, susceptibility to disease, injury, and death is not to be understood in terms of benefit to the individual organism (though they may serve a larger purpose). This susceptibility is a characteristic unavoidably connected with the materials out of which nature must make organisms, just as susceptibility to rust or breaking is not intended or desired by the craftsman who makes a saw blade for his own use. These defects are inextricably bound up with the required material

---

*These waste products do serve a useful end, however, if the whole ecology is considered. Also, in some species such as rhinoceros, dung is used to mark off territories. (See Chapter 4.)

that he chooses because of its suitability for cutting. Also, some things serve ends beyond the individual organism: reproductive organs are subordinated not to the good of the individual but to the good of the species; superfluous DNA is at the service not of the species but of the whole of life.

Animal behavior is unintelligible without reference to a goal or purpose. Griffin describes the predator-distraction behavior of certain nesting birds: "Ornithologists and ethologists have repeatedly observed the behavior of nesting plover when a large intruder, such as a person, approaches a nest where a killdeer or piping plover is incubating its eggs. At a considerable distance, long before a human observer or other mammal can see the cryptically colored bird or its eggs, the plover may stand up and walk slowly to a point a few meters from the nest. Only then does it begin the plaintive calling that gives the piping plover its name. The bird may then walk rapidly or fly in almost any direction except toward the nest. If a person approaches these birds while feeding or when they have no eggs or young, they fly away from the intruder to a safe distance, perhaps resuming their search for food. When they have no vulnerable eggs or young, the plovers almost never approach an intruder or act in a way that makes them conspicuous. [When nesting, however,] ... the bird flutters slowly but conspicuously away from the nest, staying relatively close to the intruder. It almost always makes loud piping sounds similar to those a bird makes when disturbed or mildly irritated. It may display conspicuous feather patterns that are not usually visible. ... It is common for the bird to hold its tail or wing in an abnormal position as it moves. Often the tail almost drags on the ground, and the wings slightly extended, sometimes one more than the other, strongly suggesting some weakness or injury. After running a few meters, the bird may flop about on the ground, extending one or both wings, as if injured. This is often called the 'broken-wing display,' and it requires considerable effort for an observer to believe that the bird is really quite healthy. ... Predators are extremely sensitive to minor differences in the gait and demeanor of potential prey and are much more likely to attack animals that are behaving abnormally."[40] Using these tricks, the bird entices the predator away from the nest, sometimes three hundred meters or more, and then suddenly flies off and returns to its nest by an indirect route. This is undeniably goal-oriented behavior.

Other examples abound. Ricklefs explains the elaborate courtship rituals in certain bird species as a means of identifying a mate of the right species: "Reproductive isolation prevents the formation of unfit hybrids, which are a waste of both time and effort on the part of the parents."[41] Again a clear purpose is served. One sees here also nature's efficiency and economy. The female of the South American arrow poison frog, after bearing a live tadpole, induces it onto her back and then deposits it carefully into water trapped in a bromeliad (a plant related to the pineapple). She later returns to each "aquarium" to lay in it infertile eggs as food for the youngster until it is able to fend for itself. The spider's web, the beaver's dam, and all animal artifacts also serve evident purposes. In these instances and in countless others, animals clearly act for an end. But animals do not intellectually understand the end as such. They act out of instinct, not by grasping the what or the why of things (see Chapter 3). Therefore, in cases of instinct, nature is acting for the sake of something.

The organs of plants and animals also manifest purpose. Organs are tools, and every tool is designed to accomplish a specific task. (See Figure 7.1.) Simple inspection of the bird bills and feet in Figures 7.2 and 7.3 shows how precisely each bird is equipped for the special operations it must perform to make a living.

No organ can be defined or understood without looking to its purpose, which is the activity it performs. Ayala states: "A causal [exclusively mechanistic] account of the operation of the eye is satisfactory as far as it goes, but it does not tell all that is relevant about the eye, namely that it serves to see."[42] Tributsch describes the small tropical fish *Anableps anableps* that has *two* sets of eyes, one set specifically designed for seeing in air and the other for seeing underwater.[43] The fish swims along the surface with its upper eyes just out of the water. Thus it is able to observe simultaneously prey and predators above and below the surface. Hippopotamuses, frogs, and crocodiles can submerge their entire bodies in water except for nostrils and eyes. In this way they are well hidden but can still smell, see, and, in the case of the hippo, hear what is going on around them. (See Figure 7.4.) Even apparently insignificant features often serve important ends. Hertel points out that the typical thick hair covering the body of moths absorbs high-frequency sound waves so that the moths do not appear on bat sonar.[44]

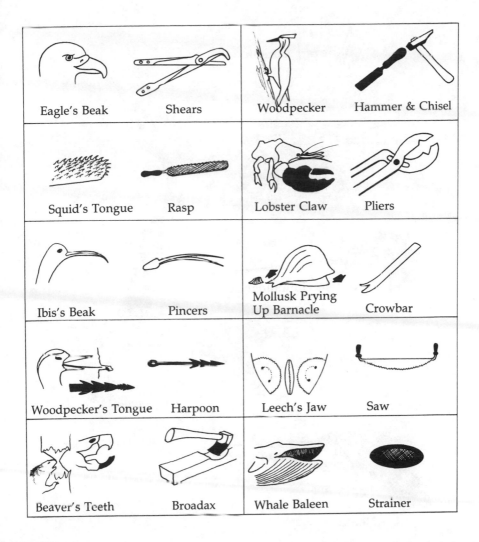

Eagle's Beak	Shears	Woodpecker	Hammer & Chisel
Squid's Tongue	Rasp	Lobster Claw	Pliers
Ibis's Beak	Pincers	Mollusk Prying Up Barnacle	Crowbar
Woodpecker's Tongue	Harpoon	Leech's Jaw	Saw
Beaver's Teeth	Broadax	Whale Baleen	Strainer

Figure 7.1. Comparison with man-made tools shows clearly the purposefulness of animal organs. (After Tributsch)

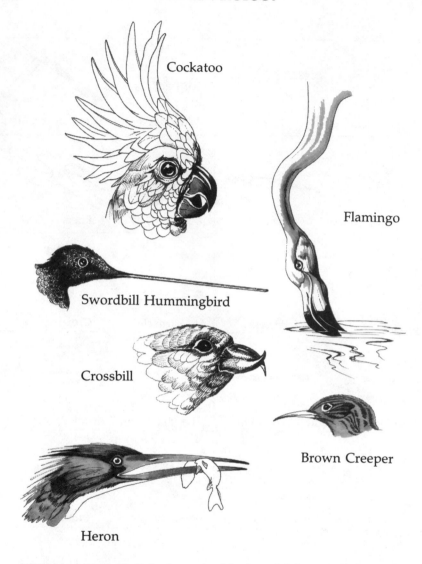

Figure 7.2. Each bird's beak is superbly designed for a special task. For example, the crossbill's strange beak allows it to pry the seeds out of evergreen cones. The flamingo strains tiny organisms from the mud with its specially fringed beak. The cockatoo's hooked beak is perfect for cracking nuts, and the swordbill hummingbird's five-inch beak gives it access to the nectar inside of deep flowers. The heron's beak is designed for spearing fish, and the brown creeper's acts as a probe and tweezers to extract insects from cracks in tree bark. These examples illustrate the principle that form is for the sake of function and can be fully understood only in terms of function.

Wading
Foot

Swimming
Foot

Climbing
Foot

Perching
Foot

Grasping
Foot

Figure 7.3. The feet of various birds show how elegantly nature suits each organ to its purpose.

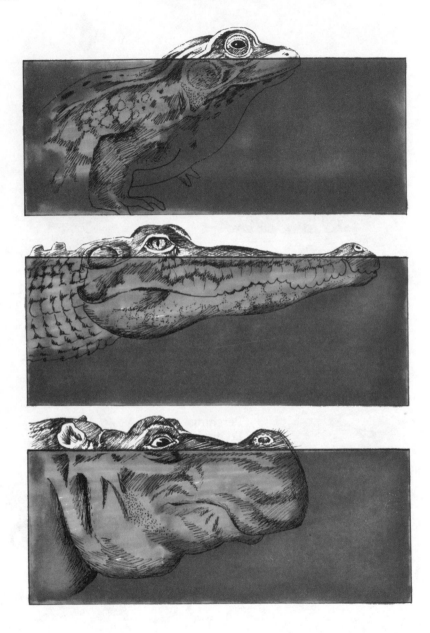

Figure 7.4. Nature's design is optimal in almost every case. Many animals, such as the frog, the crocodile, and the hippopotamus, are designed so that they can submerge their entire bodies except for eyes and nostrils, thus enabling them to hide and yet watch for predators and prey.

Nature wastes neither function nor structure. She provides all the equipment needed for each organism to live but does not burden it with useless organs. The resemblance, then, between human tools and animal tools is neither chance nor fancy. Biologist Andrée Tetry concludes a book devoted to the study of animal tools with these words: "The natural tool bears witness to an incontestable purposefulness.... The tool always carries out, sometimes more or less correctly (from our human standpoint), a determinate and limited task; it attains an end."[45]

Geneticist Lucien Cuénot sums up the marvel of organic design: "Birds that fly can do so because a thousand details converge: long wing and tail feathers, pneumatic bones, air sacs, breast bone and pectoral muscles, design of the ribs, neck, feet, spinal column, pelvis, automatic hooking of feather barbules, etc. Matisse thinks these features are joined together accidentally and that there is no need to wonder over the result, any more than over the properties of the oxygen or phosphorus atom, manifestations of a structure. I prefer to believe that the bird is made *for* flying."[46]

Some means that nature uses to achieve her goals are surprisingly ingenious. Ricklefs mentions that armadillos avoid inbreeding by always giving birth to identical quadruplets of the same sex![47] The cicada of North America live most of their lives underground. In the eastern half of the United States, the larvae emerge in adult form to reproduce only in seventeen-year cycles; in the southern states, the cycle is thirteen years. These two numbers are large enough to exceed the life cycle of any predator. Thirteen and seventeen are also prime, so that no potential predator can coordinate its life cycle with the emergence of adult cicadas.[48] The squirting cucumber, through the buildup of internal pressure, can propel its seeds with an initial velocity of thirty-five miles per hour and up to a distance of forty feet.[49] This amazing mechanism guarantees optimal distribution.

Purposes abound in living things. In many instances we can distinguish two or more purposes served by the same organ. The tongue in man, for instance, serves for speaking, tasting, and eating. Tree roots absorb water and minerals, and also anchor the tree firmly in the ground. A whale's blubber serves three distinct ends: food storage, buoyancy, and insulation.[50] Energy is stored in the blubber for the whale's long migrations when food might not always be available. The blubber's superior buoyancy neutralizes the weight of the whale's bones and internal organs so that the animal is effectively floating free in the water. And the blubber insulates the whale so efficiently that when the animal is active, it must operate a cooling system through its flippers to avoid overheating even in frigid waters (see Chapter 5). Whale blubber is a marvel of nature's simplicity, economy, and purposefulness.

The slime on a fish's body also accomplishes three goals with extraordinary efficiency: "Fish ... use a special strategy for maintaining a laminar boundary layer around their boundaries, thus reducing drag. The mechanism depends on their slimy skins. Anyone who has ever caught a fish will recall the slippery feeling of the scales. Hundreds of small glands between the scales release a mucus consisting of long-chain molecules (polysaccharides and proteins) into the water. The mucus serves several purposes—it affords protection from bacteria and microscopic parasites, and its slippery property can be useful in escaping predators. Just as significantly, it has been well established that such long-chain molecules inhibit the transition to turbulence in a boundary layer. Tests show that as few as 6 parts per million of organic substance from the slime of the Pacific barracuda are responsible for a 45 percent reduction in the friction of seawater flowing in a pipe. In fact, firemen now use tiny amounts of the synthetic polymer poly(ethylene oxide), a mucuslike substance injected into their fire hoses to obtain substantial reductions of fluid resistance. Moreover, the rulebooks of sailboat racing and crew racing now specifically prohibit the use of such substances in competition, because they are known to be effective in reducing the drag on hulls."[51] Again, three purposes and astounding efficiency.

Birds' feathers serve for flight, heat regulation, protection, and ornament. Rüppell writes: "Feathers are wonderfully light objects. Despite their lightness they are sturdy, flexible, and easy to care for; they provide a cushion, a thermal insulation, a water-repellent cover, and most importantly—they are replaceable."[52] Biologist William Montagna lists some of the ends served by skin: "Skin is a remarkable organ—the largest and by far the most versatile of the body. It is an effective shield against many forms of physical and chemical attack. It holds in the body's fluids and maintains its integrity by keeping out foreign substances and microorganisms. It acts to ward off the harsh ultraviolet rays of the sun. It incorporates mechanisms that cool the body when it is warm and retard the loss of heat when it is cold. It plays a major role in regulating blood pressure and directing the flow of blood. It embodies the sense of touch. It is the principal organ of sexual attraction. It identifies each individual, by shaping the facial and bodily contours as well as by distinctive marking such as fingerprints."[53] Curtis adds that by a "careful balance and modulation of properties—thickness versus thinness, firmness versus pliability, toughness versus sensitivity... skin is able to serve its complex double function, that is, to form a protective barrier between us and our surroundings and, at the same time, serve as the means of communication with the outside world."[54] We might add that skin is the source of hair, nails, scales, and feathers, which further serve the specialized needs of each particular animal. Blood also has several functions. It transports nutrients to each cell and carries away metabolic wastes; it distributes oxygen throughout the body and transports carbon dioxide away; it repairs injuries and attacks bacterial and viral invaders; and it distributes hormones, the body's internal chemical messengers. The intensity of purpose in these and like instances is remarkable.

In view of the purpose they are designed for, the organs produced by nature exhibit a certain perfection. For instance, the human eye operates at the physical limit of sensitivity, being able to react to a single photon.[55] Our inability to hear very low-pitched sounds (below sixteen cycles per second) is beneficial because otherwise we would be barraged with sounds caused by the movements of our own bodies conducted through our skeletons.[56]

The same holds for the organism as a whole. A bird smaller than the hummingbird would require an impossibly fast rate of metabolism. A bird larger than a condor would weigh too much to accelerate itself sufficiently to generate enough lift for flight. Thus nature has already built the smallest and the largest birds that can fly. Rüppell asks the intriguing question "Could we design a better bird?" His answer, based on simple biomechanics, is no: "If small round-winged birds are to be converted into more rapid fliers, they must become heavier so that their greater kinetic energy can help to compensate for drag. But this would be possible only at the price of a reduction in their high maneuverability.

"Another way to fly at high speed in spite of being small has been developed, for example, by the barn swallow. These birds have rather long, pointed wings. Long wings produce a greater propulsive force than short wings, since they travel over a longer path at each stroke and therefore generate a stronger airstream. Barn swallows are among the best high-speed fliers. However, they are incapable of thermal or dynamic soaring, and in dense shrubbery they are far surpassed in agility as well as in endurance by, for example, a flycatcher.

"If we wanted to turn the stork into a bird that could also fly over the ocean, its wings would have to become narrower and thicker (more wind-resistant). Then, however, it would have lost the capacity for thermal soaring and would be unable to reach its winter quarters. Chickens and pheasants could be 'remodeled' to permit long-distance flight only at the price of their sprinting ability. Then they would be easy prey for hawks.

"The combination of several skills in one model bird has also failed. As we have seen, the characteristics of different kinds of flight cannot be arbitrarily exchanged."[57] In a word, we cannot design a better bird because each species is already optimally engineered for its particular mode of life.

Purpose is so much a part of living things that it is rash to deny the utility of any major structure or function. For example, one textbook argues that the evaporation from leaves of trees is excessive and useless: "Of the materials the tree uses in photosynthesis, that taken in the greatest amount is water. However, only a small percentage of the water taken in by the tree's roots is retained; most of it is evaporated from the leaves, serving no use and being lost in the atmosphere. People usually regard successful forms of life, such as trees, as being perfectly fitted to their living conditions, all the errors in structure having been eliminated down the long road of evolution. Yet here is a tremendous loss of water that apparently serves no function. It is an unfortunate coincidence for the tree that the best way for photosynthesis to take place is to have wet cell surfaces in contact with the air for the exchange of carbon dioxide and oxygen. This results in constant and tremendous water loss. A tree requires about 55 pounds of water to form 100 pounds of cellulose, the main constituent of wood. Yet, while the tree is making 100 pounds of wood, it loses in evaporation nearly 1,000 times that weight of water!"[58]

Further investigation, however, reveals that the prodigious evaporation serves an essential purpose beyond providing the tree with water. It permits leaves to avoid overheating and drying up in hot weather, operating in a way similar to evaporative cooling in animals.[59] As temperatures cool, evaporation automatically diminishes, and as they rise, it increases. Thus there is no excess at all, but a rather precise adjustment to the needs of the tree. Without evaporative cooling, a plant would become as hot as a car parked in the sun. Also, if the ground water were never raised and recycled via evaporation in trees and other plants, huge amounts would become irretrievably locked underground. What at first glance seems to be excessive and useless turns out to be beautifully designed for both the tree and the whole ecology.

Considering the perfection of design in living things, it is not surprising that purpose is a principle of prediction and discovery in biology. Belief in purposefulness, writes Cuénot, "has shown a rare fecundity: it is because we thought that every instrument must have an end that we have discovered the roles of organs long considered enigmatic, such as internal secretory glands."[60] One famous example of the predictive power of purpose was William Harvey's discovery of the circulation of the blood. Anatomical studies showed Harvey that the valves in veins all point in one direction. Reasoning that nature does nothing without a purpose, Harvey hypothesized that the blood must circulate, a hypothesis he later confirmed by experiment and measurement.[61] In a similar way, when Crick and Watson discovered the molecular structure of DNA in 1953, they were able immediately to predict how it replicates.[62]

Purpose permeates every aspect of life. The metabolism of every cell is ordered to the organism. Growth is aiming at the completeness of form. The organ-tools of animals and plants, the capacity for self-repair, the findings of ethology and ecology, all point to purpose. With elegance and economy, nature subordinates means to end. Matter is for the sake of form, and both are for the sake of operation. Every cell, every tissue, every organ serves a purpose. Every animal, every plant directs its activities to an end. The whole of nature is ordered by purpose.

8

Hierarchy

Modern biology is characterized by a marked tendency to see all species in terms of equality. Organisms are imagined as if on a level plane with each other, differing only in complexity. Darwin entered into his notebook the general principle: "Never use the word[s] higher and lower."[1] This principle is also applied to man. Biologist Robert Trivers writes: "The chimpanzee and the human share about 99.5 per cent of their evolutionary history, yet most human thinkers regard themselves as stepping-stones to the Almighty. To an evolutionist this cannot be so. *There exists no objective basis on which to elevate one species above another.* Chimp and human, lizard and fungus, we have all evolved over some three billion years by a process known as natural selection."[2]

On this view, to attribute any sort of superiority to man is to fall victim to what Monod calls the "anthropocentric illusion."[3] Only because of his foolish vanity does man insist on ranking himself higher than other natural creatures. But, says this philosophy, the facts belie man's self-congratulatory pride: nothing planned his appearance. From the point of view of the universe, man is a relatively minor, accidental result worth about $1.50 in chemicals. In this context, Simpson praises the honesty of one modern writer although "he is a little petulant with scientists for discovering that the world is purposeless and for thus forcing abandonment of religions that require the postulate of purpose. He can only face the fact that childish dreams of a meaningful universe must be laid aside, and he exhorts mankind to become adult and to live as honorably as may be in a stark and bleak world."[4] In the same line, Lynn Margulis and Dorion Sagan write: "There is little, in the end, that is very different about human beings. For all our imagination, fecundity, and power, we are no more than communities of bacteria, modular manifestations of the nucleated cell."[5]

Three reasons lie behind the egalitarian tendency of modern

biology. First, the rejection of purpose entails the denial that anything in nature can be subordinated to anything else. Second, from the perspective of adaptationism all species are equal. Natural selection does not distinguish between animal, plant, or man. No species is higher or better, just different. Simpson writes, "On the basis of adaptation alone there is no reason to consider one adaptive type higher or lower than another."[6] Third is the denial of species implied in gradualism. Darwin thought that varietal differences in a population eventually accumulate to produce differences of species: "Varieties are species in the process of formation, or are, as I have called them, incipient species.... the lesser difference between varieties... augmented into the greater difference between species." Consequently, Darwin saw the notion species as a human contrivance: "I look at the term species as one arbitrarily given, for the sake of convenience, to a set of individuals closely resembling each other, and that it does not essentially differ from the term variety."[7] If this is true, all organisms would differ from each other only in degree, not fundamentally in kind. A man would be just a more complex arrangement of matter than an amoeba. Simpson reflects this consequence: "In a sense the mammals, and the birds too, are simply glorified reptiles. But in a similar sense the reptiles are glorified amphibians, the amphibians glorified fishes, and so on back until all forms of life might be called glorified amoebas."[8] Stanley observes that "the persistence of Darwin's gradualistic view...downplays the role of speciation."[9]

Rejection of purpose, adaptationism, and gradualism, then, are responsible for modern biology's homogenization of species. But as we saw in Chapter 7, adaptationism is not a cause of evolution, and purpose is an essential part of the way living things are put together. Moreover, in Chapter 6 it was shown that modifications in varieties do not lead to new species.

The argument from adaptation says that since each organism is equally suited to its lifestyle, none can be better or higher than any other. But this is like pointing out that the foot does not walk better than the eye sees; each is equally suited to its own task. This kind of equality *is* found in living things; it follows from their optimal design. However, this kind of proportional equality (as when we say $2/4 = 3/6$) does not prove that any of the members are equal (as the example shows, for $2 \neq 3$ and $4 \neq 6$). Therefore, even granted that each organism does its job equally well, it does not follow that every job is equal. The plant has a vegetative job; the animal, a perceptual and emotional one; and man, an intellectual and moral one.

Moreover, it is ironic that natural selection, a theory purporting to explain the *origin* of species, ends up denying the *existence* of species. Without the notion of species, biology would be impossible, since there would be no way to identify what one was talking about, no way to verify that two independent observations dealt with the same kind of organism. Science aims not at knowledge of individuals but at knowledge of *kinds*. As Patterson states, "Species are real, not a human concept that we try to impose on nature."[10] As a definition of species, absence of interbreeding is not a bad rule of thumb, but it has its deficiencies. For example, it cannot be used to distinguish fossil species. Also, sibling species, though isolated reproductively, are recognized as essentially one in kind.[11] Infertility with other kinds is more a property of species than a definition. Systematic differentiation suggests that a species is distinguished by its genetically different body plan. This agrees with Darwin at least to the extent that he assumed that whatever causes speciation should also define what a species is. That is why his gradualism led him to assert that species are only arbitrarily distinguishable.

Having cleared away these obstacles, we will next try to determine whether any subordination or hierarchy exists in nature. Then we will examine the fossil record to see if any hierarchic order is reflected in the history of life.

In Chapter 2 we discussed the natural hierarchy of physical, chemical, and organic form. An unbiased consideration of the natural creatures on our planet reveals a clear order from lower to higher: minerals, plants, animals, man. Each level incorporates the capacities of the lower levels plus exhibits other capacities unique to itself. Animals, for instance, not only grow, nourish themselves, and reproduce as plants do but also perceive the world through their senses, move about, and experience emotions, which plants cannot do. This order is not a human invention but reflects an essential inequality in the organisms themselves. What is more, this order is hierarchical, proceeding from less perfect forms to more perfect forms, from good to better to best. Each stage is qualitatively superior to its predecessor.

The claim that nothing in nature is better than anything else is unsound. Health is not merely *different* from disease; it is *better*. Sight is better than blindness: in a word, life is better than nonlife. Anyone who maintains that a plant is no better than a rock must also hold that having a power is no better than lacking it. But this is unreasonable. The ability to move is undeniably better than paralysis; the ability to digest food is certainly better than the inability. And even the lowest organism is able to grow, something no virus or nonliving thing can do (see Chapter 2). Therefore, life is better than nonlife.

Furthermore, directing one's own activities is better than having them directed from the outside. Otherwise the life activities of an adult would in no way be higher or better than those of an infant. The free man would have no advantage over the slave, and the mentally incompetent would be put on a par with the person of normal faculties. But as we saw in Chapter 2, life is defined by its capacity for self-directed activities. This mode of action is not attained by nonliving things. "What organisms *do* is different from what *happens* to stones," observes Thorpe.[12] Therefore, even the lowest living being, because of its ability to direct its own operations from within, is superior to all things not alive.

Again, the end is always better than the means, since the means is sought for the sake of the end. But plants make use of nonliving things, putting them into the service of life in many ways. Trees, for example, use sunlight to drive the works of photosynthesis, and they convert minerals in the soil and gases of the air into their own substance. If nonliving things are means in relation to life, then living beings are superior.

Darwin himself recognized the superiority of life over nonlife: "The most humble organism is something much higher than the inorganic dust under our feet; and no one with an unbiased mind can study any living creature, however humble, without being struck with enthusiasm at its marvelous structure and properties."[13]

By the same standards, animals are superior to plants. For animals have more powers and activities than plants do, as stated above. And the animal has a more perfect kind of self-direction than the plant since the animal moves itself, not only through growth but through local motion as directed by a sense awareness of the world around it. Animals also use plants for food, shelter, and other purposes. Thus the animal is higher than the plant.

By the same standards, man is unmistakably superior to other animals, having the capacities of plants and animals plus intellect and will. By these latter powers man moves himself more perfectly than any other natural creature since he understands and can select his own ends as well as means. Man also uses most fully the whole of nature—nonliving things, plants, and animals—for his own purposes.

The essential inequality built into the order from nonliving things to plants, to animals, to man, is not adequately expressed by terms such as *simpler* and *more complex*. These terms imply a mere rearrangement of what is already there. The series plant–animal–man represents a progressive order in the fullness of life. At each level the lower powers are transformed and elevated, and new capacities emerge, different in kind from anything that goes before. Just as the individual organism is a beautifully subordinated hierarchy of cells, tissues, organs, and systems, so too, all organisms taken together fall into a natural order from lower to higher. Thus Thorpe declares, "Any general theory of biology...must include the concept of hierarchy."[14]

The subordination of matter to life extends beyond the use that plants make of nonliving things. There is now abundant evidence from physics, chemistry, and cosmology that our universe, its history, and its material laws are uniquely suited to life in general. Physicist Paul Davies, for example, points out how the existence of Earth-like planets depends on the capacity of stars to explode in supernovae:

"Supernovae play an important part in the chemical evolution of galaxies. The galactic material of primeval origin is almost entirely hydrogen and helium. This raises the question of where all the other heavier elements came from. It is now known that they are synthesized inside of stars. But how do they get out? The aging star that explodes is rich in heavy elements that have been synthesized in its interior by successive nuclear reactions. The supernova explosion disperses this element-rich material around the galaxy. When subsequent generations of stars and planets form they incorporate the debris of these long-dead stars. We owe the presence of the carbon in our bodies, the iron core of our planet and the uranium in our nuclear reactors to supernovae that occurred before the solar system formed. Without supernovae, Earth-like planets would not exist."[15]

But supernovae would be impossible if weak interactions were slightly altered: "If the weak interaction were much weaker, the neutrinos would not be able to exert enough pressure on the outer envelope of the star to cause the supernova explosion. On the other hand, if it were much stronger, the neutrinos would be trapped inside the core, and rendered impotent."[16] Either way the heavy elements manufactured in the core of stars could not form second-generation stars like our sun and planets capable of supporting life. Hence, the weak interaction of physics appears uniquely suited to making life possible in the universe.

This is not a mere coincidence. The same pattern recurs with many other fundamental constants in physics. For instance, if the strong force that binds protons and neutrons in the atomic nucleus were half its present strength, the chemical elements would decay rapidly. Even iron and carbon would be unstable. If, on the other hand, the strong force were only slightly greater, the di-proton could exist, rendering ordinary hydrogen catastrophically explosive. In this way all the hydrogen in the universe would have been burned before stars could form. Again, either no stable elements or no hydrogen. Either way life is rendered impossible.[17]

Davies speaks of "the same balancing act" with respect to the rate of the universe's expansion: "For a given density of cosmic material, the universe has to explode from the creation event with a precisely defined degree of vigour to achieve its present structure. If the bang is too small, the cosmic material merely falls back again after a brief dispersal, and crunches itself to oblivion. On the other hand, if the bang is too big, the fragments get blasted completely apart at high speed, and soon become isolated, unable to clump together into galaxies. In reality, the bang that occurred was of such exquisitely defined strength that the outcome lies precisely on the boundary between these alternatives."[18]

Many other constants in physics—such as the "strangely fortunate" resonances that make possible the synthesis of heavy elements in stars—are comprehensible in terms of their subordination to the possibility of life. Physicists Dicke, Carter, Dyson, Hawking, and Wheeler have all used the goal of life to illuminate the history of the universe and many of its fundamental properties. This procedure, called the Strong Anthropic Principle,* is the subject of a

*See The New Story of Science, chap. 4.

recent comprehensive study by John Barrow and Frank Tipler. They argue that "the Universe must have those properties which allow life to develop within it at some stage in its history."[19]

Surveying this evidence, molecular biologist George Wald concludes, "If any one of a considerable number of physical properties of the universe...were other than it is... life...would become impossible, here or anywhere."[20] He declares, "This is a life-breeding universe."[21] In the same spirit geneticist Lucien Cuénot writes that in the universe "everything happens as if Life were necessary; but the mechanist can never understand why, since we can easily imagine a lifeless Cosmos; uninhabited and uninhabitable planets are certainly not lacking."[22]

The hierarchy we have discovered is also reflected in the history of life on earth as seen in the fossil record. The order of appearance of various organisms (shown in Figure 8.1) makes sense ecologically, since bacteria, so important in recycling, appear first, and plants appear before animals, land plants before land animals, and insects before plants requiring insect pollination. The sequence also represents a development toward higher organization. Patterson remarks: "In the main groups there is an orderly progression: those which are simplest in organization, like bacteria and simple seaweeds, appear before more highly-organized things like fungi and worms, and these, in turn, appear before seed (flowering) plants or land vertebrates. Thus the fossil record demonstrates progression in geological time, whether progression is defined as the development and further modification of homologous features, or as increase in information content of DNA."[23]

The lower forms set the stage for the higher forms, just as a foundation supports a building. Dobzhansky adds, "Viewing evolution of the living world as a whole, from the hypothetical primeval self-reproducing substance to higher plants, animals and man, one cannot avoid the recognition that progress, or advancement, or rise, or ennoblement, has occurred."[24]

With respect to man specifically, we must inquire whether the intellect is a product of evolution. The received opinion is that the human mind evolved to aid survival and that intellectual powers might just as well have appeared in any other species. Darwin thought that "the mind of man...developed from a mind as low as that possessed by the lowest animal."[25] But if our intellectual

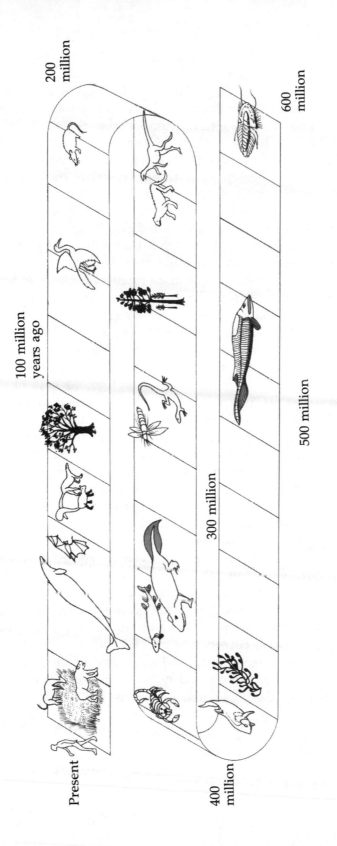

Figure 8.1. The history of life as revealed by the fossil record, marking the time of first appearance of various organisms. The overall picture shows progress from lower to higher. (After Lambert et al.)

abilities "evolved to let us get along in the cave, how can it be that they permit us to obtain deep insights into cosmology, elementary particles, molecular genetics, number theory?" asks molecular biologist Max Delbrück.[26] None of these abstract enterprises has any direct relation to survival. Physicist Louis de Broglie argues that man's ability to develop such things as relativity and quantum theory is not the result of primitive survival adaptation since these theories are "absolutely contrary to all the data of our usual intuition." Thus, he adds, "Our mind can find in itself . . . ideas of space and time quite different from that which the experience of daily life suggests."[27] Such an ability would have been of no use to early man. Furthermore, the human intellect is not an extension of any power in animals (see Chapter 3). Therefore, it cannot occur in just any species and is not the result of gradualistic evolution.

If gradualism cannot account for the origin of the human intellect, then did it perhaps first appear by one sudden evolutionary jump? We saw in Chapter 6 that all the greatest differences among organisms came first in the history of life. No new phyla have emerged since the Cambrian period.[28] By the time man comes along, only lesser differences of body plan are genetically available (such as those that differentiate man from gorilla). But the mental difference between man and the other animals by far exceeds the differences between any other species. Dobzhansky writes, "Man's structural peculiarities only suffice to place him in a monotypic zoological family, with a single living species. His mental abilities are far more distinctive. If the zoological classification were based on psychological instead of mainly morphological traits, man would have to be considered a separate phylum or even kingdom."[29] In sum, the greatest differences among organisms occurred earliest in the history of life. But man is one of the latest species to appear and yet is separated from animals by an enormous gap. Therefore, the human intellect was not produced by natural evolutionary saltation.

These conclusions corroborate the discoveries of modern neuroscience.* If the human intellect and will are nonmaterial and have no bodily organs, then they could not evolve out of matter by any natural process. Consequently, they must have been produced by immediate creation, just as matter had to be created to make the Big

*See *The New Story of Science*, chap. 2.

Bang possible, and just as we saw that the intervention of the Mind behind nature was necessary to create the first living organism (Chapter 6). Neuroscientist Sir John Eccles concludes, "Since materialist solutions fail to account for our experienced uniqueness, I am constrained to attribute the uniqueness of the psyche or soul to a supernatural spiritual creation. To give the explanation in theological terms: each soul is a new Divine creation which is 'attached' to the growing foetus at some time between conception and birth."[30] And this fits the larger pattern of nature: oaks come from oaks, horses from horses, and so only a Mind can produce a mind. Nothing prevents the human body from being prepared by natural causes, however.

Both the hierarchy of nature and the history of the universe culminate in man, who appears at the end of the evolutionary process as a flower appears at the end of a stalk. Some would call this conclusion insufferable egotism and consider anyone who holds it to be a victim of "speciesism." From the mosquito's point of view, they would contend, *it* is the center of the universe. They would argue man's insignificance by pointing out how tiny he is in such a vast universe and how short-lived in relation to the age of stars and galaxies.

But these reasons are spurious. First, the mosquito has no general perspective. Its perception of the world is extremely narrow, as is that of every other animal (see Chapter 3). Man's understanding, on the other hand, incorporates these narrower worlds: he can know them and their limits. If the mosquito could reflect—which it cannot—it would have no *reason* to claim a central position in the world. We have seen above the reasons for the natural hierarchy in which man occupies the highest position because of his superior faculties. Further, physicists Wheeler and Hawking have demonstrated that the universe must have the great age and size it does for life to be possible. The age and size of the universe are not evidence of man's insignificance, but on the contrary are subordinated to his existence.

As for the cliché that belittles man by calling him $1.50 worth of chemicals, molecular physicist Harold Morowitz refutes it on its own terms. Observing that hemoglobin costs $2.95 per gram from chemical supply houses, trypsin $36 a gram, human DNA $768 a gram, and follicle-stimulating hormone $4,800,000 a gram, he calculated the chemical value of a 168-pound man to be $6,000,015.44! But chemicals are not a human body. Morowitz continues: "If I wanted to price the human body in terms of synthesized cellular substructures, I would have to think in terms of six hundred billion or perhaps six trillion dollars." Organizing those parts into cells he estimated would cost another six thousand trillion dollars, *if* we had the technology to do it. But cells are still not organs or an organism: "How would we assemble the cells into tissues, tissues into organs, and organs into a person? The very task staggers the imagination. Our ability to ask the question in dollars and cents has immediately disappeared. We suddenly and sharply face the realization that each human being is priceless. We are led cent by dollar from a lowly pile of common materials to a grand philosophical conclusion—the infinite preciousness of each person."[31]

This is a resounding refutation of simplistic reductionism on its own ground. But we must not lose sight of the real worth of each human person, which resides not in the body but in the mind. Other natural creatures might be just as costly to manufacture from scratch, but only human beings possess intellectual understanding and the capacity to choose freely, both of which faculties confer upon each individual an immeasurable dignity.

We have seen how the universe as a whole aims at life and how the history of life has established a hierarchy in which the lower is for the sake of the higher. Will this procedure continue forever in nature or is there some natural term? Is evolution going to continue after man?

The theme of evolution has been to intensify life by producing forms with progressively higher and more universal powers, forms that exhibit life more fully and completely. To ask what is the natural term of evolution, then, is to ask what is the maximum way to intensify life and still remain in the natural order. The answer is mind. Only a mind can have life—that is, self-direction—most fully and perfectly. For even the highest animals do not have control over the ends they pursue. Further, the mind contains through knowl-edge all other forms of life and nonlife. In addition, it has something no other natural creature has: it can understand the what and the why of things. In man for the first time, nature is able to know itself. If nature is like a work of art, it must be for the contemplation of a mind different from the Mind that produced it. The Divine Artist of nature will not only want to reflect His mind in His work but also have a spectator-participant: man. Thus the realm of physical nature is completed by man and the human mind. Any step beyond man would exceed the natural order entirely and therefore could not be a product of evolution even in part.

9

Toward a New Biology

In the preceding chapters we have explored several problem areas in contemporary biology. We shall now compare as whole systems the present regime and the new biology we have attempted to outline.

One central shortcoming of the present regime is disunity. In many biological disciplines there is disagreement over starting points, such as whether life can be defined, whether animals experience any sort of consciousness, whether natural selection is all, part, or none of the explanation for new species. Moreover, modern biology, though unable to distinguish itself from physics, is oddly out of step with modern physics, which has broken the monopoly of mechanistic explanations. One also finds an unlikely reversal in the attitude toward mind. Physicist Paul Davies notes that "It is ironical that physics, which led the way for all other sciences, is now moving towards a more accommodating view of mind, while the life sciences, following the path of last century's physics, are trying to abolish mind altogether."[1] Harold Morowitz perceives the same incongruity: "What has happened is that biologists, who once postulated a privileged role for the human mind in nature's hierarchy, have been moving relentlessly toward the hard-core materialism that characterized nineteenth-century physics. At the same time, physicists, faced with compelling experimental evidence, have been moving away from strictly mechanical models of the universe to a view that sees the mind as playing an integral role in all physical events. It is as if the two disciplines were on fast-moving trains, going in opposite directions and not noticing what is happening across the tracks."[2]

The present biology also gives rise to conflicts with disciplines outside of science. Lionel Stevenson writes that with "the appearance of the Darwinian theory ... one of the most painful elements to the poetic mind was the revelation of cruelty in nature. The ruthless struggle for survival, the wasteful fecundity that entailed inevitable destruction, went counter to the belief in beneficence which had colored all previous poetry about nature. If any god existed, he could not be endowed with both omnipotence and benevolence— one or other attribute must be discarded. And if no god existed, nature was but a vast machine indifferent to the sufferings of living beings."[3] Natural selection denied to the poets the image of a wise, benign nature and also raised grave theological, philosophical, and ethical questions. J. W. Burrow, an editor of a recent reprint of the first edition of *The Origin of Species*, reflects on the early reaction to Darwin's theory: "To some the implications of the theory seemed negative and desolating. The whole earth no longer proclaimed the glory of the Lord. Paradoxically, in revealing the closeness of man's links with the rest of creation, Darwin seemed to have cut the emotional ties between man and nature. The world was not, apparently, the rational design in every detail of a superintending Being, whose purposes, though infinitely beyond man's full comprehension, were in some sense akin to the purposes and feelings of man himself—at least they *were* purposes. Nature, according to Darwin, was the product of blind chance and a blind struggle, and man a lonely, intelligent mutation, scrambling with the brutes for his sustenance. To some the sense of loss was irrevocable; it was as if an umbilical cord had been cut, and men found themselves part of 'a cold passionless universe.' Unlike nature as conceived by the Greeks, the Enlightenment and the rationalist Christian tradition, Darwinian nature held no clues for human conduct, no answers to human moral dilemmas."[4]

Nearly a century ago T. H. Huxley saw a conflict between Darwin's image of nature and the principles of ethics: "The practice of that which is ethically best—what we call goodness or virtue— involves a course of conduct which, in all respects, is opposed to that which leads to success in the cosmic struggle for existence. In place of ruthless self-assertion it demands self-restraint; in place of thrusting aside, or treading down, all competitors, it requires that the individual shall not merely respect, but shall help his fellows; its influence is directed, not so much to the survival of the fittest, as to the fitting of as many as possible to survive. It repudiates the gladiatorial theory of existence."[5]

Consequently, Huxley argued that man must not use nature as a model in ethics. But just as many theorists argue to the contrary, that ruthless struggle must be the human paradigm since it is nature's mode. Biologist Garrett Hardin: "As a species becomes increasingly 'successful,' its struggle for existence ceases to be one of struggle with the physical environment or with other species and comes to be almost exclusively competition with its own kind. *We call that species most successful that has made its own kind its worst enemy.* Man enjoys this kind of success. Intraspecific competition may be as crude as cannibalism or infanticide, as 'romantic' as chivalrous jousting or dueling, or as subtle as Stephen Potter's 'one-upmanship,' but it all has the same end in view: the securing of advantage of one's self at the expense of one's neighbor."[6] Thus from the Darwinian perspective the principles of ethics must be ruthless or they must contradict nature.

Finally, modern biology has occasioned a most unfortunate polarization of opinion between materialist evolutionists on the one hand and fundamentalist creationists on the other. Both sides tend to conflate evolution with Darwinism. The evolutionists argue that to attack Darwin is to attack evolution itself, while the creationists argue that since Darwin is faulty, evolution is wrong.

By contrast with the present regime, the new biology offers significant unity at many levels. For example, the definition of life as self-directed activity unites physiology, natural population regulation, and the mechanisms of evolution (see Chapters 2 and 6). Systematic differentiation also brings into harmony data from ecology, genetics, and paleontology. Further, the new biology accords with the new physics which in the Anthropic Principle asserts purpose. And if nature incorporates wisdom, purpose, and beauty, then the artist and poet can use it as a model. Ethics also can look to nature for a foundation of its principles.* Finally, the new perspective in biology resolves the unnecessary conflict between religion and science. Darwin thought that his theory destroyed the evidence of purpose in nature and hence the argument based on it for a Mind directing all of life: "The old argument from design in nature, as given by Paley, which formerly seemed to me so conclusive, fails, now that the law of natural selection has been discovered. We can no longer argue that, for instance, the beautiful hinge of a bivalve shell must have been made by an intelligent being,

---

*We intend to develop and explain this connection in a sequel to *The New Biology*.

like the hinge of a door by man. There seems to be no more design in the variability of organic beings and in the action of natural selection, than in the course which the winds blows. Everything in nature is the result of fixed laws."[7]

But we have seen the inadequacy of Darwin's theory (Chapter 6). And the reality of purpose (Chapter 7) argues a Mind behind nature since things lacking intelligence do not act for a purpose unless directed by a separate intelligence. Again, we saw evidence for a Mind in the origin of life. The natural hierarchy of living things also points to the same conclusion. Thus astronomer Fred Hoyle declares, "A commonsense interpretation of the facts suggests that a superintellect has monkeyed with physics, as well as chemistry and biology, and that there are no blind forces worth speaking about in nature."[8]

Today some who affirm the necessity of an intelligent cause of all living beings think they must deny that plants and animals also have natural causes. And some who affirm evolution, on the other hand, feel constrained to deny any cause of living things but matter. One side rejects purpose and divine causality while the other rejects the role of natural causes. But if the whole of nature, both living and nonliving, is a tool in the hands of God, nothing prevents nature *and* God from being the causes of new species, just as both Shakespeare and his pen wrote the sonnets, one moving the other. In the fifth century, the great theologian Saint Augustine argued from the text of Genesis that in the beginning God created all living things not immediately as actual individuals, but "potentially in their causes, as things that will be in the future."[9] Expounding an evolutionary development of what he called seminal principles, Augustine, in this way, preserved both the causality of nature and the causality of the Creator. Another great theologian, Saint Thomas Aquinas, assigned the reason for this dual causality: "Nor is it superfluous, even if God can by Himself produce all natural effects, for them to be produced by certain natural causes. For this is not a result of the inadequacy of divine power, but of the immensity of His goodness, whereby He also willed to communicate His likeness to things, not only so that they might exist, but also that they might be causes for other things. Indeed all creatures generally attain the divine likeness in these two ways ... By this, in fact, the beauty of order in created things is evident."[10]

Contemporary biology suffers from narrowness because of its strong inclination to various kinds of reductionism. In Chapter 1 we discussed the tendency to reduce everything to atoms, and in Chapter 2 the attempt to reduce all life to biochemistry and molecular activity. Another form of reductionism considers the cell to be the basic unit of life rather than the organism. But a liver cell, for example, cannot live on its own, and its activities make sense only when their subordination to the whole organism is understood. Yet another form of narrowness tries to reduce consciousness to physiology. Reductionism is deceptive because it emphasizes a half truth. Even the study of a whole organism can be reductionistic if it ignores habitat, niche, and relation to other living things. Physiologist Erich von Holst distinguishes two approaches to animal studies. One concentrates on investigating the function of a single organ, dissected and isolated from all else; the other studies the organ's function in the whole intact organism. Von Holst argues that both approaches, only when taken together, "will yield a complete picture."[11] No organism makes sense in abstraction from its natural living conditions. The environment is part of its definition. Study by dissection alone, like reading a sentence out of context, will necessarily yield only partial results. Because of the inclination to reductionism, certain fields in biology were discredited or abandoned. The study of animal behavior, for example, did not develop until the 1930s, yet behavior is a starting point for all zoology.

With its emphasis on populations and whole environments, the new biology offers an effective antidote to reductionism. In acknowledging purpose and mind, biology can free itself from the tyranny of mechanistic explanations. And the ordered hierarchy of living things counters the tendency to democratize organisms.

The new biology begins with what is known and observable now. It does not require us to impose anything artificial onto nature. Too much of the present regime, however, begins with an *imaginary* nature. It searches nature for things it expects to see but which are not there, such as ill-adapted organisms, competition, and rational thought and language in animals. "Still to be explained is why competition dominates ecological thinking, given the paucity of hard data to support it," writes Simberloff.[12]

The chronic expectation of what is not there induces a kind of blindness to what is found in nature: cooperation among organisms, purposefulness, efficiency, and harmony with the environment. These are either ignored or resolved to their opposites by recourse to an unobservable hypothetical past. Beauty and hierarchy are overlooked or obscured. One indicative example is the elaborate linguistic subterfuge called teleonomy, invented to deny the evidence of purpose in natural things.

Thus we are unable to see what nature is, and we imagine her to be many things she is not. This is the antithesis of good science. Hypotheses are legitimate and necessary in natural science but with one proviso: they must be based on experience and not contradict the evidence of induction. Long ago, Newton enunciated the rule for experimental science: "In experimental philosophy we are to look upon propositions inferred by general induction from phenomena as accurately or very nearly true, notwithstanding any contrary hypotheses that may be imagined, till such time as other phenomena occur by which they may either be made more accurate or liable to exceptions."[13] The purpose, economy, and cooperation of living beings is inductively certain.

The new biology is born of a new sense of nature. Conventional opinion holds that "the wisdom of nature is a sentimental notion,"[14] or worse yet, that nature incorporates an antiwisdom. Darwin exclaims, "What a book a devil's chaplain might write on the clumsy, wasteful, blundering, low and horribly cruel works of nature!"[15]

But the nature we have discovered in the preceding chapters is a model for both engineer and artist. Her attributes of simplicity, economy, beauty, purpose, and harmony make her a model for ethics and politics. This rediscovery of nature's wisdom calls for a new biology.

Notes

INTRODUCTION

1. Edmund W. Sinnott, *Cell and Psyche: The Biology of Purpose* (New York: Harper & Row, 1961), p. 15.
2. Henry Margenau, *The Miracle of Existence* (Woodbridge, Conn.: Ox Bow Press, 1984), p. 32.
3. Ludwig von Bertalanffy, *Modern Theories of Development: An Introduction to Theoretical Biology*, trans. J. H. Woodger (New York: Harper & Row, 1962), p. 22.
4. Ibid., p. 190.
5. Steven M. Stanley, "Darwin Done Over," *The Sciences* 21 (October 1981): 18.
6. Stephen Jay Gould, "Is a New and General Theory of Evolution Emerging?," *Paleobiology* 6 (1980): 120.
7. Ernst Mayr, *The Growth of Biological Thought: Diversity, Evolution, and Inheritance* (Cambridge: Harvard University Press, 1982), p. 73.

1. PHYSICS AS THE PARADIGM

1. Peter Medawar, "A Geometric Model of Reduction and Emergence," in *Studies in the Philosophy of Biology*, ed. F. J. Ayala and T. Dobzhansky (Los Angeles & Berkeley: University of California Press, 1974), p. 62.
2. E. H. Mercer, *The Foundations of Biological Theory* (New York: John Wiley, 1981), p. 1.
3. Similar charts are found in Mercer, p. 15, and Medawar, p. 61.
4. Mercer, p. 14.
5. Heinz R. Pagels, *The Cosmic Code: Quantum Physics as the Language of Nature* (New York: Bantam, 1983), p. 109.
6. Mercer, p. 1.
7. René Descartes, letter to Claude Picot, the French translator of *Principles of Philosophy*, in *Philosophical Works of Descartes*, trans. E. S. Haldane and G. R. T. Ross (Cambridge: Cambridge University Press, 1911), I, p. 211.
8. René Descartes, *Discourse on Method* in *Philosophical Works of Descartes*, I, p. 115.
9. Thomas Hobbes, *Body, Man, and Citizen: Selections from Thomas Hobbes*, ed. Richard S. Peters (New York: Collier, 1962), pp. 77–78.
10. Henry Oldenburg, Letter to Baruch Spinoza, dated London, 27 September 1661, in *The Correspondence of Spinoza*, trans. A. Wolf (London: Allen & Unwin, 1928), p. 80.
11. Isaac Newton, *Principia*, trans. Florian Cajori (Berkeley & Los Angeles: University of California Press, 1934), p. xviii.
12. Pierre Simon Laplace, *A Philosophical Essay on Probabilities*, trans. F. W. Truscott and F. L. Emory (New York: Dover, 1951), p. 4.
13. Mercer, p. 15.

14. Thomas Robert Malthus, *An Essay on the Principle of Population* (1798), ed. Philip Appleman (New York: Norton, 1976), p. 120.
15. Newton, p. 13.
16. Malthus, pp. 118–119.
17. Karl Marx and Friedrich Engels, *Basic Writings on Politics and Philosophy*, trans. Lewis Feuer (Garden City, N.Y.: Doubleday, 1959), p. 43.
18. Sigmund Freud, *A General Introduction to Psychoanalysis*, trans. Joan Riviere (New York: Washington Square Press, 1963), p. 25.
19. Sigmund Freud, *The Future of an Illusion*, trans. W. D. Robson-Scott (Garden City, N.Y.: Doubleday, 1961), p. 80.
20. Freud, *General Introduction*, p. 251.
21. Sigmund Freud, *Civilization and Its Discontents*, trans. James Strachey (New York: Norton, 1962), p. 59.
22. B. F. Skinner, *About Behaviorism* (New York: Knopf, 1974), p. 189.
23. Skinner, p. 104.
24. Edward O. Wilson, *On Human Nature* (Cambridge: Harvard University Press, 1978), p. 16.
25. Ibid., p. 195.
26. Ibid., p. 204.
27. Edward O. Wilson, *Sociobiology: The New Synthesis* (Cambridge: Harvard University Press, 1978), p. 575.
28. Richard Dawkins, *The Selfish Gene* (New York: Oxford University Press, 1976), p. 21.
29. Albert Einstein and Leopold Infeld, *The Evolution of Physics* (New York: Simon & Schuster, 1966), p. 121.
30. Margenau, *Miracle of Existence*, p. 8.
31. William H. Thorpe, *Purpose in a World of Chance* (London: Oxford University Press, 1978), pp. 9–10.
32. Freeman Dyson, *Disturbing the Universe* (New York: Harper & Row, 1979), p. 248.
33. Richard P. Feynman, *QED* (Princeton, New Jersey: Princeton University Press, 1985), p. 84.
34. Isaac Newton, *Opticks* (New York: Dover, 1952), Query 31, p. 400; Newton, "Rules of Reasoning in Philosophy," in *Principia*, p. 399.
35. Werner Heisenberg, *Physics and Philosophy* (New York: Harper & Row, 1958), p. 28.
36. Eugene Wigner, *Symmetries and Reflections* (Bloomington: Indiana University Press, 1967), p. 189.
37. Max Born, *Physics in My Generation* (London & New York: Pergamon, 1956), p. 48.
38. Dyson, p. 249.
39. Carl F. von Weizsäcker, *The World View of Physics*, trans. Marjorie Grene (Chicago: University of Chicago Press, 1952), p. 33.
40. Heisenberg, p. 186.
41. Margenau, p. 11.

42. Weizsäcker, p. 31.

43. Pagels, p. xiii.

44. Ibid., p. 72.

45. Heisenberg, p. 145.

46. Werner Heisenberg, *Philosophical Problems of Nuclear Science* (Greenwich, Conn.: Fawcett, 1966), p. 98.

47. Dyson, p. 249.

48. Weizsäcker, p. 203.

49. Heisenberg, *Physics and Philosophy*, p. 106.

50. François Jacob, *The Logic of Life: A History of Heredity*, trans. Betty E. Spillman (New York: Pantheon, 1973), p. 307.

2. LIFE

1. J. E. Lovelock, *Gaia: A New Look at Life on Earth* (New York: Oxford University Press, 1979), p. 3.

2. William S. Beck, *Modern Science and the Nature of Life* (New York: Harcourt, 1957), p. 130.

3. Jacob, *The Logic of Life*, p. 299.

4. John Kendrew, *The Thread of Life* (Cambridge: Harvard University Press, 1966), p. 91.

5. N. W. Pirie, "The Meaninglessness of the Terms Life and Living," in *Perspectives in Biochemistry*, ed., J. Needham and D. Green (Cambridge: University of Cambridge Press, 1937).

6. Barry Commoner, "In Defense of Biology," in *Interrelations: The Biological and Physical Sciences*, ed. Robert Blackburn (Chicago: Scott, Foresman, 1966), p. 133.

7. Descartes, *Discourse on Method*, p. 115.

8. René Descartes, from a letter to Henry More, February 5, 1649, quoted by Mirko D. Grmek, "A Survey of the Mechanical Interpretations of Life from the Greek Atomists to the Followers of Descartes," in *Biology, History and Natural Philosophy*, ed. Allen Breck and Wolfgang Yourgau (New York: Plenum, 1972), p. 186; Descartes, *Meditations on First Philosophy*, p. 195.

9. Ludwig von Bertalanffy, "The Model of Open Systems: Beyond Molecular Biology," in *Biology, History and Natural Philosophy*, p. 20.

10. Jacques Monod, BBC Interview, July 1970, quoted in *Beyond Chance and Necessity: A Critical Inquiry into Professor Jacques Monod's Chance and Necessity*, ed. John Lewis (London: Teilhard Centre for the Future, 1974), p. ix.

11. Jacob, *The Logic of Life*, p. 89.

12. Peter Farb, *The Insects* (New York: Time-Life, 1962), p. 58.

13. Edmund Sinnott, *Matter, Mind and Man* (London: Allen & Unwin, 1958), p. 36.

14. Bertalanffy, *Modern Theories of Development*, p. 67.

15. Sinnott, *Matter, Mind and Man*, p. 36.

16. J. S. Haldane, quoted in Sinnott, *Matter, Mind and Man*, p. 38.

17. A. I. Oparin, "The Nature of Life," in *Interrelations: The Biological and Physical Sciences*, p. 200.

18. Ibid., pp. 191–192.

19. Ibid., p. 200.

20. Ibid., pp. 200–201.

21. Jacques Monod, *Chance and Necessity: An Essay on the Natural Philosophy of Modern Biology* , trans. Autryn Wainhouse (New York: Knopf, 1971), pp. 10–11.

22. Oparin, "The Nature of Life," pp. 203–204.

23. Georges Cuvier, letter to Mortrud, *Leçons d'anatomie comparée* (Brussels: Culture et Civilisation, 1969), I, p. xvii.

24. J. Shaxel, *Grundzuge der Theorienbildung in der Biologie* (Jena: Fischer, 1922), p. 308.

25. Paul Weiss, "The Living System," in *Beyond Reductionism: New Perspectives in the Life Sciences,* ed. A. Koestler and J. R. Smythies (Boston: Beacon, 1964), pp. 7–8.

26. Oparin, "The Nature of Life," p. 200.

27. Weiss, "The Living System," pp. 19–20.

28. Jacob, *The Logic of Life,* p. 272.

29. Jakob von Uexküll, quoted by Lucien Cuénot in *Invention et finalité en biologie* (Paris: Flammarion, 1941), p. 222.

30. Weiss, "The Living System," pp. 20–21.

31. Jacob, *The Logic of Life,* pp. 270–271.

32. Bertalanffy, *Modern Theories,* p. 108.

33. Ibid., p. 31.

34. Oparin, "The Nature of Life," p. 201.

35. Ibid., p. 187.

36. Bertalanffy, *Modern Theories,* p. 38.

37. Jacob, *The Logic of Life,* p. 271.

38. Erwin Schrödinger, *Science and Humanism: Physics in Our Time* (Cambridge: Cambridge University Press, 1961), pp. 16–17.

39. Ibid., pp. 20–21.

40. Heisenberg, *Physics and Philosophy,* p. 160. Italics added.

41. Ibid.

42. Harold Hart and Robert Schuetz, *Organic Chemistry: A Short Course* (Boston: Houghton Mifflin, 1972), p. 8.

43. Dyson, *Disturbing the Universe,* p. 248.

44. Mayr, *The Growth of Biological Thought,* p. 63.

45. Ibid.

46. P. B. Medawar and J. S. Medawar, *The Life Sciences: Current Ideas of Biology* (New York: Harper & Row, 1977), p. 165.

47. Ibid.

48. Mayr, *The Growth of Biological Thought,* p. 63.

49. Feynman, *QED,* p. 5.

50. Oparin, "The Nature of Life," p. 199.

51. Jacob, *The Logic of Life,* p. 303.

52. Elizabeth Wood, *Crystals and Light* (Princeton, New Jersey: Van Nostrand, 1964), p. 53.

53. Linus Pauling and Peter Pauling, *Chemistry* (San Francisco: Freeman, 1975), p. 443.

54. Ibid., p. 444.
55. Jacob, *The Logic of Life*, p. 296.
56. Salvador Luria, *Life—The Unfinished Experiment* (New York: Scribner's, 1973), p. 92.
57. Mercer, *The Foundations of Biological Theory*, p. 132.
58. Niels Bohr, "Light and Life," in *Interrelations: The Biological and Physical Sciences*, p. 112.
59. Niko Tinbergen, *Animal Behavior* (New York: Time-Life, 1965), p. 90.
60. David M. Gates, "Heat Transfer in Plants," *Scientific American* 213 (December 1965): 79.
61. Sinnott, *Matter, Mind and Man*, p. 38.

3. ANIMALS AND MAN

1. Donald R. Griffin, "Animal Thinking," *American Scientist* 72 (September–October 1984): 456.
2. Descartes, letter to Henry More: see note 8, chap. 2. Italics added.
3. René Descartes, *Treatise on Man*, trans. Thomas S. Hall (Cambridge: Harvard University Press, 1972), pp. 21, 28–29.
4. Ibid., pp. 71, 21.
5. Descartes, *Discourse on Method*, p. 115.
6. Descartes, *Treatise on Man*, pp. 36–37.
7. Thomas H. Huxley, *Method and Results* (New York & London: 1925), pp. 216, 217.
8. Ibid., p. 156.
9. Ibid.
10. *Brain Mechanisms and Consciousness: A Symposium*, ed. Edgar D. Adrian, Frederic Brenner, and Herbert H. Jasper (Oxford: Blackwell, 1956), pp. 404, 446, 423–424.
11. Gordon W. Allport, *Becoming* (New Haven: Yale University Press, 1955), p. 37.
12. Ragnar Granit, "Reflections on the Evolution of the Mind and Environment," in *Mind in Nature: Nobel Conference XVII*, ed. Richard Q. Elvee (San Francisco: Harper & Row, 1982), p. 97.
13. Mayr, *The Growth of Biological Thought*, p. 64.
14. Charles Sherrington, *Man on His Nature* (Cambridge: Cambridge University Press, 1975), p. 230.
15. Gunter S. Stent, "Limits to the Scientific Understanding of Man," *Science* 187 (21 March 1975): 1057.
16. John Eccles, *Facing Reality* (Berlin & New York: Springer-Verlag, 1970), p. 55.
17. Erwin Schrödinger, *What Is Life? & Mind and Matter* (Cambridge: Cambridge University Press, 1967), p. 101.
18. Ibid., pp. 167, 167–168.
19. Eccles, p. 162.
20. Niko Tinbergen, *The Animal in Its World: Explorations of an Ethologist* (Cambridge: Harvard University Press, 1972), I, pp. 123–144.
21. Ibid., pp. 146–195.

22. Otto Koehler, "Non-verbal Thinking," in *Man and Animal: Studies in Behavior*, ed. Friedrich Heinz, trans. M. Nawiasky (New York: St. Martin's Press, 1968), p. 98.

23. Richard K. Davenport and Charles M. Rogers, "Intermodal Equivalence of Stimuli in Apes," *Science* 168 (10 April 1970): 279.

24. Helena Curtis, *Biology* (New York: Worth, 1968), p. 564.

25. Wolfgang Kohler, *The Mentality of Apes*, trans. Ella Winter (New York: Harcourt, Brace, 1931), pp. 305–306.

26. Tinbergen, *Animal Behavior*, p. 21.

27. Donald R. Griffin, *Animal Thinking* (Cambridge: Harvard University Press, 1984), p. 203.

28. Tinbergen, *Animal Behavior*, p. 45.

29. Jacob von Uexküll, quoted by Josef Pieper, *Leisure: The Basis of Culture*, trans. Alexander Dru (New York: Mentor, 1963), pp. 85–86.

30. Niko Tinbergen, *The Study of Instinct* (Folcroft, Pa.: Folcroft Editions, 1969), pp. 25–27.

31. J. Y. Lettvin, H. R. Maturana, W. S. McCulloch, and W. H. Pitts, "What the Frog's Eye Tells the Frog's Brain," *Proceedings of the Institute of Radio Engineers* 47 (November 1959): 1940.

32. Ibid., p. 1940.

33. E. S. Russell, "The Limitations of Analysis in Biology," in *Interrelations: The Biological and Physical Sciences*, p. 59. Italics added.

34. Helmut Tributsch, *How Life Learned to Live: Adaptation in Nature*, trans. Miriam Varon (Cambridge: MIT Press, 1982), p. 204.

35. Ibid., p. 90.

36. Ibid., p. 48.

37. Ibid., p. 58.

38. Ibid., p. 34.

39. Ibid., p. 60.

40. Tinbergen, *The Animal in Its World*, p. 113.

41. W. S. Bristowe, *The World of Spiders* (London: Collins, 1958), p. 240.

42. Richard D. Estes, "Territory's Invisible Walls," in *The Marvels of Animal Behavior*, ed. Thomas B. Allen (Washington, D.C.: National Geographic, 1972), p. 240.

43. Dian Fossey, "Living with Mountain Gorillas," in *The Marvels of Animal Behavior*, ed. Allen, p. 212.

44. Jane Goodall, "My Life Among Wild Chimpanzees," *National Geographic* 124 (August 1963): 296.

45. Tinbergen, *The Study of Instinct*, p. 76.

46. Keller Breland and Marian Breland, "A Field of Applied Animal Psychology," *American Psychologist* 6 (1951): 202–204.

47. Keller Breland and Marian Breland, "The Misbehavior of Organisms," *American Psychologist* 16 (1961): 681.

48. Ibid., p. 682.

49. Ibid., p. 683.

50. Ibid.

51. Ibid., pp. 683, 683–684.

52. Ibid., p. 684.

53. Ibid.

54. Ibid.

55. Keith J. Hayes and Catherine H. Nissen, "Higher Mental Functions of a Home-Raised Chimpanzee," in *Behavior of Nonhuman Primates*, vol. 4, ed. Allan M. Shrier and Fred Stollnitz (New York: Academic Press, 1971), vol. 4, pp. 78–100.

56. H. W. Nissen, "Phylogenetic Comparison," in *Handbook of Experimental Psychology*, ed. S. S. Stevens (New York: Wiley, 1951), p. 377.

57. Griffin, *Animal Thinking*, p. 140.

58. Kohler, pp. 73, 138, 48–49.

59. Jane van Lawick-Goodall, *In the Shadow of Man* (Boston: Houghton Mifflin, 1971), pp. 35–37.

60. W. Kawai, "Newly Acquired Precultural Behavior of the Natural Troop of Japanese Monkeys on Koshima Islet," *Primates* 6 (1965): 1–30.

61. R. Allen Gardner and Beatrice T. Gardner, "Teaching Sign Language to a Chimpanzee," *Science* 165 (15 August 1969): 664–672.

62. Francine G. Patterson, "Linguistic Capabilities of a Lowland Gorilla," in *Language Intervention from Ape to Child*, ed. Richard L. Schiefelbush and John H. Hollis (Baltimore: University Park Press, 1979), pp. 325–356.

63. Herbert S. Terrace, *Nim* (New York: Knopf, 1979). See our bibliography for other references.

64. David Premack, "Language in Chimpanzee?," *Science* 172 (21 May 1971): 808–822.

65. Duane M. Rumbaugh, ed., *Language Learning by a Chimpanzee: The Lana Project* (New York: Academic Press, 1977).

66. Brian B. Boycott, "Learning in the Octopus," *Scientific American* 212 (March 1965): 42–50.

67. Jean Piaget, *Six Psychological Studies*, trans. Anita Tenzer (New York: Vintage, 1968), p. 52.

68. Ibid., p. 10.

69. Jean Piaget, "The Child and Modern Physics," *Scientific American* 196 (March 1957): 47.

70. Ibid., pp. 47–48.

71. Konrad Lorenz, *King Solomon's Ring* (New York: Crowell, 1952), p. 140.

72. Ibid., p. 142.

73. Ibid.

74. Konrad Lorenz, *On Aggression* (New York: Harcourt, & World, 1963), pp. 117–118.

75. Kohler, pp. 320–321.

76. Francine G. Patterson, "Conversations with a Gorilla," *National Geographic* 154 (October 1978): 456, 459.

77. Piaget, "The Child and Modern Physics," p. 49.

78. Ibid., p. 50.

79. Kohler, pp. 28, 30.

80. Herbert G. Birch, "The Role of Motivational Factors in Insightful Problem-Solving," *Journal of Comparative Psychology* 38 (30 May 1945): 298, 302–303.

81. Kohler, p. 30.

82. Ibid., pp. 37, 53.

83. Birch, pp. 298, 302–303.

84. Ibid., p. 314.

85. Kohler, p. 194.

86. Ibid., p. 196.

87. Ibid.

88. Ibid., p. 197.

89. Ibid.

90. E. Sue Savage-Rumbaugh, Duane Rumbaugh, and Sally Boysen, "Linguistically Mediated Tool Use and Exchange by Chimpanzees (*Pan Troglodytes*)," in *Speaking of Apes: A Critical Anthology of Two-Way Communication with Man*, ed. Thomas Sebeok and Jean Umiker-Sebeok (New York: Plenum, 1980), p. 357.

91. Kohler, p. 273.

92. Ibid., pp. 41–42.

93. Robert M. Yerkes, *Chimpanzees: A Laboratory Colony* (New Haven: Yale University Press, 1943).

94. Piaget, *Six Psychological Studies*, p. 12.

95. Benjamin B. Beck, "Cooperative Tool Use by Captive Hamadryas Baboons," *Science* 182 (November 1973): 594.

96. David E. H. Jones, "The Stability of the Bicycle," *Physics Today* 23 (April 1970): 34.

97. Ibid., p. 40.

98. Jane van Lawick-Goodall, "A Preliminary Report on Expressive Movements and Communication in the Gombe Stream Chimpanzees," in *Primate Patterns*, ed. Phyllis Dohlinow (New York: Holt, Rinehart & Winston, 1972), pp. 25–84.

99. Emil W. Menzel, "Spontaneous Invention of Ladders in a Group of Young Chimpanzees," *Folia Primatoligica* 17 (1972): 87–106.

100. David Premack, "The Education of Sarah, a Chimp," *Psychology Today* 4 (September 1970): 55.

101. Herbert S. Terrace, "How Nim Chimpsky Changed My Mind," *Psychology Today* 13 (November 1979): 65–76.

102. Herbert S. Terrace, L. A. Petitto, R. J. Sanders, and T. G. Bever, "Can an Ape Create a Sentence?," *Science* 206 (23 November 1979): 900.

103. Ibid., p. 891.

104. Ibid., pp. 894–895.

105. Terrace, "How Nim Chimpsky Changed My Mind," p. 72.

106. Terrace, *Nim*, pp. 222–223.

107. Ibid., p. 212.

108. Ibid., pp. 150–153.

109. Jean Piaget, *The Construction of Reality in the Child*, trans. Margaret Cook (New York: Basic, 1954), pp. 359–360.

110. Terrace, "Can an Ape Create a Sentence?," p. 900.

111. Thomas A. Sebeok and Jean Umiker-Sebeok, "Performing Animals: Secrets of the Trade," *Psychology Today* 13 (November 1979): 91.

112. Noam Chomsky, quoted in *Time*, 10 March 1980, p. 57.

113. Sheri Lynn Gish, quoted by Leslie Roberts, "Insights into the Animal Mind," *BioScience* 33 (June 1983): 363.

114. Piaget, *Six Psychological Studies*, p. 11.

115. Born, *Physics in My Generation*, p. 48.

116. John Wheeler, "Genesis and Observership," in *Foundational Problems in the Special Sciences*, ed. Robert E. Butts and Jaakko Hintikka (Dordrecht, Holland: Reidel, 1977), pp. 5–6.

117. Wigner, *Symmetries and Reflections*, p. 189.

118. E. S. Russell, *The Interpretation of Development and Heredity: A Study in Biological Method* (Oxford: Oxford University Press, 1930), p. 138.

119. Weizsäcker, *The World View of Physics*, p. 23.

120. Donald R. Griffin, ed., *Animal Mind—Human Mind: Report of the Dahlem Workshop, Berlin 1981* (Berlin & New York: Springer-Verlag, 1982), p. 3.

121. Kathleen Perrin, Assistant Professor of Nursing, private communication, 1984. See also Lois J. Davitz and Joel R. Davitz, "How Do Nurses Feel When Patients Suffer?," *American Journal of Nursing* 75 (September 1975): 1505–1510.

4. COOPERATION

1. Charles Darwin, "The Linnean Society Papers," in *Darwin: A Norton Critical Edition*, ed. Philip Appleman (New York: Norton, 1970), p. 83.

2. Alfred R. Wallace, "The Linnean Society Papers," p. 92.

3. Thomas H. Huxley, "The Struggle for Existence in Human Society," in *Evolution and Ethics and Other Essays* (New York: Appleton, 1896), p. 200.

4. Alfred, Lord Tennyson, *In Memoriam*, ed. Robert Ross (New York: Norton, 1973), stanza 56, p. 36.

5. Charles Darwin, *The Origin of Species*, 6th ed. (London, 1872; rpt. New York: Mentor, 1958), p. 74.

6. Daniel Simberloff, "The Great God of Competition," *The Sciences* 24 (July–August 1984): 20.

7. John A. Wiens, "Competition or Peaceful Coexistence?," *Natural History* 92 (March 1983): 34.

8. Ibid.

9. Ibid., p. 30.

10. P. S. Messenger, "Biotic Interactions," *Encyclopaedia Britannica: Macropaedia* (15th ed.), vol. 2, p. 1048.

11. E. J. Kormondy, *Concepts of Ecology* (Englewood Cliffs, N.J.: Prentice-Hall, 1976), p. 143.

12. W. C. Allee, Alfred Emerson, Orlando Park, Thomas Park, and Karl Schmidt, *Principles of Animal Ecology* (Philadelphia: Saunders, 1959), p. 699.

13. Robert Ricklefs, *Ecology* (Newton, Mass.: Chiron Press, 1974), p. 204.

14. Paul Colinvaux, *Introduction to Ecology* (New York: Wiley, 1973), p. 300.

15. Lorenz, *On Aggression*, p. 33.

16. Eugene P. Odum, *Fundamentals of Ecology* (Philadelphia: Saunders, 1971), p. 214.

17. Ibid., p. 216.

18. Frits W. Went, *The Plants* (New York: Time-Life, 1963), p. 168.

19. Frits W. Went, "The Ecology of Desert Plants," *Scientific American* 192 (April 1955): 74.

20. Ibid.

21. Paul Colinvaux, *Why Big Fierce Animals Are Rare: An Ecologist's Perspective* (Princeton: Princeton University Press, 1978), p. 146.

22. Peter Farb, *The Forest* (New York: Time-Life, 1969), p. 116.

23. P. Klopfer, *Habitats and Territories* (New York: Basic Books, 1969), p. 9.

24. Colinvaux, *Introduction to Ecology*, pp. 343–344.

25. G. D. Hale Carpenter, *A Naturalist on Lake Victoria* (London: Unwin, 1920), p. 39.

26. Colinvaux, *Introduction to Ecology*, p. 346.

27. Curtis, *Biology*, p. 747.

28. Charles Elton, *Animal Ecology* (London: Methuen, 1968), p. 86.

29. Ibid., p. 84.

30. Lorenz, p. 35.

31. M. Philip Kahl, "The Stork: A Taste for Survival," in *The Marvels of Animal Behavior*, ed. Allen, p. 267.

32. Nickolas M. Waser and Leslie A. Real, "Effective Mutualism between Sequentially Flowering Plant Species," *Nature* 281 (25 October 1979): 670.

33. Ricklefs, p. 206.

34. Ibid., p. 215.

35. Darwin, *The Origin of Species*, p. 78.

36. Colinvaux, *Why Big Fierce Animals Are Rare*, p. 149.

37. James L. Gould, *Ethology: Mechanisms and Evolution of Behavior* (New York: Norton, 1982), p. 467.

38. Gordon H. Orians, "The Strategy of the Niche," in *Marvels of Animal Behavior*, ed. Allen, p. 171.

39. Colinvaux, *Why Big Fierce Animals Are Rare*, p. 145.

40. Robert H. MacArthur, "Population Ecology of Some Warblers of Northeastern Coniferous Forests," *Ecology* 39, (October 1958): 599, 617.

41. Colinvaux, *Why Big Fierce Animals Are Rare*, pp. 144, 149.

42. Herbert R. Ross, "Principles of Natural Coexistence Indicated by Leafhopper Populations," *Evolution* 11, (June 1957): 113–129.

43. P. Feinsinger, "Organization of a Tropical Guild of Nectarivorous Birds," *Ecological Monographs* 46 (1976): 275–291.

44. R. V. O'Neill, "Niche Segregation in Seven Species of Diplopods," *Ecology* 48 (1967): 983.

45. Ricklefs, p. 204.

46. David Lack, "Competition for Food by Birds of Prey," *Journal of Animal Ecology* 15 (1946): 123–129.

47. H. G. Andrewartha and L. C. Birch, *The Distribution and Abundance of Animals* (Chicago: University of Chicago Press, 1954), pp. 464–465.

48. Lorenz, p. 11.

49. Gould, p. 468. See photograph.

50. Allee et al., p. 699.

51. Colinvaux, *Why Big Fierce Animals Are Rare*, p. 144.

52. Andrewartha and Birch, p. 25.

53. Odum, p. 222.

54. L. David Mech, *The Wolves of Isle Royale: Fauna of the National Parks of the United States* (Washington, D.C.: Government Printing Office, 1966), p. xiii.

55. Adolph Murie, *The Wolves of Mount McKinley: Fauna of the National Parks of the United States* (Washington, D.C.: Government Printing Office, 1944), p. xvii.

56. David Kirk, ed., *Biology Today* (New York: Random House, p. 659.

57. L. B. Slobodkin, "Experimental Populations of Hydrida," in *British Ecological Society Jubilee Symposium* (Oxford: Blackwell, 1964), pp. 131–148. (Also in supplements to *Journal of Ecology*, no. 52, and *Journal of Animal Ecology*, no. 33).

58. Lorenz, p. 25.

59. Mech, p. xii.

60. Murie, pp. 123–124.

61. Thomas C. Cheng, *Symbiosis: Organisms Living Together* (New York: Pegasus, 1970), p. 32.

62. Jean G. Baer, *Animal Parasites*, trans. Kathleen Lyons (New York: McGraw-Hill, 1971), p. 10.

63. Robert L. Smith, *Ecology and Field Biology* (New York: Harper & Row, 1974), p. 370.

64. Thomas C. Cheng, ed., *Aspects of the Biology of Symbiosis* (Baltimore: University Park Press, 1971), p. 103.

65. David Linicome, "The Goodness of Parasitism: A New Hypothesis," in *Aspects of the Biology of Symbiosis*, pp. 139–227; see also pp. 103–137.

66. G. F. Gause, "Competition for Common Food in Protozoa," in *Readings in Ecology*, ed. Edward J. Kormondy (New York: Prentice-Hall, 1965), pp. 82–85.

67. Robert Axelrod and William D. Hamilton, "The Evolution of Cooperation," *Science* 211 (27 March 1981): 1391.

68. Robert M. May, "A Test of Ideas about Mutualism," *Nature* 307 (February 1984): 410.

69. Lynn Margulis, *Symbiosis in Cell Evolution* (San Francisco: Freeman, 1981), p. 164.

70. Kirk, p. 648.

71. Ibid., p. 649.

72. Cheng, *Aspects of the Biology of Symbiosis*, p. 229; Odum, p. 228.

73. George L. Clarke, *Elements of Ecology* (New York: Wiley, 1954), p. 377.

74. Peter Farb, *Ecology* (New York: Time-Life, 1963), p. 103.

75. Kirk, pp. 658–659.

76. David W. Inouye, "The Ant and the Sunflower," *Natural History* 93 (June 1984): 49.

77. Farb, *Ecology*, p. 104.

78. Clarke, p. 390.

79. George O. Poinar, Jr., "Sealed in Amber," *Natural History* 91 (June 1982): 26, 29–30.

80. Mea Allen, *Darwin and His Flowers: The Key to Natural Selection* (New York: Taplinger, 1977), p. 202

81. Lee R. Dice, *Natural Communities* (Ann Arbor: University of Michigan Press, 1962), p. 300.

82. "Dodo Ecology," *Scientific American* 237 (October 1977): 81–82.

83. Clarke, p. 368.

84. Paul Bucher, *Endosymbiosis of Animals with Plant Microorganisms*, trans. Bertha Mueller (New York: Wiley, 1965), p. 3.

85. Clarke, p. 376.

86. Margulis, p. 167.

87. Odum, p. 232.

88. Curtis, p. 172.

89. Paul R. Burkholder, "Cooperation and Conflict among Primitive Organisms," in *Readings in Ecology*, ed. Kormondy, p. 81.

90. Dice, p. 302.

91. Conrad Limbaugh, "Cleaning Symbiosis," *Scientific American* 205 (August 1961): 42.

92. Ibid. Also see Wolfgang Wickler, *Mimicry in Plants and Animals* (New York: McGraw-Hill, 1968), p. 158.

93. Ibid., p. 48.

94. Ibid., p. 49.

95. Nicolette Perry, *Symbiosis* (Poole, England: Blanford Press, 1983), p. 61.

96. Ricklefs, p. 757.

97. Allen, *Marvels of Animal Behavior*, pp. 174–175.

98. Ibid., p. 195–197.

99. Dice, p. 290.

100. Clarence J. Hylander, *Wildlife Communities: From Tundra to Tropics in North America* (Boston: Houghton Mifflin, 1966), p. 55.

101. Burkholder, p. 77.

102. Margulis, p. 163.

103. Lewis Thomas, "On the Uncertainty of Science," Phi Beta Kappa *Key Reporter* (1980), no. 6, p. 1.

104. Darwin, *The Origin of Species*, p. 83.

105. Tinbergen, *Animal Behavior*, p. 175.

106. Curtis, p. 737.

107. Hans Kruuk, "The Warring Clans of the Hyena," in *Marvels of Animal Behavior*, ed. Allen, p. 252.

108. Kirk, p. 636.

109. Ibid., p. 637.

110. Farb, *Ecology*, p. 41.

111. Lorenz, p. 109.

112. Kirk, p. 637.

113. Norman Owen-Smith, "Territoriality in the White Rhinoceros (*Ceratotherium simum*) Burchell," *Nature* 231 (4 June 1971): 295.

114. Kirk, p. 642.

115. Lorenz, p. 129.

116. Dale F. Lott, "The Way of the Bison: Fighting to Dominate," in *Marvels of Animal Behavior*, ed. Allen, p. 326.

117. Lorenz, p. 123.

118. Ibid., p. 119.

119. Farb, *Ecology*, p. 146.

120. W. C. Allee, *Cooperation among Animals* (New York: Schuman, 1938), p. 212.

121. Darwin, *The Origin of Species*, p. 75.

122. Ibid., p. 77.

123. Ibid., p. 75.

124. Ibid., p. 76.

125. Ibid., p. 79.

126. Ibid., pp. 78–79.

127. Ibid., p. 76.

128. Ibid.

129. Elton, p. 118; Andrewartha and Birch, pp. 22, 464; David Lack, *The Natural Regulation of Animal Numbers* (Oxford: Oxford University Press, 1954), p. 169.

130. Richard M. Laws, "Experiences in the Study of Large Mammals," in *Dynamics of Large Mammal Populations*, ed. Charles Fowler and Tim Smith (New York: Wiley, 1981), p. 27.

131. Charles Fowler, "Comparative Population Dynamics in Large Animals," in *Dynamics of Large Mammal Populations*, ed. Fowler and Smith, pp. 444–445.

132. Kirk, p. 673.

133. Darwin, *The Origin of Species*, p. 76.

134. Owen-Smith, p. 294.

135. Robert Stewart and John Aldrich, "Removal and Repopulation of Breeding Birds in a Spruce-Fir Community," *Auk* 75 (1951): 474.

136. Ibid., p. 481.

137. A. J. Pontin, *Competition and Coexistence of Species* (London: Pitman, 1982), p. 68.

138. Ricklefs, p. 491.

139. Elton, p. 119.

140. Lack, *The Natural Regulation of Animal Numbers*, pp. 29–30, 46.

141. Susan Grant, *Beauty and the Beast* (New York: Scribner's, 1984), pp. 47–49.

142. Y. Ito, *Comparative Ecology*, trans. Jiro Kikkawa (Cambridge: Cambridge University Press, 1978), p. 1.

143. Ibid., p. 53.

144. V. C. Wynne-Edwards, "Self-Regulating Systems in Populations of Animals," *Science* 147 (26 March 1965): 1543.

5. HARMONY

1. Darwin, *The Origin of Species*, p. 75. Italics added.
2. Ibid.
3. John E. Weaver and Frederic E. Clements, *Plant Ecology* (New York: McGraw-Hill, 1938), p. 148.
4. Larry S. Underwood, "Outfoxing the Arctic Cold," *Natural History* 92 (December 1983): 46.
5. Ibid.
6. Ibid.
7. Laurence Irving, "Adaptations to the Cold," *Scientific American* 214 (January 1966): 97.
8. Ibid., p. 96.
9. Lynn Rogers, "A Bear in Its Lair," *Natural History* 90 (October 1981): 64.
10. Knut Schmidt-Nielsen, *Animal Physiology* (Cambridge: Cambridge University Press, 1975), p. 281.
11. Cynthia Carey and Richard L. Marsh, "Shivering Finches," *Natural History* 90 (October 1981): 58–59.
12. Bernd Heinrich, "The Energetics of the Bumblebee," *Scientific American* 228 (April 1973): 97.
13. Carey and Marsh, pp. 63, 60.
14. Charles B. Bogert, "How Reptiles Regulate Their Body Temperature," *Scientific American* 200 (April 1959): 105, 107, 112–114.
15. Knut Schimdt-Nielsen and Bodil Schmidt-Nielsen, "The Desert Rat," *Scientific American* 189 (July 1953): 76.
16. George A. Bartholomew and Jack W. Hudson, "Desert Ground Squirrels," *Scientific American* 205 (November 1961): 110, 111, 112.
17. Knut and Bodil Schmidt-Nielsen, p. 73.
18. Ibid., pp. 110–112.
19. William G. Eickmeier, "Desert Resurrection," *Natural History* 93 (January 1984): 41.
20. Went, "The Ecology of Desert Plants," p. 71.
21. Ibid., p. 72.
22. Tributsch, *How Life Learned to Live*, p. 187.
23. Went, *The Plants*, p. 80.
24. Tributsch, p. 28.
25. Elbert L. Little, *The Audubon Society Field Guide to North American Trees: Eastern Region* (New York: Knopf, 1985), p. 326.
26. Charles F. Cooper, "The Ecology of Fire," *Scientific American* 204 (April 1961): 154.
27. Ibid., pp. 154–158.
28. Tributsch, p. 23.
29. D'Arcy Thompson, *On Growth and Form* (Cambridge: Cambridge University Press, 1959), II, pp. 969, 970.

30. Peter N. Witt, "Do We Live in the Best of All Worlds? Spiders Suggest an Answer," *Perspectives in Biology and Medicine* 8 (Summer 1965): 479.

31. Kirk, *Biology Today*, p. 309.

32. Tributsch, p. 147.

33. George Wald, "Life and Light," *Scientific American* 201 (October 1959): 99.

34. Kirk, p. 252.

35. Thomas A. McMahon and John Tyler Bonner, *On Size and Life* (New York: Scientific American Books, 1983), p. 171.

36. Carl Welty, "Birds as Flying Machines," *Scientific American* 192 (March 1955): 88–89.

37. P. B. S. Lissaman and Carl A. Shollenberger, "Formation Flight of Birds," *Science* 168 (22 May 1970): 1003. Also see the excellent article by Peter P. Wegener, "The Science of Flight," *American Scientist* 74 (May–June 1986): 268–278.

38. Mohamed Gad-el-Hak, quoted by Ivars Peterson, "On the Wings of a Dragonfly," *Science News* 128 (10 August 1985): 91.

39. Richard C. Lewontin, "Adaptation," *Scientific American* 239 (September 1978): 220.

40. Milton Hildebrand, "How Animals Run," *Scientific American* 202 (May 1960): 151.

41. Welty, p. 96.

42. P. F. Scholander, "The Wonderful Net," *Scientific American* 196 (April 1957): 102–104.

43. Lewontin, p. 225.

44. Scholander, pp. 98–99.

45. Thompson, p. 950.

46. McMahon and Bonner, pp. 104–105.

47. Keith Copeland, ed., *Aids for the Severely Handicapped* (New York: Grune & Straton, 1974), p. 7.

48. Werner Heisenberg, "The Meaning of Beauty in the Exact Sciences," in *Across the Frontier* (New York: Harper & Row, 1974), p. 175.

49. James Watson, *The Double Helix* (New York: Mentor, 1968), pp. 131, 134.

50. Matthew Scott, quoted by Terence Monmaney, "Life Taking Shape: A Developing View," *Science 85* 6 (September 1985): 15.

51. David Bohm, in *Towards a Theoretical Biology*, ed. C. H. Waddington (Chicago: Aldine, 1969), p. 50.

52. Thompson, p. 981.

53. Welty, p. 90.

54. Kirk, p. 637.

55. John W. Smith, *Theory of Evolution* (Middlesex, England: Penguin, 1958), p. 148.

56. W. H. Thorpe, *Animal Nature and Human Nature* (New York: Doubleday, 1974), p. 204.

57. Joseph Wood Krutch, *The Great Chain of Life* (Boston: Houghton Mifflin, 1978), pp. 99–100.

58. Ibid., p. 102.

59. Hugh Johnson, *The International Book of Trees* (New York: Simon & Schuster, 1973), front flyleaf, p. 9.

60. Sinnott, *Matter, Mind and Man*, p. 141.

61. Adolf Portmann, *Animal Forms and Patterns* (New York: Schocken, 1967), pp. 25, 19–20, 31–32.

62. Charles Darwin, *The Origin of Species*, p. 185.

63. Henri Poincaré, *The Value of Science* (New York: Dover, 1958), p. 8.

64. Charles Darwin, *The Voyage of the Beagle* (New York: Dutton, 1967), p. 11.

65. Edward O. Wilson, "The Biological Diversity Crisis: A Challange to Science," *Issues in Science and Technology* 2 (Fall 1985): 21.

66. Ibid.

67. Preston Cloud, "The Biosphere," *Scientific American* 249 (September 1983): 176.

68. Associated Press Story, Caracas, Venezuela, March 1985.

69. Robert D. Ballard and J. Frederick Grassle, "Return to the Oases of the Deep," *National Geographic* 156 (November 1979): 698.

70. Tributsch, p. 5.

71. Bohm, p. 104.

6. ORIGINS

1. Gould, "Is a New and General Theory of Evolution Emerging?," p. 120.

2. Colin Patterson, quoted by Tom Bethell, "Agnostic Evolutionists," *Harper's*, February 1985, p. 50.

3. G. Ledyard Stebbins and Francisco J. Ayala, "The Evolution of Darwinism," *Scientific American* 253 (July 1985): 72.

4. Richard Dawkins, "What's All the Fuss About?," review of Niles Eldredge's *Time Frames*, *Nature* 316 (22 August 1985): 683.

5. Darwin, *The Origin of Species*, p. 120.

6. Ibid., p. 29.

7. Niles Eldredge, *Time Frames: The Rethinking of Darwinian Evolution and the Theory of Punctuated Equilibria* (New York: Simon & Schuster, 1985), p. 82.

8. Axelrod and Hamilton, p. 1390.

9. Kinji Imanishi, quoted by Beverly Halstead, "Anti-Darwinism in Japan," *Nature* 317 (17 October 1985): 587.

10. Darwin, *The Origin of Species*, p. 111.

11. Francis Hitching, *The Neck of the Giraffe* (New Haven: Ticknor & Fields, 1982), p. 54.

12. Luther Burbank, quoted by Wilbur Hall, *Partner of Nature* (New York: Appleton-Century, 1939), pp. 97–98.

13. Hitching, p. 54.

14. Colin Patterson, *Evolution* (Ithaca, N.Y.: Cornell University Press, 1978), p. 11.

15. Theodosius Dobzhansky, *Genetics of the Evolutionary Process* (New York: Columbia University Press, 1970), p. 67.

16. See *The Origin of Species*, chap. 10.

17. Eldredge, p. 28.

18. David M. Raup, "Conflicts between Darwin and Paleontology," *Bulletin Field Museum of Natural History* 50 (January 1979): 24.

19. Steven Stanley, *The New Evolutionary Timetable: Fossils, Genes, and the Origin of Species* (New York: Basic Books, 1981), p. 71.

20. Heribert Nilsson, *Synthetische Artbildung* (Lund, Sweden: Gleerup, 1954), English Summary, p. 1212.

21. Eldredge, p. 145.

22. Darwin, *The Origin of Species*, p. 287.

23. Charles Darwin, *Charles Darwin's Natural Selection: Being the Second Part of His Big Species Book Written from 1856 to 1858*, ed. from manuscript by R. C. Stauffer (Cambridge: Cambridge University Press, 1975), p. 208.

24. Niles Eldredge and Stephen Jay Gould, "Punctuated Equilibria: An Alternative Approach to Phyletic Gradualism," in *Models in Paleobiology*, ed. T. J. M. Schopf (San Francisco: Freeman, Cooper & Co., 1972), pp. 82–115.

25. G. Ledyard Stebbins and Francisco Ayala, "Is a New Evolutionary Synthesis Necessary?," *Science* 213 (28 August 1981): 969.

26. Ernst Mayr, *Population, Species and Evolution* (Cambridge: Harvard University Press, 1970), p. 279.

27. Patterson, *Evolution*, p. 69.

28. Ibid., p. 70.

29. Søren Løvtrup, "On the Falsifiability of Neo-Darwinism," *Evolutionary Theory* 1 (December 1976): 280.

30. Leopold Infeld, *Albert Einstein* (New York: Scribner's, 1950), p. 21.

31. Stanley, *New Evolutionary Timetable*, p. 174.

32. James Valentine, in T. Dobzhansky, F. Ayala, G. L. Stebbins, and J. Valentine, *Evolution* (San Francisco: Freeman, 1977), p. 349.

33. Charles Darwin, *Charles Darwin and T. H. Huxley: Autobiographies*, ed. Gavin de Beer (London: Oxford University Press, 1974), p. 85.

34. David B. Kitts, "Paleontology and Evolutionary Theory," *Evolution* 28 (September 1974): 465.

35. L. C. Birch and P. Ehrlich, "Evolutionary History and Population Biology," *Nature* 214 (22 April 1967): 350.

36. Stanley, *New Evolutionary Timetable*, pp. 6–7.

37. Patterson, *Evolution*, pp. 128–129.

38. Stephen Jay Gould, "Nature's Great Era of Experiments," *Natural History* 92 (July 1983): 18.

39. James Brough, "Time and Evolution," in *Studies on Fossil Vertebrates*, ed. T. Stanley Westoll (London: University of London, 1958), p. 36.

40. Ibid., pp. 27–29, 32–33, 38.

41. Gould, "Nature's Great Era of Experiments," p. 20.

42. Stanley, *New Evolutionary Timetable*, p. xv.

43. G. R. Coope, "Late Cenozoic Fossil Coleoptera: Evolution, and Ecology," *Annual Review of Ecology and Systematics* 10 (1979): 264.

44. Stanley, *New Evolutionary Timetable*, pp. 83–84.

45. Steven Stanley, "Evolution of Life: Evidence of a New Pattern," in *Great Ideas Today 1983*, (Chicago: Encyclopaedia Britannica, 1983), pp. 15–16.
46. Gabriel Dover, quoted by Roger Lewin, "Evolutionary Theory under Fire," *Science* 210 (21 November 1980): 884.
47. Darwin, *The Origin of Species*, p. 90.
48. Stanley, *New Evolutionary Timetable*, p. 85.
49. Eldredge, p. 120.
50. Stanley, "Evolution of Life," p. 20.
51. Charles Darwin, letter to J. D. Hooker, 22 July 1879, in *More Letters of Charles Darwin*, ed. Francis Darwin and A. C. Seward (London: Murray, 1903), II, pp. 20–21.
52. Darwin, *The Origin of Species*, p. 310.
53. Steven Stanley, "Darwin Done Over," *The Sciences* 21 (October 1981): 21.
54. George Gaylord Simpson, *Fossils and the History of Life* (New York: Scientific American Library, 1983), p. 167.
55. Stanley, *New Evolutionary Timetable*, p. 101.
56. Raup, p. 25.
57. Eldredge, p. 144.
58. G. Ledyard Stebbins, Jr., "Cataclysmic Evolution," *Scientific American* 184 (April 1951): 55.
59. Patterson, *Evolution*, p. 51.
60. Stebbins, "Cataclysmic Evolution," p. 58.
61. Ricklefs, *Ecology*, pp. 93–96.
62. Allan C. Wilson, "The Molecular Basis of Evolution," *Scientific American* 253 (October 1985): 170.
63. Roy J. Britten and Eric H. Davidson, "Repetitive and Nonrepetitive DNA Sequences and a Speculation on the Origins of Evolutionary Origins," *Quarterly Review of Biology* 46 (June 1971): 112.
64. Ibid.
65. Ibid.
66. A. C. Wilson, L. R. Maxon, and V. M. Sarich, "Two Types of Molecular Evolution: Evidence from Studies of Interspecific Hybridization," *Proceedings of the National Academy of Sciences (USA)* 71 (July 1974): 2847.
67. Bernard Davis, quoted by Roger Lewin, "Molecules Come to Darwin's Aid," *Science* 216 (4 June 1982): 1091.
68. Walter J. Gehring, "The Molecular Basis of Development," *Scientific American* 253 (October 1985): 160.
69. Charles G. Sibley and Jon E. Ahlquist, "Reconstructing Bird Phylogeny by Comparing DNA's," *Scientific American* 254 (February. 1986): 82–92.
70. S. J. O'Brien, W. G. Nash, D. E. Wildt, M. E. Bush, and R. E. Benveniste, "A Molecular Solution to the Riddle of the Giant Panda's Phylogeny," *Nature* 317 (12 September 1985): 140–144.
71. Britten, p. 111.
72. Ibid., p. 112.
73. Ibid., p. 129.

74. Peter Oppenheimer, "Fractals, Computers and DNA," *Semaine internationale de l'image electronique/Deuxième colloque image* (Nice, April 1986).

75. Peter Oppenheimer, "The Genesis Algorithm," *The Sciences* 25 (September–October 1985): 44–47.

76. James W. Valentine and Cathryn A. Campbell, "Genetic Regulation and the Fossil Record," *American Scientist* 63 (November–December 1975): 678.

77. Pere Alberch and R. D. K. Thomas, remarks at the annual meeting of the American Association for the Advancement of Science (1986), reported by Julie Ann Miller and Lisa Davis, *Science News* 129 (7 June 1986): 365.

78. F. J. Ayala, in Dobzhansky, Ayala, Stebbins, and Valentine, *Evolution*, pp. 266–267.

79. Theodosius Dobzhansky, in Dobzhansky, Ayala, Stebbins, and Valentine, *Evolution*, pp. 443–444.

80. A. G. Cairns-Smith, *Genetic Takeover* (Cambridge: Cambridge University Press, 1982), pp. 34–35.

81. Darwin, *The Origin of Species*, p. 129.

82. Eldredge, p. 45.

83. Ibid., p. 13

84. Julian Huxley, from the television program "At Random," transcript in *Evolution after Darwin: Issues in Evolution*, ed. Sol Tax and Charles Callender (Chicago: University of Chicago, 1960), p. 45.

85. François Jacob, *The Possible and the Actual* (Seattle: University of Washington Press, 1982), p. 14.

86. George G. Simpson, *The Meaning of Evolution* (New Haven: Yale University Press, 1949), p. 15.

87. Patterson, *Evolution*, p. 26.

88. Stanley L. Miller and Leslie E. Orgel, *The Origins of Life on the Earth* (New York: Prentice-Hall, 1974), pp. 81–87.

89. Cairns-Smith, pp. 56–59.

90. Robert Shapiro, *Origins: A Skeptic's Guide to the Creation of Life* (New York: Summit Books, 1986), pp. 104, 116.

7. PURPOSE

1. Charles Darwin, letter to J. D. Hooker, 18 March 1862, in *More Letters of Charles Darwin*, I, p. 198.

2. Dover, "Molecular Drive through Evolution," p. 527.

3. H. Frederick Nijhout, "The Color Patterns of Butterflies and Moths," *Scientific American* 245 (November 81): 140.

4. Lewontin, "Adaptation," p. 215.

5. Norman Newell, "Crises in the History of Life," *Scientific American* 208 (February 1963): 79.

6. Stephen Jay Gould, "The Cosmic Dance of Siva," *Natural History* 93 (August 1984): 14.

7. Ibid., p. 18.

8. Newell, p. 79.

9. Raup, "Conflicts between Darwin and Paleontology," p. 23.

10. Tinbergen, *Animal Behavior*, p. 12.

11. Stephen Jay Gould and Richard Lewontin, "The Spandrels of San Marco and the Panglossian Paradigm: A Critique of the Adaptationist Programme," *Proceedings of the Royal Society London Series B* 205 (1979): 587–588.

12. Jens Clausen, *Stages in the Evolution of Plant Species* (New York & London: Hafner, 1967), pp. 11–53.

13. Eldredge, *Time Frames*, p. 140.

14. Coope, "Late Cenozoic Fossil Coleoptera," p. 264.

15. Alex B. Novikoff, "The Concept of Integrative Levels and Biology," *Science* 101 (2 March 1945): 212–213.

16. Oparin, "The Nature of Life," in *Interrelations*, ed. Blackburn, p. 194.

17. Ayala, "The Autonomy of Biology as a Natural Science," in *Biology, History and Natural Philosophy*, ed. Breck and Yourgrau, p. 7.

18. Julian Huxley, *Evolution in Action* (New York: Harper & Row, 1953), p. 7.

19. Luria, *Life—The Unfinished Experiment*, p. 80.

20. Thomas. H. Huxley, *Lectures and Essays* (New York: Macmillan, 1904), pp. 178–179.

21. Medawar and Medawar, *The Life Sciences*, pp. 11, 12.

22. Monod, *Chance and Necessity*, p. 9.

23. Sinnott, *Cell and Psyche*, p. 46; Sinnott, *Matter, Mind and Matter*, p. 41.

24. Jacob, *The Logic of Life*, pp. 8, 88.

25. Theodosius Dobzhansky, "Chance and Creativity in Evolution" in *Studies in the Philosophy of Biology*, ed. Ayala and Dobzhansky, p. 330.

26. Thorpe, *Animal Nature and Human Nature*, p. 17.

27. George Gaylord Simpson, "Biology and the Nature of Science," in *Interrelations*, ed. Blackburn, p. 159.

28. Niels Bohr, *Atomic Physics and Human Knowledge* (New York & London: Wiley, 1958), p. 92.

29. Niko Tinbergen, *Social Behavior in Animals* (London & New York: Methuen and Wiley, 1962), p. 2.

30. Ricklefs, *Ecology*, p. 21.

31. Tributsch, *How Life Learned to Live*, p. 22.

32. Tinbergen, *Animal Behavior*, p. 128.

33. Ricklefs, p. 250.

34. John Crook, "The Rites of Spring," in *Marvels of Animal Behavior*, ed. Allen, p. 294

35. Georg Rüppell, *Bird Flight* (New York: Van Nostrand Reinhold, 1975), p. 49.

36. Farb, *The Forest*, p. 13.

37. Adolph Portmann, *Animal Camouflage* (Ann Arbor: University of Michigan Press, 1959), p. 79.

38. Bohr, p. 92.

39. Lorenz, *On Aggression*, p. 231.

40. Griffin, *Animal Thinking*, pp. 88–89.

41. Ricklefs, p. 236.

42. Ayala, in Dobzhansky, Ayala, Stebbins, and Valentine, *Evolution*, p. 503.

43. Tributsch, p. 151.

44. Heinrich Hertel, *Structure—Form—Movement* (New York: Reinhold, 1966), pp. 23–24.

45. Andrée Tetry, *Les outils chez les êtres vivants* (Paris: Gallimard, 1948), p. 312. Our translation.

46. Lucien Cuénot, *Invention et finalité en biologie*, pp. 240–241. Our translation.

47. Ricklefs, p. 319.

48. Stephen Jay Gould, *Ever Since Darwin* (New York: Norton, 1977), pp. 99, 102.

49. Tributsch, p. 59.

50. John W. Kanwisher and Sam H. Ridgway, "The Physiological Ecology of Whales and Porpoises," *Scientific American* 248 (June 1983): 113.

51. McMahon and Bonner, *On Size and Life*, p. 187.

52. Rüppell, p. 43.

53. William Montagna, "The Skin," *Scientific American* 212 (February 1965): 56.

54. Curtis, *Biology*, p. 497.

55. George Wald, "Eye and Camera," *Scientific American* 183 (August 1950): 35.

56. Curtis, p. 607.

57. Rüppell, p. 140.

58. Farb, p. 99.

59. Gates, "Heat Transfer in Plants," pp. 77, 79.

60. Cuénot, p. 245.

61. Mayr, *Growth of Biological Thought*, p. 72.

62. Watson, *The Double Helix*, p. 139.

8. HIERARCHY

1. Darwin, *More Letters of Charles Darwin*, I, p. 114.

2. Robert Trivers, Foreword to *The Selfish Gene* by Richard Dawkins, p. v. Italics added.

3. Monod, *Chance and Necessity*, p. 41.

4. Simpson, *The Meaning of Evolution*, p. 346.

5. Lynn Margulis and Dorion Sagan, "Stange Fruit on the Tree of Life," *The Sciences* 26 (May–June 1986): 43.

6. Simpson, p. 249.

7. Darwin, *The Origin of Species*, pp. 111, 67.

8. Simpson, p. 62.

9. Stanley, "Evolution of Life," p. 5.

10. Patterson, *Evolution*, p. 4.

11. Dobzhansky, in Dobzhansky, Ayala, Stebbins, and Valentine, *Evolution* , pp. 182–185.

12. Thorpe, *Animal Nature and Human Nature*, p. 17.

13. Charles Darwin, *Descent of Man and Selection in Relation to Sex*, 2nd ed. (1874; rpt. New York: Burt, n.d.), p. 188.

14. Thorpe, p. 20.

15. Paul Davies, *The Accidental Universe* (Cambridge: Cambridge University Press, 1982), pp. 67–68.

16. Ibid., p. 68.

17. Ibid., pp. 70–71.

18. Ibid., p. 91.

19. John D. Barrow and Frank J. Tipler, *The Anthropic Cosmological Principle* (New York: Oxford University Press, 1986), p. 21.

20. George Wald, "Life and Mind in the Universe," *International Journal of Quantum Chemistry: Quantum Biology Symposium* 11 (New York: Wiley, 1984), p. 2.

21. Ibid., p. 7.

22. Cuénot, *Invention et finalité en biologie*, p. 86. Our translation.

23. Patterson, p. 129.

24. Dobzhansky, "Chance and Creativity in Evolution," in *Studies in the Philosophy of Biology*, ed. Ayala and Dobzhansky, p. 310.

25. Darwin, *Charles Darwin and T. H. Huxley: Autobiographies*, p. 54.

26. Max Delbrück, "Mind from Matter?," *American Scientist* 47 (Summer 1978): 353.

27. Louis de Broglie, *Physics and Microphysics* (New York: Pantheon, 1955), p. 210.

28. Brough, "Time and Evolution," p. 27.

29. Dobzhansky, p. 333.

30. John C. Eccles, "Self-Consciousness and the Human Person," Accademia Nazionale dei Lincei Memorie Science Fisiche Mathematiche E Natural, Series 8, forthcoming.

31. Harold Morowitz, *The Wine of Life* (New York: St. Martin's, 1979), pp. 3–6.

9. TOWARD A NEW BIOLOGY

1. Paul Davies, *God and the New Physics* (New York: Simon & Schuster, 1983), p. 8.

2. Harold Morowitz, "Rediscovering the Mind," *Psychology Today* 14 (August 1980): 12.

3. Lionel Stevenson, *Darwin among the Poets* (New York: Russell & Russell, 1963), p. 45.

4. J. W. Burrow, ed., *The Origin of Species*, 1st ed. (1859; rpt. Middlesex, England; Penguin, 1968), pp. 42–43.

5. Huxley, *Evolution and Ethics and Other Essays*, pp. 81–82.

6. Garrett Hardin, *Nature and Man's Fate* (New York: Mentor, 1959), p. 220.

7. Darwin, *Charles Darwin and T. H. Huxley: Autobiographies*, pp. 50–51.

8. Fred Hoyle, quoted by Davies, *The Accidental Universe*, p. 118.

9. Saint Augustine, *The Literal Meaning of Genesis*, trans. John Hammond Taylor (New York: Newman Press, 1982), I, p. 185.

10. St. Thomas Aquinas, *Summa Contra Gentiles*, ed. Vernon Burke, (Notre Dame, Ind.: University of Notre Dame Press, 1975), Bk. 3, Pt. 1, pp. 236–237.

11. Erich von Holst, "The Physiologist and His Experimental Animals," in *Man and Animal*, ed. Friedrich, p. 74.

12. Simberloff, "The Great God of Competition," p. 22.

13. Newton, "Rules of Reasoning in Philosophy" in *Principia*, p. 400.

14. Curtis, *Biology*, p. 10.

15. Darwin, letter to J. D. Hooker, 13 July 1856, in *More Letters of Charles Darwin*, I, p. 94.

References

Adrian, Edgar D.; Frederic Brenner; and Herbert H. Jasper, eds. *Brain Mechanisms and Consciousness*. Oxford: Blackwell, 1956.

Allee, W. C. *Cooperation among Animals*. New York: Schuman, 1938.

_____, Alfred Emerson, Orlando Park, and Karl Schmidt. *Principles of Animal Ecology*. Philadelphia: Saunders, 1959.

Allen, Mea. *Darwin and His Flowers: The Key to Natural Selection*. New York: Taplinger, 1977.

Allen, Thomas B. *The Marvels of Animal Behavior*. Washington, D.C.: National Geographic, 1972.

Allport, Gordon W. *Becoming*. New Haven: Yale University Press, 1955.

Andrewartha, H. G., and L. C. Birch. *The Distribution and Abundance of Animals*. Chicago: University of Chicago Press, 1954.

Appleman, Philip, ed. *Darwin: A Norton Critical Edition*. New York: Norton, 1970.

Aquinas, Thomas. *Summa Contra Gentiles*. Ed. Vernon Burke. 5 vols. Notre Dame, Ind.: University of Notre Dame Press, 1975.

Augros, Robert M., and George N. Stanciu. *The New Story of Science: Mind and the Universe*. New York: Bantam Books, 1986.

Augustine. *The Literal Meaning of Genesis*. Trans. John Hammond Taylor. 2 vols. New York: Newman Press, 1982.

Axelrod, Robert, and William D. Hamilton. "The Evolution of Cooperation." *Science* 211 (27 March 1981): 1390–1396.

Ayala, F. J., and Theodosius Dobzhansky, eds. *Studies in the Philosophy of Biology*. Los Angeles & Berkeley: University of California Press, 1974.

Baer, Jean G. *Animal Parasites*. Trans. Kathleen Lyons. New York: McGraw-Hill, 1971.

Ballard, Robert D., and J. Frederick Grassle. "Return to the Oases of the Deep." *National Geographic* 156 (November 1979): 689–703.

Barrow, John D., and Frank J. Tipler. *The Anthropic Cosmological Principle*. New York: Oxford University Press, 1986.

Bartholomew, George A., and Jack W. Hudson. "Desert Ground Squirrels." *Scientific American* 205 (November 1961): 107–116.

Beck, Benjamin B. "Cooperative Tool Use by Captive Hamadryas Baboons." *Science* 182 (9 November 1973): 594–597.

Beck, William S. *Modern Science and the Nature of Life*. New York: Harcourt, 1957.

Bertalanffy, Ludwig von. *Modern Theories of Development: An Introduction to Theoretical Biology*. Trans. J. H. Woodger. New York: Harper, 1962.

Bethell, Tom. "Agnostic Evolutionists." *Harper's*, February 1985.

Birch, Herbert G. "The Role of Motivational Factors in Insightful Problem-Solving." *Journal of Comparative Psychology* 38 (30 May 1945): 295–317.

Birch, L. C., and P. Ehrlich. "Evolutionary History and Population Biology." *Nature* 214 (22 April 1967): 349–352.

Blackburn, Robert T., ed. *Interrelations: The Biological and Physical Sciences.* Chicago: Scott, Foresman, 1966.

Bogert, Charles B. "How Reptiles Regulate Their Body Temperature." *Scientific American* 200 (April 1959): 105–120.

Bohr, Niels. *Atomic Physics and Human Knowledge.* New York & London: Wiley, 1958.

Boreske, J. R. *Museum of Comparative Zoology Bulletin* 146 (1974): 1–87.

Born, Max. *Physics in My Generation.* London & New York: Pergamon, 1956.

Boycott, Brian B. "Learning in the Octopus." *Scientific American* 212 (March 1965): 42–50.

Breck, Allen D., and Wolfgang Yourgau, eds. *Biology, History, and Natural Philosophy.* New York: Plenum Press, 1972.

Breland, Keller, and Marian Breland. "A Field of Applied Animal Psychology." *American Psychologist* 6 (1951): 202–204.

————, and Marian Breland. "The Misbehavior of Organisms." *American Psychologist* 16 (1961): 681–684.

Bristowe, W. S. *The World of Spiders.* London: Collins, 1958.

Britten, Roy J., and Eric H. Davidson. "Repetitive and Nonrepetitive DNA Sequences and a Speculation on the Origins of Evolutionary Origins." *Quarterly Review of Biology* 46 (June 1971): 111–133.

Broglie, Louis de. *Physics and Microphysics.* New York: Pantheon, 1955.

Brough, James. "Time and Evolution." In *Studies on Fossil Vertebrates,* ed. T. Stanley Westoll. London: University of London, 1958, pp. 16–38.

Bucher, Paul. *Endosymbiosis of Animals with Plant Microorganisms.* Trans. Bertha Mueller. New York: Wiley, 1965.

Burrow, J. W., ed. *The Origin of Species.* 1st ed. 1859; rpt. Middlesex, England: Penguin, 1968.

Cairns-Smith, A. G. *Genetic Takeover.* Cambridge: Cambridge University Press, 1982.

Carey, Cynthia, and Richard L. Marsh. "Shivering Finches." *Natural History* 90 (October 1981): 58–63.

Carpenter, G. D. Hale. *A Naturalist on Lake Victoria.* London: Unwin, 1920.

Cheng, Thomas C. *Symbiosis: Organisms Living Together.* New York: Pegasus, 1970.

————, ed. *Aspects of the Biology of Symbiosis.* Baltimore: University Park Press, 1971.

Clarke, George L. *Elements of Ecology.* New York: Wiley, 1954.

Clausen, Jens. *Stages in the Evolution of Plant Species.* New York & London: Hafner, 1967.

Cloud, Preston. "The Biosphere." *Scientific American* 249 (September 1983): 176–187.

Colinvaux, Paul. *Why Big Fierce Animals Are Rare: An Ecologist's Perspective.* Princeton: Princeton University Press, 1978.

————. *Introduction to Ecology.* New York: Wiley, 1973.

Coope, G. R. "Late Cenozoic Fossil Coleoptera: Evolution, Biogeography and Ecology." *Annual Review of Ecology and Systematics* 10 (1979): 247–267.

Cooper, Charles F. "The Ecology of Fire." *Scientific American* 204 (April 1961): 150–160.

Copeland, Keith, ed. *Aids for the Severely Handicapped*. New York: Grune & Straton, 1974.

Cuénot, Lucien. *Invention et finalité en biologie*. Paris: Flammarion, 1941.

Curtis, Helena. *Biology*. New York: Worth, 1968.

Cuvier, Georges. *Leçons d'anatomie comparée*. Brussels: Culture et Civilisation, 1969.

Darwin, Charles. *The Voyage of the Beagle*. New York: Dutton, 1967.

_____. *The Origin of Species* (1872). 6th ed. New York: Mentor, 1958.

_____. *The Descent of Man and Selection in Relation to Sex* (1874). 2nd ed. New York: Burt, n.d.

_____. *Charles Darwin's Natural Selection: Being the Second Part of His Big Species Book Written from 1856 to 1858*. Ed. from manuscript by R. C. Stauffer. Cambridge: Cambridge University Press, 1975.

_____. *More Letters of Charles Darwin*. 2 vols. Ed. Francis Darwin and A. C. Seward. London: Murray, 1903.

_____. *Charles Darwin and T. H. Huxley: Autobiographies*. Ed. Gavin de Beer. London: Oxford University Press, 1974.

Davenport, Richard K., and Charles M. Rogers. "Intermodal Equivalence of Stimuli in Apes." *Science* 168 (10 April 1970): 279–281.

Davies, Paul. *The Accidental Universe*. Cambridge: Cambridge University Press, 1982.

_____. *God and the New Physics*. New York: Simon & Schuster, 1983.

Davitz, Lois J., and Joel R. Davitz, "How Do Nurses Feel When Patients Suffer?" *American Journal of Nursing* 75 (September 1975): 1505–1510.

Dawkins, Richard. *The Selfish Gene*. New York: Oxford University Press, 1976.

_____. "What's All the Fuss About?" *Nature* 316 (August 1985): 683–684.

Delbrück, Max. "Mind from Matter?" *American Scholar* 47 (Summer 1978): 339–353.

Descartes, René. *The Philosophical Works of Descartes*. 2 vols. Trans. E. S. Haldane and G. R. T. Ross. Cambridge: Cambridge University Press, 1911.

_____. *Treatise of Man*. Trans. Thomas S. Hall. Cambridge: Harvard University Press, 1972.

Dice, Lee R. *Natural Communities*. Ann Arbor: University of Michigan Press, 1962.

Dobzhansky, Theodosius. *Genetics of the Evolutionary Process*. New York: Columbia University Press, 1970.

_____, F. Ayala, G. L. Stebbins, and J. Valentine. *Evolution*. San Francisco: Freeman, 1977.

Dover, Gabriel. "A Molecular Drive through Evolution." *BioScience* 32 (June 1982): 526–533.

Dyson, Freeman. *Disturbing the Universe*. New York: Harper & Row, 1979.

Eccles, John. *Facing Reality*. Berlin & New York: Springer-Verlag, 1970.

_____. "Self-Consciousness and the Human Person." Accademia Nazionale dei Lincei Memorie Science Fisiche Mathematiche E Natural, Series 8. Forthcoming.

Eickmeier, William G. "Desert Resurrection." *Natural History* 93 (January 1984): 36–41.

Einstein, Albert, and Leopold Infeld. *The Evolution of Physics.* New York: Simon & Schuster, 1966.

Eldredge, Niles. *Time Frames: The Rethinking of Darwinian Evolution and the Theory of Punctuated Equilibria.* New York: Simon & Schuster, 1985.

———, and Stephen Jay Gould. "Punctuated Equilibria: An Alternative Approach to Phyletic Gradualism." In *Models in Paleobiology,* ed. T. J. M. Schopf. San Francisco: Freeman, Cooper & Co., 1972, pp. 82–115.

Elton, Charles. *Animal Ecology.* London: Methuen, 1968.

Elvee, Richard Q., ed. *Mind in Nature: Nobel Conference XVII.* San Francisco: Harper & Row, 1982.

Farb, Peter. *Ecology.* New York: Time-Life, 1963.

———. *The Insects.* New York: Time-Life, 1962.

———. *The Forest.* New York: Time-Life, 1969.

Feinsinger, P. "Organization of a Tropical Guild of Nectarivorous Birds." *Ecological Monographs* 46 (1976): 275–291.

Feynman, Richard P. *QED.* Princeton, N.J.: Princeton University Press, 1985.

Fowler, Charles, and Tim Smith, eds. *Dynamics of Large Mammal Populations.* New York: Wiley, 1981.

Freud, Sigmund. *The Future of an Illusion.* Trans. W. D. Robson-Scott. Garden City, N.Y.: Doubleday, 1961.

———. *Civilization and Its Discontents.* Trans. James Strachey. New York: Norton, 1962.

———. *A General Introduction to Psychoanalysis.* Trans. Joan Riviere. New York: Washington Square Press, 1963.

Friedrich, Heinz, ed. *Man and Animal: Studies in Behavior.* Trans. M. Nawiasky. New York: St. Martin's, 1968.

Gardner, R. Allen, and Beatrice T. Gardner. "Teaching Sign Language to a Chimpanzee." *Science* 165 (15 August 1969): 664–672.

Gates, David M. "Heat Transfer in Plants." *Scientific American* 213 (December 1965): 76–84.

Gehring, Walter J. "The Molecular Basis of Development." *Scientific American* 253 (October 1985): 152B–162.

Goodall, Jane. "My Life among Wild Chimpanzees." *National Geographic* 124 (August 1963): 272–308.

Gould, James L. *Ethology: Mechanisms and Evolution of Behavior.* New York: Norton, 1982.

Gould, Stephen Jay. *Ever Since Darwin.* New York: Norton, 1977.

———. "Is a New and General Theory of Evolution Emerging?" *Paleobiology* 6 (1980): 119–130.

———. "Nature's Great Era of Experiments." *Natural History* 92 (July 1983): 12–21.

———. "The Cosmic Dance of Siva." *Natural History* 93 (August 1984): 14–19.

_____, and Richard Lewontin. "The Spandrels of San Marco and the Panglossian Paradigm: A Critique of the Adaptationist Programme." *Proceedings of the Royal Society London Series B* 205 (1979): 581–598.

Grant, Susan. *Beauty and the Beast*. New York: Scribner's, 1984.

Griffin, Donald R. *Animal Thinking*. Cambridge: Harvard University Press, 1984.

_____. "Animal Thinking." *American Scientist* 72 (September–October 1984): 456–464.

_____, ed. *Animal Mind—Human Mind: Report of the Dahlem Workshop, Berlin 1981*. Berlin & New York: Springer-Verlag, 1982.

Hall, Wilbur. *Partner of Nature*. New York: Appleton-Century, 1939.

Halstead, Beverly. "Anti-Darwinism in Japan." *Nature* 317 (17 October 1985): 587–589.

Hardin, Garrett. *Nature and Man's Fate*. New York: Mentor, 1959.

Hart, Harold, and Robert D. Schuetz. *Organic Chemistry: A Short Course*. Boston: Houghton Mifflin, 1972.

Hayes, Keith J., and Catherine H. Nissen. "Higher Mental Functions of a Home-Raised Chimpanzee." In *Behavior of Nonhuman Primates*, vol. 4, ed. Allan M. Shrier and Fred Stollnitz. New York: Academic Press, 1971, pp. 78–100.

Heinrich, Bernd. "The Energetics of the Bumblebee." *Scientific American* 228 (April 1973): 97–102.

Heinz, Friedrich, ed. *Man and Animal: Studies in Behavior*. Trans. M. Nawiasky. New York: St. Martin's Press, 1968.

Heisenberg, Werner. *Physics and Philosophy*. New York: Harper & Row, 1958.

_____. *Philosophical Problems of Nuclear Science*. Greenwich, Conn.: Fawcett, 1966.

_____. *Across the Frontier*. New York: Harper & Row, 1974.

Hertel, Heinrich. *Structure—Form—Movement*. New York: Reinhold, 1966.

Hildebrand, Milton. "How Animals Run." *Scientific American* 202 (May 1960): 148–157.

Hitching, Francis. *The Neck of the Giraffe*. New Haven: Ticknor & Fields, 1982.

Hobbes, Thomas. *Body, Man, and Citizen: Selections from Thomas Hobbes*. Ed. Richard S. Peters. New York: Collier, 1962.

Huxley, Julian. *Evolution in Action*. New York: Harper & Row, 1953.

Huxley, Thomas H. "The Struggle for Existence in Human Society." In *Evolution and Ethics and Other Essays*. New York: Appleton, 1896.

_____. *Method and Results*. New York & London: Appleton, 1925.

_____. *Lectures and Essays*. New York: Macmillan, 1904.

Hylander, Clarence J. *Wildlife Communities: From Tundra to Tropics in North America*. Boston: Houghton Mifflin, 1966.

Infeld, Leopold. *Albert Einstein*. New York: Scribner's, 1950.

Inouye, David W. "The Ant and the Sunflower." *Natural History* 93 (June 1984): 49–52.

Irving, Laurence. "Adaptations to the Cold." *Scientific American* 214 (January 1966): 94–101.

Ito, Y. *Comparative Ecology*. Trans. Jiro Kikkawa. Cambridge: Cambridge University Press, 1978.

Jacob, François. *The Logic of Life: A History of Heredity*. Trans. Betty E. Spillman. New York: Pantheon Books, 1973.

————. *The Possible and the Actual*. Seattle: University of Washington Press, 1982.

Johnson, Hugh. *The International Book of Trees*. New York: Simon & Schuster, 1973.

Jones, David E. H. "The Stability of the Bicycle." *Physics Today* 23 (April 1970): 34–40.

Kanwisher, John W., and Sam H. Ridgway. "The Physiological Ecology of Whales and Porpoises." *Scientific American* 248 (June 1983): 110–120.

Kawai, W. "Newly Acquired Precultural Behavior of the Natural Troop of Japanese Monkeys on Koshima Islet," *Primates* 6 (1965): 1–30.

Kendrew, John. *The Thread of Life*. Cambridge: Harvard University Press, 1966.

Kirk, David, ed. *Biology Today*. New York: Random House, 1975.

Kitts, David B. "Paleontology and Evolutionary Theory." *Evolution* 28 (September 1974): 458–472.

Klopfer, P. *Habitats and Territories*. New York: Basic Books, 1969.

Koestler, Arthur, and J. R. Smythies, eds. *Beyond Reductionism: New Perspectives in the Life Sciences*. Boston: Beacon Press, 1971.

Kohler, Wolfgang. *The Mentality of Apes*. Trans. Ella Winter. New York: Harcourt, Brace, 1931.

Kormondy, Edward J. *Concepts of Ecology*. Englewood Cliffs, N.J.: Prentice-Hall, 1976.

————, ed. *Readings in Ecology*. New York: Prentice-Hall, 1965.

Krutch, Joseph Wood. *The Great Chain of Life*. Boston: Houghton Mifflin, 1978.

Lack, David. "Competition for Food by Birds of Prey." *Journal of Animal Ecology* 15 (1946): 123–129.

————. *The Natural Regulation of Animal Numbers*. Oxford: Oxford University Press, 1954.

Lambert, David, and the Diagram Group. *Field Guide to Prehistoric Life*. New York: Facts on File, 1985.

Laplace, Pierre Simon. *A Philosophical Essay on Probabilities*. Trans. F. W. Truscott and F. L. Emory. New York: Dover, 1951.

Lawick-Goodall, Jane van. *In the Shadow of Man*. Boston: Houghton Mifflin, 1971.

————. "A Preliminary Report on Expressive Movements and Communication in the Gombe Stream Chimpanzees." In *Primate Patterns*, ed. Phyllis Dohlinow. New York: Holt, Rinehart & Winston, 1972, pp. 25–84.

Lettvin, J. Y.; H. R. Maturana; W. S. McCulloch; and W. H. Pitts. "What the Frog's Eye Tells the Frog's Brain." *Proceedings of the Institute of Radio Engineers* 47 (November 1959): 1940–1951.

Lewin, Roger. "Evolutionary Theory Under Fire." *Science* 210 (21 November 1980): 883–887.

————. "Molecules Come to Darwin's Aid." *Science* 216 (4 June 1982): 1091–1092.

Lewis, John, ed. *Beyond Chance and Necessity: A Critical Inquiry into Professor Jacques Monod's Chance and Necessity*. London: Teilhard Centre for the Future, 1974.

Lewontin, Richard C. "Adaptation." *Scientific American* 239 (September 1978): 212–230.

Limbaugh, Conrad. "Cleaning Symbiosis." *Scientific American* 205 (August 1961): 42–49.

Lissaman, P. B. S., and Carl A. Shollenberger. "Formation Flight of Birds." *Science* 168 (22 May 1970): 1003–1005.

Little, Elbert L. *The Audubon Society Field Guide to North American Trees: Eastern Region.* New York: Knopf, 1985.

Lorenz, Konrad. *King Solomon's Ring.* New York: Crowell, 1952.

_____. *On Aggression.* New York: Harcourt, Brace & World, 1963.

Lovelock, J. E. *Gaia: A New Look at Life on Earth.* New York: Oxford University Press, 1979.

Løvtrup, Søren. "On the Falsifiability of Neo-Darwinism." *Evolutionary Theory* 1 (December 1976): 267–283.

Luria, Salvador E. *Life—The Unfinished Experiment.* New York: Scribner's, 1973.

MacArthur, Robert H. "Population Ecology of Some Warblers of Northeastern Coniferous Forests." *Ecology* 39 (October 1958): 599–619.

McMahon, Thomas A., and John Tyler Bonner. *On Size and Life.* New York: Scientific American Books, 1983.

Malthus, Thomas Robert. *An Essay on the Principle of Population* (1798). Ed. Philip Appleman. New York: Norton, 1976.

Margenau, Henry. *The Miracle of Existence.* Woodbridge, Conn.: Ox Bow Press, 1984.

Margulis, Lynn. *Symbiosis in Cell Evolution.* San Francisco: Freeman, 1981.

_____, and Dorion Sagan. "Strange Fruit on the Tree of Life." *The Sciences* 26 (May–June 1986): 38–45.

Marx, Karl, and Friedrich Engels. *Basic Writings on Politics and Philosophy.* Trans. Lewis Feuer. Garden City, N.Y.: Doubleday, 1959.

May, Robert M. "A Test of Ideas about Mutualism." *Nature* 307 (2 February 1984): 410–411.

Mayr, Ernst. *Population, Species and Evolution.* Cambridge: Harvard University Press, 1970.

_____. *The Growth of Biological Thought: Diversity, Evolution, and Inheritance.* Cambridge: Harvard University Press, 1982.

Mech, David L. *The Wolves of Isle Royale: Fauna of the National Parks of the United States.* Washington, D.C.: Government Printing Office, 1966.

Medawar, P. B., and J. S. Medawar. *The Life Sciences: Current Ideas of Biology.* New York: Harper & Row, 1977.

Menzel, Emil W. "Spontaneous Invention of Ladders in a Group of Young Chimpanzees." *Folia Primatoligica* 17 (1972): 87–106.

Mercer, E. H. *The Foundations of Biological Theory.* New York: Wiley, 1981.

Messenger, P. S. "Biotic Interactions." In *Encyclopaedia Britannica: Macropaedia* (15th ed.), vol. 2, pp. 1044–1052.

Miller, Stanley L., and Leslie E. Orgel. *The Origins of Life on the Earth.* New York: Prentice-Hall, 1974.

Monmaney, Terence. "Life Taking Shape: A Developing View." *Science 85* 6 (September 1985): 14–16.

Monod, Jacques. *Chance and Necessity: An Essay on the Natural Philosophy of Modern Biology.* Trans. Autryn Wainhouse. New York: Knopf, 1971.

Montagna, William. "The Skin." *Scientific American* 212 (February 1965): 56–66.

Morowitz, Harold. *The Wine of Life.* New York: St. Martin's, 1979.

——. "Rediscovering the Mind." *Psychology Today* 14 (August 1980).

Murie, Adolph. *The Wolves of Mount McKinley: Fauna of the National Parks of the United States.* Washington, D.C.: Government Printing Office, 1944.

Newell, Norman. "Crises in the History of Life." *Scientific American* 208 (February 1963): 76–92.

Newton, Isaac. *Principia.* Trans. Florian Cajori. Berkeley & Los Angeles: University of California Press, 1934.

——. *Opticks.* New York: Dover, 1952.

Nijhout, Frederick H. "The Color Patterns of Butterflies and Moths." *Scientific American* 245 (November 1981): 139–151.

Nilsson, Heribert. *Synthetische Artbildung.* Lund, Sweden: Gleerup, 1954.

Nissen, H. W. "Phylogenetic Comparison." In *Handbook of Experimental Psychology,* ed. S. S. Stevens. New York: Wiley, 1951, pp. 347–386.

Novikoff, Alex B. "The Concept of Integrative Levels and Biology." *Science* 101 (2 March 1945): 209–215.

O'Brien, S. J.; W. G. Nash, D. E. Wildt; M. E. Bush; and R. E. Benveniste. "A Molecular Solution to the Riddle of the Giant Panda's Phylogeny." *Nature* 317 (12 September 1985): 140–144.

Odum, Eugene P. *Fundamentals of Ecology.* Philadelphia: Saunders, 1971.

O'Neill, R. V. "Niche Segregation in Seven Species of Diplopods." *Ecology* 48 (1967): 983.

Oppenheimer, Peter. "The Genesis Algorithm." *The Sciences* 25 (September–October 1985): 44–47.

——. "Fractals, Computers and DNA." *Semaine internationale de l'image electronique/ Deuxième colloque image.* Nice, April 1986.

Owen-Smith, Norman. "Territoriality in the White Rhinoceros (*Ceratotherium simum*) Burchell." *Nature* 231 (4 June 1971): 294–296.

Pagels, Heinz R. *The Cosmic Code: Quantum Physics as the Language of Nature.* New York: Bantam Books, 1983.

Patterson, Colin. *Evolution.* Ithaca, N.Y.: Cornell University Press, 1978.

Patterson, Francine G. "Conversations with a Gorilla." *National Geographic* 154 (October 1978): 438–465.

——. "Linguistic Capabilities of a Lowland Gorilla." In *Language Intervention from Ape to Child,* ed. Richard L. Schiefelbusch and John H. Hollis. Baltimore: University Park Press, 1979, pp. 325–356.

Pauling, Linus, and Peter Pauling. *Chemistry.* San Francisco: Freeman, 1975.

Peterson, Ivars. "On the Wings of a Dragonfly." *Science News* 128 (10 August 1985): 90–91.

Perry, Nicolette. *Symbiosis.* Poole, England: Blanford Press, 1983.

Piaget, Jean. *The Construction of Reality in the Child.* Trans. Margaret Cook. New York: Basic, 1954.

_____. *Six Psychological Studies.* Trans. Anita Tenzer. New York: Vintage, 1968.

_____. "The Child and Modern Physics." *Scientific American* 196 (March 1957): 46–51.

Pieper, Josef. *Leisure: The Basis of Culture.* Trans. Alexander Dru. New York: Mentor, 1963.

Pirie, N. W. "The Meaninglessness of the Terms Life and Living." In *Perspectives in Biochemistry,* ed. J. Needham and D. Green. Cambridge: Cambridge University Press, 1937.

Poinar, George O. Jr. "Sealed in Amber." *Natural History* 91 (June 1982): 26–30.

Poincaré, Henri. *The Value of Science.* New York: Dover, 1958.

Pontin, A. J. *Competition and Coexistence of Species.* London: Pitman, 1982.

Portmann, Adolph. *Animal Camouflage.* Ann Arbor: University of Michigan Press, 1959.

_____. *Animal Forms and Patterns.* New York: Schocken, 1967.

Premack, David. "The Education of Sarah, a Chimp." *Psychology Today* (September 1970).

_____. "Language in Champanzee?" *Science* 172 (21 May 1971): 808–822.

Raup, David M. "Conflicts between Darwin and Paleontology." *Bulletin Field Museum of Natural History* 50 (January 1979): 22–29.

Ricklefs, Robert. *Ecology.* Newton, Mass.: Chiron Press, 1974.

Roberts, Leslie. "Insights into the Animal Mind." *BioScience* 33 (June 1983): 362–364.

Rogers, Lynn. "A Bear in Its Lair." *Natural History* 90 (October 1981): 64–70.

Ross, Herbert R. "Principles of Natural Coexistence Indicated by Leafhopper Populations." *Evolution* 11 (June 1957): 113–129.

Rumbaugh, Duane, ed. *Language Learning by a Chimpanzee: The Lana Project.* New York: Academic Press, 1977.

Rüppell, Georg. *Bird Flight.* New York: Van Nostrand Reinhold, 1975.

Russell, E. S. *The Interpretation of Development and Heredity: A Study in Biological Method.* Oxford: Oxford University Press, 1930.

Savage-Rumbaugh, E. Sue; Duane Rumbaugh; and Sally Boysen. "Linguistically Mediated Tool Use and Exchange by Chimpanzees (Pan Troglodytes)." In *Speaking of Apes: A Critical Anthology of Two-Way Communication with Man,* ed. Thomas Sebeok and Jean Umiker-Sebeok. New York: Plenum, 1980.

Schmidt-Nielsen, Knut. *Animal Physiology.* Cambridge: Cambridge University Press, 1975.

_____, and Bodil Schmidt-Nielsen. "The Desert Rat." *Scientific American* 189 (January 1953): 73–78.

Scholander, P. F. "The Wonderful Net." *Scientific American* 196 (April 1957): 96–107.

Schrödinger, Erwin. *Science and Humanism: Physics in Our Time.* Cambridge: Cambridge University Press, 1961.

_____. *What Is Life? and Mind and Matter.* Cambridge: Cambridge University Press, 1967.

Sebeok, Thomas A., and Jean Umiker-Sebeok. "Performing Animals: Secrets of the Trade." *Psychology Today* 13 (November 1979).

Shapiro, Robert. *Origins: A Skeptic's Guide to the Creation of Life.* New York: Summit Books, 1986.

Shaxel, J. *Grundzuge der Theorienbildung in der Biologie.* Jena: Fischer, 1922.

Sherrington, Charles. *Man on His Nature.* Cambridge: Cambridge University Press, 1975.

Sibley, Charles G., and Jon E. Ahlquist. "Reconstructing Bird Phylogeny by Comparing DNA's." *Scientific American* 254 (February 1986): 82–92.

Simberloff, Daniel. "The Great God of Competition." *The Sciences* 24 (July–August 1984): 17–22.

Simpson, George G. *The Meaning of Evolution.* New Haven: Yale University Press, 1949.

_____. *Fossils and the History of Life.* New York: Scientific American Library, 1983.

Sinnott, Edmund W. *Cell and Psyche: The Biology of Purpose.* New York: Harper & Row, 1961.

_____. *Matter, Mind and Man.* London: Allen & Unwin, 1958.

Skinner, B. F. *About Behaviorism.* New York: Knopf, 1974.

Slobodkin, L. B. "Experimental Populations of Hydrida." In *British Ecological Society Jubilee Symposium.* Oxford: Blackwell, 1964, pp. 131–148.

Smith, John W. *Theory of Evolution.* Middlesex, England: Penguin, 1958.

Smith, Robert L. *Ecology and Field Biology.* New York: Harper & Row, 1974.

Spinoza, Baruch. *The Correspondence of Spinoza.* Trans. A. Wolf. Allen & Unwin, 1928.

Stanley, Steven. *The New Evolutionary Timetable: Fossils, Genes, and the Origin of Species.* New York: Basic Books, 1981.

_____. "Darwin Done Over." *The Sciences* 21 (October 1981): 18–23.

_____. "Evolution of Life: Evidence of a New Pattern." In *Great Ideas Today 1983.* Chicago: Encyclopaedia Britannica, 1983, pp. 2–54.

Stebbins, G. Ledyard. "Cataclysmic Evolution." *Scientific American* 184 (April 1951): 54–59.

_____, and Francisco Ayala. "Is a New Evolutionary Synthesis Necessary?" *Science* 213 (28 August 1981): 967–971.

_____, and Francisco J. Ayala. "The Evolution of Darwinism." *Scientific American* 253 (July 1985): 72–82.

Stent, Gunther S. "Limits to the Scientific Understanding of Man." *Science* 187 (21 March 1975): 1052–1057.

Stevenson, Lionel. *Darwin among the Poets.* New York: Russell & Russell, 1963.

Stewart, Robert, and John Aldrich. "Removal and Repopulation of Breeding Birds in a Spruce-Fir Community." *Auk* 75 (1951): 471–482.

Tax, Sol, and Charles Callender, eds. *Evolution after Darwin: Issues in Evolution.* Chicago: University of Chicago Press, 1960.

Tennyson, Alfred Lord. *In Memoriam.* Ed. Robert Ross. New York: Norton, 1973.

Terrace, Herbert S. *Nim.* New York: Knopf, 1979.

_____. "How Nim Chimpsky Changed My Mind." *Psychology Today* 13 (November 1979).

_____, L. A. Petitto, R. J. Sanders, and T. G. Bever. "Can an Ape Create a Sentence?." *Science* 206 (23 November 1979): 891–901.

Tetry, Andrée. *Les outils chez les êtres vivants.* Paris: Gallimard, 1948.

Thomas, Lewis. "On the Uncertainty of Science." *Key Reporter,* no. 6 (1980).

Thompson, D'Arcy. *On Growth and Form.* 2 vols. Cambridge: Cambridge University Press, 1959.

Thorpe, W. H. *Animal Nature and Human Nature.* New York: Doubleday, 1974.

_____. *Purpose in a World of Chance.* London: Oxford University Press, 1978.

Tinbergen, Niko. *Social Behavior in Animals.* London & New York: Methuen and Wiley, 1962.

_____. *The Study of Instinct.* Folcroft, Pa.: Folcroft Editions, 1969.

_____. *Animal Behavior.* New York: Time-Life, 1965.

_____. *The Animal in Its World: Explorations of an Ethologist.* 2 vols. Cambridge: Harvard University Press, 1972.

Tributsch, Helmut. *How Life Learned to Live: Adaptation in Nature.* Trans. Miriam Varon. Cambridge: MIT Press, 1982.

Underwood, Larry S. "Outfoxing the Arctic Cold." *Natural History* 92 (December 1983): 38–46.

Valentine, James W., and Cathryn A. Campbell. "Genetic Regulation and the Fossil Record." *American Scientist* 63 (November–December 1975): 673–689.

Waddington, C. H., ed. *Towards a Theoretical Biology.* Chicago: Aldine, 1969.

Wald, George. "Eye and Camera." *Scientific American* 183 (August 1950): 32–41.

_____. "Life and Light." *Scientific American* 201 (October 1959): 92–108.

_____. "Life and Mind in the Universe." *International Journal of Quantum Chemistry: Quantum Biology Symposium* 11 New York: Wiley, 1984, pp. 1–15.

Waser, Nickolas M., and Leslie A. Real. "Effective Mutualism between Sequentially Flowering Plant Species." *Nature* 281 (25 October 1979): 670–672.

Watson, James. *The Double Helix.* New York: Mentor, 1968.

Weaver, John E., and Frederic E. Clements. *Plant Ecology.* New York: McGraw-Hill, 1938.

Wegener, Peter P. "The Science of Flight." *American Scientist* 74 (May–June 1986): 268–278.

Weizsäcker, Carl F. von. *The World View of Physics.* Trans. Marjorie Grene. Chicago: University of Chicago Press, 1952

Wells, H. G., Julian S. Huxley; and G. P. Wells. *The Science of Life.* London: Doubleday, Doran and Co., 1931

Welty, Carl. "Birds as Flying Machines." *Scientific American* 192 (March 1955): 88–96.

Went, Frits W. "The Ecology of Desert Plants." *Scientific American* 192 (April 1955): 68–75.

_____. *The Plants.* New York: Time-Life, 1963.

Wheeler, John. "Genesis and Observership." In *Foundational Problems in the Special Sciences,* ed. Robert E. Butts and Jaakko Hintikka. Dordrecht, Holland: Reidel, 1977.

Wickler, Wolfgang. *Mimicry in Plants and Animals.* New York: McGraw-Hill, 1968.

Wiens, John A. "Competition or Peaceful Coexistence?" *Natural History* 92 (March 1983): 30–34.

Wigner, Eugene. *Symmetries and Reflections.* Bloomington: Indiana University Press, 1967.

Wilson, Allan C. "The Molecular Basis of Evolution." *Scientific American* 253 (October 1985): 164–173.

———, L. R. Maxon, and V. M. Sarich. "Two Types of Molecular Evolution: Evidence from Studies of Interspecific Hybridization." *Proceedings of the National Academy of Sciences (USA)* 71 (July 1974): 2843–2847.

Wilson, Edward O. *Sociobiology: The New Synthesis.* Cambridge: Harvard University Press, 1978.

———. *On Human Nature.* Cambridge: Harvard University Press, 1978.

———. "The Biological Diversity Crisis: A Challenge to Science." *Issues in Science and Technology* 2 (Fall 1985): 20–29.

Witt, Peter N. "Do We Live in the Best of All Worlds? Spiders Suggest an Answer." *Perspectives in Biology and Medicine* 8 (Summer 1965): 475–487.

Wood, Elizabeth. *Crystals and Light.* Princeton, N.J.: Van Nostrand, 1964.

Wynne-Edwards, V. C. "Self-Regulating Systems in Populations of Animals." *Science* 147 (26 March 1965): 1543–1548.

Yerkes, Robert M. *Chimpanzees: A Laboratory Colony.* New Haven: Yale University Press, 1943.

Index

ALSO IN NEW SCIENCE LIBRARY